If you wish to move to the top of your profession in terms of income, success, clientele, and prestige, Bob Bly brings decades of street honed experience to this game with the clarity and work ethic of a professional engineer. As you employ Bob's method, you'll realize you narrowly avoided diving into an empty swimming pool. I can't count how many businesses will file Chapter 11 or go "404–PAGE NOT FOUND" because they should have read this book. And I respect Bob all the more for advising you in this book to put measurements in place before you do anything else. Stephen Covey says "Begin with the end in mind," but Bob Bly says, "Begin by deciding how you're going to measure your happy ending."

—PERRY MARSHALL, AUTHOR OF *ULTIMATE GUIDE TO GOOGLE ADWORDS*, *ULTIMATE GUIDE TO FACEBOOK ADVERTISING*, AND *80/20 SALES & MARKETING*

Bob Bly says his book is about marketing plans, but it's really about planning a business. With this step-by-step guide, small business owners can think through their products, their market opportunity and their potential profits, to choose the most productive actions for achieving their goals. Filled with practical, hands-on advice, *The Marketing Plan Handbook* is a one-stop source for business success.

—RUTH P. STEVENS, AUTHOR OF *B2B DATA-DRIVEN MARKETING: SOURCES, USES, RESULTS*

If you're convinced that marketing your business is difficult or time-consuming, or you believe you don't have the "right" knowledge, then you need Bob Bly's book. He gives you an easy-to-implement plan for growing your business consistently over time.

— DIANNA HUFF, FOUNDER AND PRESIDENT OF HUFF INDUSTRIAL MARKETING, INC.

If you've been looking for a marketing book that "goes the extra mile" and over-delivers on its promises, then pay close attention to the book now resting in your hands. *The Marketing Plan Handbook* is the most comprehensive, concentrated and concise course I have even seen on the subject of building a business from the ground up. It covers every modern day nuance of entrepreneurship as well as the actions that cause your eventual success. Whether you're interested in starting or growing a business, or becoming a top tier marketing consultant, Robert W. Bly lays gold before your eyes, giving you the keys to a kingdom he knows inside and out.

— MATT FUREY, AUTHOR OF *COMBAT CONDITIONING*, MATTFUREY.COM

I'm a pretty good ad writer, but when it comes to planning marketing strategy and tactics, Bob Bly is at the top of my list—all his best secrets are revealed in this valuable book.

—ROBERT RINGER, *THE NEW YORK TIMES* #1 BESTSELLING AUTHOR

Marketing is becoming more complex, even for professional marketers. Bob's time-saving 12 steps make it easy for small business owners to market more effectively and prosper.

—JOAN DAMICO, B2B COPYWRITER & MARCOM CONSULTANT, @COPYWRITER4U

The very idea of crafting your marketing plan can be absolutely terrifying, if you've got no idea where to start . . . or incredibly liberating, once you realize what a huge edge it gives you, if you craft it well. Bob does an amazing job, in his new book, of showing us how to craft it well. Within the first 20 pages, he lays out a 12-step plan that takes all the mystery—and anxiety—out of trying to figure out exactly what a good marketing plan is and what's next. Bob decodes all that stuff so many long-time marketers are afraid to admit they don't know—from how to use Google Analytics to get better marketing feedback, to how to slog your way through every online marketing metric you need to know. All this is no longer optional. You can't survive today without making a plan like this. The good news—great news, in fact—is that Bob just made it easy.

— JOHN FORDE, EDITOR AND FOUNDER OF
THE COPYWRITER'S ROUNDTABLE

The Marketing Plan Handbook

Develop Big-Picture Marketing Plans for Pennies on the Dollar

Second Edition

Robert W. Bly

EP
Entrepreneur
PRESS®

Entrepreneur Press, Publisher
Cover Design: Kaochoy Saeteurn
Production and Composition: Eliot House Productions

This publication is designed to provide accurate and authoritative information
in regard to the subject matter covered. It is sold with the understanding that
the publisher is not engaged in rendering legal, accounting or other professional
services. If legal advice or other expert assistance is required, the services of a
competent professional person should be sought.

Library of Congress Cataloging-in-Publication Data
Bly, Robert W.
    The marketing plan handbook : develop big-picture marketing plans for
pennies on the dollar/Robert W. Bly.—Second Edition.
    pages cm.
    ISBN-13: 978-1-59918-559-0 (paperback)
    ISBN-10: 1-59918-559-8 (paperback)
    1. Marketing—Management—Handbooks, manuals, etc. 2. Small
business—Handbooks, manuals, etc. I. Title.
    HF5415.13.B559 2015
    658.8—dc23   2015029004

Printed in the United States of America

19 18 17 16 15   10 9 8 7 6 5 4 3 2 1

This book is for
Jed Rosen

CONTENTS

ACKNOWLEDGMENTS

First, thanks to Lura Harrison for researching, writing, and editing significant portions of this book. This is truly our book, not just my book—a total collaboration.

Second, as always, thanks to Bob Diforio, my literary agent, for finding a great publisher to produce this book with us.

Third, thanks to Jill McTigue and Karen Billipp, editors of this updated second edition, for giving the book new life and new value.

Thanks also to Mark Amtower, Roger C. Parker, and others who permitted me to reprint their writings or otherwise share their marketing expertise in this book.

A tip of the hat to Jennifer Holmes for her work on chapter 13, and the same to Kim Stacey for her help on chapters 14 and 15.

And thanks to my editor on the first edition, Jere Calmes, for believing in our idea and for making the book much better than it was when it first crossed his desk.

PREFACE

America is not only the land of the free, but also of the entrepreneur: There are almost 28 million small businesses in the United States. Of these, over 22 million are self-employed solopreneurs, and a little over half work at home. By comparison, a mere 17,700 firms in America have 500 employees or more. Small business is where it's at.

More than half a million new businesses are started each month. Of these, 1 out of 4 will stay in business 16 years or more. Small businesses employ half of all people who work in the private sector and have generated up to 80 percent of the net growth in jobs in the United States over the last decade or so.

Most people, when they go into a business, think that if they are good at what they do, they will be successful. For instance, if they are a photographer, they believe that all they have to do is take good pictures and they will have more business than they can handle. Unfortunately, it usually doesn't work out that way at all.

There are legions of small-business owners, especially in service industries, who are technically competent or even excellent at their professions, yet earn only a modest living at best. That's because they don't know the ultimate secret to achieving outrageous success in any business: Those who make the most money in any profession or service business, from accountants and ad agencies to window washers and web designers, are those who are the best at *marketing and selling themselves*—not at performing the actual function or service.

Doctors, attorneys, and other professionals have traditionally held the opposite point of view. They criticize competitors who advertise, saying, "If your product or service was any good, you wouldn't have to promote it with such hype." Nice to think so, but naïve. Sad to say, it doesn't work that way in the real world. "The expression 'If you build it, they will come' is not true," said Steve Murphy, former CEO of publisher Rodale Inc., in an interview with *Fast Company* magazine. "We had lots of great properties at Rodale, but not enough of them were known. We needed to expose them to the mass market."

So, how do you make the transition from struggling or average entrepreneur to the top of your profession in terms of income, success, clientele, and prestige? Well, you can start with the simple, commonsense 12-step process for creating and implementing a winning marketing plan presented in this book! Over the years, I've shared my battle-tested marketing methods—in books, articles, blogs, seminars, webinars, consultations, and countless promotions and campaigns—with thousands of copywriters, graphic designers, consultants, self-employed service professionals, manufacturers, small-business owners, marketing professionals, and corporate clients. Those who apply these techniques consistently enjoy a number of benefits, including increased income, elimination of slow periods, greater cash flow, and enhanced prestige and status within their market or industry.

This second edition follows but also expands on the proven 12-step process introduced in the first. It gives you more in-depth advice and coverage on the hottest marketing trends to emerge within the last decade, including data analytics, content marketing, mobile marketing, social networking, infographics, search engine optimization, and more.

I do have one favor to ask. If you have a marketing method or campaign that has worked particularly well for your business, why not send it to me so I can share it with readers of the next edition of this book? You can reach me at:

Bob Bly
Copywriter/Consultant
31 Cheyenne Dr.
Montville, NJ 07045
Phone: (973) 263-0562; Fax: (973) 263-0613
Email: rwbly@bly.com
Web: www.bly.com

INTRODUCTION

According to the U.S. Small Business Administration (SBA), about half of al new small businesses survive only five years or less. The SBA and others who specialize in helping small businesses succeed tell us that lack of capital is seldom the main reason.

Rather, most small businesses fail because they don't have a plan for getting customers or clients. Yes, we're experts in the products and services we offer, but too many of us open our doors absolutely clueless about how we're going to make money.

Who are the top earners, the most successful business owners, in their markets and niches? More often than not, those at the top got there not because they are the best at what they do (e.g., financial planning, web design, accounting), but because they are the best at marketing and selling themselves.

The aim of this book is to show small-business owners, managers, and entrepreneurs how to write a marketing plan to grow your business every month. If you've researched your marketplace in the past and know your business well, you'll be able to complete the 12 simple steps to creating a winning marketing plan in a couple of days or so. If you don't have the answers you need in each step, it will take longer because you'll need to gather more information about your business, competition, marketplace, and customers.

Learning to create and execute a successful marketing plan can mean the difference between living well vs. just scraping by—or even between

enjoying many years of success in business vs. watching your enterprise dwindle and disappear, a casualty of tough competition, changing marketplace, recession, or a weak economy. So it's a skill worth your while to master, and by using this book, you can do just that.

What's in a Marketing Plan?

When your small business is profitable, the money allows you to continue operations and enjoy the freedom and fulfillment of being your own boss. Should your small business fail, you will likely be forced to take a nine-to-five job working for someone else—which is sometimes a bitter pill for us to swallow after we've tasted the independence of entrepreneurship.

That makes reversing the high failure rate of new businesses a priority for all of us. If you think being in business would be great if only you didn't have to market it, you're not going to get that wish. To succeed, you must market and sell what you make or do. Setting goals and having a written plan to implement your marketing campaigns is a major determinant of whether we meet with success or failure.

Yet too many small-business owners think creating a marketing plan is either too difficult, too time-consuming, or too distant from the day-to-day reality of running their businesses. Nothing could be further from the truth. The value of a marketing plan is it forces you to think through how you're going to make money in concrete, detailed action steps. Marketing plans lead to purposeful action.

Marketing plans lay out the steps you'll take to create the business you want. Think of your plan as a blueprint for success, a major to-do list—one that's based on the vision and strategy you crafted for your business. It ties your strategy for succeeding with the actions you'll take to make it happen. In your plan, you'll assign specific tasks to individuals (even if it's just you) and give them deadlines for achieving them. To create a marketing plan that has true value, you must be willing to examine your business from top to bottom to ensure that everything in it is working toward achieving your ultimate vision.

A marketing plan spells out:

◆ What you want your business to accomplish over the next year
◆ How you're going to do it
◆ The resources you'll need
◆ The monthly, weekly, and daily actions you'll take to do it

No one has perfect knowledge of what will or won't work in growing a particular business. That's why you need a plan. It will give you a system that lets you measure which strategies and tactics work best for growing your business. The clearer you are on which actions bring you desired results, the more you'll be able to duplicate successful results. You'll also see a more efficient use of your resources and a greater return on your investment, because you won't be wasting them on tactics that don't work.

Benefits of Creating a Marketing Plan

A marketing plan offers several advantages to a business; it can help you:

◆ Determine whether there is a demand for your product or service
◆ Identify segments of potential customers most likely to buy the product or service from you
◆ Uncover your clients' and prospects' needs and wants
◆ Understand the advantages you offer clients over your competitors
◆ Generate more leads, orders, sales, and profits
◆ Research and reach out to new markets you might want to serve
◆ Test and measure your marketing campaign results
◆ Find and fix weaknesses in your assumptions and tactics

Typical questions that your marketing plan will help you answer include:

- ◆ "I just started my new business. How do I market?"
- ◆ "I've gone as far as I can. How do I expand my client base?"
- ◆ "What used to work isn't working anymore. What should I do?"
- ◆ "Should I increase my marketing during the recession or cut back?"
- ◆ "A new competitor is stealing my clients. What can I do?"
- ◆ "How do I market my new service or product to my current clients?"
- ◆ "My industry is changing. How do I compete in the new internet age?"
- ◆ "Outsourcing to overseas competitors and price competition is killing us. Should we lower our prices to fight back?"
- ◆ "How can we command a premium price in an industry where our product or service is increasingly viewed as a commodity?"
- ◆ "More companies are doing what we offer in-house to save money. How can we get them to hire us to do some of the work?"

The actual process of writing your marketing plan will help you answer these questions. In examining your business thoroughly, you'll learn what you know about the business and what else you need to learn to succeed.

The object here is not to create a perfect plan, and this too is not a small point. I see too many marketing consultants and corporate marketing professionals who treat writing the plan as the end in itself, and not the means to an end, which it is. Often these "overplanners" spend months creating the perfect plan, which ends up being the perfect unused plan.

Good marketing plans are simple and dynamic. Your marketing plan is a document that will change as your business evolves. The marketing tactics within it will not survive the yearlong period for which you wrote it. Why not? Because the first time you implement various campaigns, you will quickly know which promotions were good ideas and which aren't going to pay off.

Smart marketers do not stubbornly stick with the written plan. Instead, they continue those strategies that generate a big return on marketing dollars (ROMD). The ones that don't work are rethought, and new ideas are tested in their place.

So why bother writing a marketing plan for an entire year if it's going to change? If you were planning a cross-country trip in your RV, you'd certainly carry a road atlas to supplement Siri and your GPS. The map is a guide to point the way. If one of the routes on the map is washed out, you don't turn around and go back home. It's much the same with a marketing plan. A marketing plan is your road map, and the point is to get started. As you learn more about your business, you'll update your plan.

This book walks you through the 12 simple steps to launch your business into a new phase of success. It's set up to allow you to complete your plan in as little as one weekend, though it may take you longer. So, make an appointment with yourself, and plan to spend Saturday and Sunday—or any other days or evenings you prefer—mapping out your road to success for your business. By the time we come to Step 10: Write Your Plan, most of your plan will be completed; you'll simply need to combine your results from Steps 1 through 9.

We assume that you're already in business and have a basic knowledge of your clients. If you don't or you're a new business, you'll still find the information you need to create your marketing plan. Just know that you're going to need to invest—yes, invest!—more than a day or two to produce a plan that works for you.

How This Book Works

To make our advice more specific and clear, we'll follow a fictional company, Chiropractic Marketing Plans Inc. (CMP), as it works through the steps to update its own marketing plan. CMP is a four-year-old sole proprietorship, owned by Chandra Martin Perez. It's located in the Los Angeles area. As its name indicates, the company specializes in writing marketing plans for chiropractic practices. CMP wants to increase its billings from $150,000 to $200,000 over the next year. Follow along as Ms. Perez conducts an annual review of her own marketing plan to determine how to achieve this growth.

Quick-Start Guide

Here are the 12 steps to writing a winning marketing plan at a glance. Each is covered in detail in its own chapter in the book. By reading this quick-start guide first, you can understand the market planning process in less than five minutes. The 12 steps are as follows:

Step 1: Harness the Power of Vision. If you're like most small business owners, you'll have days when you wonder why you ever thought running your own business was a great idea. On those days, you'll need the power of your vision for your business to infuse you with the excitement you once knew. Don't even think about going further until you have a clear vision of what you want this business to be. Step 1 is all about gaining that clarity.

Step 2: Decide What Business You're In. The purpose of this step is to define the primary market you'll focus on. By the end, you'll describe your chosen well-defined niche.

Step 3: Get to Know Everything about Your Ideal Customer. Who is your ideal client? This step will help you define that for your business so you can focus your efforts and resources where they're most likely to succeed.

Step 4: Who Is the Competition? Because you don't do business in a vacuum, you need to know what other options your ideal client has to solve his or her problem. This step walks you through defining and evaluating your competition.

Step 5: Strategize: Position Your Business. Here's where you'll lay out the strategy for accomplishing your goals for the business. First, you need to position the business in the minds of your prospects and clients.

Step 6: Build Out Your Product Line. The main cost in business is the marketing expended to acquire a new customer. The main profits are in selling additional products and services to your base of existing customers. Without a broad line of related products and services, you leave most of these profits on the table.

Step 7: Assess Your Tactics. With your strategy spelled out, you'll evaluate the best tools for implementing it. Because marketing usually requires more than one type of effort, you'll choose three to five tactics to begin your implementation.

Step 8: Integrate Online and Offline Marketing. Small businesses that are not on the internet need to enter the 21st century, and internet marketers that do no offline promotion are missing opportunities to grow. Some marketers call this integration O2O for "offline to online," because the offline tactics are increasingly oriented (though not exclusively oriented by any means) to driving the consumer online.

Step 9: Put Your Measurements in Place. You'll need to assess whether the tactics you choose are working. That means you must have a standard for evaluating "success." In this step, you'll spell out how you intend to measure success.

Step 10: Write Your Plan. In this step, you'll pull together all the decisions you made in Steps 1 through 9 to create your plan.

Step 11: Work It! Implementation. The point of creating this plan is to hit the ground running with focused action. In this step, you'll map out your actions for the next 30 days.

Step 12: Review and Troubleshoot Your Plan. In business, every day is a learning experience. But most of us miss the benefits of those lessons because we don't take the time to understand what we've experienced. In this step, you'll plan your reviews and decide how you'll troubleshoot when things don't go according to plan. Then, start working your plan all over again.

Appendices. Here you'll find a sample marketing plan for Chiropractic Marketing Plans and the forms created throughout the book. Consultants will also find information on how to charge for writing marketing plans; if you're a business owner and choose not to write your own plan, you'll know what to expect to pay someone else to write it.

In addition, since the publication of the first edition of this book, three relatively new marketing channels are undergoing explosive growth, and we have added a chapter on each in this second edition:

Chapter 13: Content Marketing. Using free information to help educate consumers and sell them your products.

Chapter 14: Mobile Marketing. Millions of consumers now consume content and read advertising on their smartphones rather than desktop devices, and marketers now create promotions specifically optimized for display and reading on mobile devices.

Chapter 15: Social Networking. Though there is huge disagreement among marketers as to the effectiveness and ROI of social media, it is undeniably one of the biggest and fastest growing marketing channels today.

There you have the 12 steps to creating and implementing a marketing plan that will help you grow your business every month plus guidance on three of the most important new marketing channels: content, mobile, and social.

Napoleon Hill wrote, "First comes thought; then organization of that thought into ideas and plans; then transformation of those plans into reality. The beginning, as you will observe, is in your imagination." And so we begin with imagination and the creation of your powerful vision, mission, or central goal.

Chapter 1
HARNESS THE POWER OF VISION

There is a key aspect to the planning of marketing campaigns that differs depending on whether you are a corporate marketing manager or a small business owner or solopreneur. The former has to please only his employer; the latter seeks to create a business that rewards him personally as well as financially, delivering both the income and the lifestyle he seeks.

For the marketing manager at a corporation or a small business of which she is not the owner, the objective of the marketing plan is pretty much the same for every company: Create and implement a campaign that maximizes return on marketing dollars (ROMD). In other words, generate the maximum sales and profits for every dollar spent on marketing.

But for the marketing planner who is also the business owner, there is an added dimension to the planning process: vision. By this, we mean creating a marketing plan that not only maximizes ROMD, but also delivers the lifestyle the solopreneur or owner wants to get from her business.

To create a marketing plan that enables you to live this lifestyle, you need a clear vision of what your ideal lifestyle would be. For instance, I am a workaholic who puts in 12-hour days and has a relatively large work output. But I have colleagues in the businesses I am in—freelance copywriting and information products—for whom working only a few hours each day is paramount. Naturally, our businesses look wildly different, with our marketing plans tailored to achieving our goals and vision.

When I was a corporate marketing manager, my marketing plans were written strictly to maximize my employer's ROMD. But if you own outright or are a partner or shareholder in a small business, you are writing a marketing plan that not only achieves the company's goal but your personal vision of how you want to live your life. There are also many bigger companies that integrate a vision or mission statement into a marketing plan designed to make the vision a reality.

What Is Your Vision?

Too many business owners and managers have no clue about which way to go next. Are you one of them?

If so, what you need is a clear picture of your destination. You need a vision. Your vision—or in the parlance of corporate America, your "mission statement"—declares where your business is headed and what it will look like when it has arrived.

A mission statement tells you what success (for you) looks like. How else will you know when you've achieved it? Your marketing plan refocuses everything you do in your business into a series of planned, coordinated actions to create your vision.

Why are goals important? You've heard the old saying: "If you don't know where you're going, you'll never get there." This is true for travel, for life, and in business. People say, "I want a business in which I make a lot of money," but they can't tell you what "a lot of money" is and have no specific income goal. They say, "I want to be successful in business," but when you ask them exactly what that means, they can't say.

The conventional definition of business success is money and size: how much money you earn per year, the gross annual sales of the business, number of employees, number of customers served, number of locations, and the net worth of the owner. But is that really accurate? Does it work for you? Or are your values different?

There is no right or wrong answer. Choose what works for you, and then design a marketing plan that enables your business to deliver both the income and the lifestyle you seek from it.

Design Your Business to Deliver the Lifestyle You Seek

The ideal business is one that delivers the income and lifestyle you desire, while enabling you to attain it doing work you enjoy and find both meaningful and satisfying, with and for people you care about.

Many businesspeople spend their days doing work they either actively dislike or do not care about so that they can own a big home or drive a luxury car. But during the workweek, you spend more than half your waking hours working. True happiness comes from being happy both at work and in the life you enjoy from the fruits of your labors.

To write a marketing plan for your business that enables you to achieve optimum reward both at work and at home, you need to visualize what you want in both venues. At work, do you want to be part of a team of bright, creative, enthusiastic professionals? Or do you dream of spending the day alone at your PC, in quiet and solitude, writing programs or balancing numbers on spreadsheets? At home, is it important that you are the envy of your friends and neighbors for your obvious wealth, living in the biggest, fanciest home on the block, or driving the most expensive cars? Do you desire with all your being to dine in five-star restaurants and join the best clubs? Or is your idea of happiness grilling franks and hamburgers with neighbors in your backyard? Think about your ideal day. What does it look like? How would you envision your tasks, your overall productivity? Taking some time to map that concept out can be worthwhile to your venture in the long run.

Does this exercise of writing down your ideal day pay any dividends, or is it just theoretical, touchy-feely nonsense? When I did it, I was skeptical, as I have never been a fan of self-talk or journaling. Just the act of doing this small bit of planning energized me, and that's another advantage creating a marketing plan for your business can give you: the act alone of thinking about your marketing and putting your thoughts down on paper can get you excited and enthusiastic about going out there and promoting your product or service to the hilt.

Even better for me, somehow the goals contained within my ideal day description implanted themselves in my brain. Not everything in my ideal-day essay has come true, but I have moved toward it in several significant directions. A couple of years ago, I started an internet marketing business that generates a six-figure income and gives me significantly greater financial freedom than I had as a freelance writer. With the profits, we bought a weekend home with a dock on a beautiful lake in northwestern New Jersey, making the dream of living on the water come partially true.

> The key to happiness is to figure out your ideal lifestyle and design a business that enables you to live that lifestyle, or as close to it as you can get.

My personal definition of success is *a business that allows me to do what I want to do, when I want to do it—and conversely, avoid the things I don't like to do—and get paid very, very well for it.*

The key to happiness, in my view, is to figure out your ideal lifestyle and design a business that enables you to live that lifestyle, or as close to it as you can get. That includes both what you do to earn a living and how you spend your time outside of work.

Begin with the End in Mind

In the book *Counterintuitive Marketing,* authors Kevin Clancy and Peter Krieg define a vision as "a dream" and write that a "powerful vision looks outward. . . . [it] expresses *the end.*" Visions speak to our most passionate, deeply felt reasons for why we do what we do.

Your vision is your mental "big picture" of what your business can become. It clarifies your direction and presents clearly what the business is striving to become. In the process, it should instill a sense of purpose in everyone within your business. If it doesn't, either the vision is not vivid enough or you have failed to express it clearly and passionately enough.

Paint a Picture of the Possible

Let's look briefly at what you need to create a powerful vision statement:

- *Paint a picture of the possible.* Paint your vision powerfully. Shakespeare wrote, "In dreams begin our possibilities." Ask yourself, "If I could create my business to be anything (and you can), what would it look like? When I dream about this business, what do I see? Why am I so passionate about this business?" Answer these questions in as much detail as you can, and then write it down.

- *Describe your vision as if it has already come true.* Write it in the present tense. Describe what you see as you look around. How does it feel? You're developing a mental picture of your business as a success, so make it as vivid as possible. Describe whom you see, the sounds and smells around you, and the colors you're experiencing. What are you thinking? What words capture this experience for you? Are you working alone? If not, describe the people who surround you. How has your company contributed to society or your local community? Have you tackled and changed a particular problem in your industry or community?

- *Search yourself to gain an understanding of your main values.* In corporate language, these are called your "core values." Your vision should not only inspire you, but it must stretch you beyond your comfort zone as well. If necessary, rewrite your vision statement to ensure that it is consistent with these values.

♦ *Communicate your vision to everyone involved in growing your business.* Do it in a manner that inspires people and builds their commitment to the goals of the vision. As they share in the vision, it will evolve from something that is just your vision to "our vision."

♦ *Realize that your vision isn't cast in stone.* Expect it to evolve as your business evolves.

Why is a vision important for a small or solo professional business? Because it forces you to really know your ambitions for your business. A vision cannot be vague. It declares the outcomes you expect and becomes a guiding light that will lead your business forward. So make sure your vision statement clearly states the outcomes you intend to create.

The more vivid your experience, the greater permission you give your subconscious to dream big on your behalf. Webster defines a dream as "something that fully satisfies." Is your vision fully satisfying? It will be your secret weapon on those days when you feel frustrated or are sure you can't go any further with this business.

Here are a few examples of actual vision statements:

♦ *Microsoft (original)*: "A personal computer in every home running Microsoft software."

♦ *eBay*: "To provide a global trading platform where practically anyone can trade practically anything."

♦ *North Point Church*: "To create a church that unchurched people love to attend."

♦ *Canadian Cancer Society*: "Creating a world where no Canadian fears cancer."

♦ *Amazon*: "To be Earth's most customer-centric company; to build a place where people can come to find and discover anything they might want to buy online."

♦ *EABS Bank*: "A bank account for every Kenyan."

- *Milwaukee Public Library*: "Every person's gateway to an expanding world of information. Providing the best in library service, we guide Milwaukeeans in their pursuit of knowledge, enjoyment, and lifelong learning, ultimately enriching lives and our community as a whole."
- *Sunset Playhouse*: "[To be] the distinction between community and professional theater and . . . the region's destination for experiences of artistic excellence, whether traditional in nature or daring and innovative in choice."
- *Bowling Inc.*: "More people, bowling more often, having more fun."
- *American Red Cross*: "We are the pacesetter and benchmark for excellence in nonprofit management and human service delivery for charitable organizations around the world."
- *Chiropractic Marketing Plans Inc. (our fictional company)*: "To be the planning resource chiropractors in Southern California think of first when looking for tools to grow their practice, because they know we know their industry even better than they do."

Use a Vision Board to Make It Clearer

If you're still having problems, try creating a "vision board." Gather about a dozen magazines that you don't mind ripping apart. Now, go through the magazines looking for pictures and words that speak to you. Don't overanalyze this. If it speaks to you, rip it out and set it aside. (And if you don't feel like going old school, create a Pinterest vision board.) Remember, our subconscious minds work in images, so all you're doing here is working with something that comes naturally to your built-in problem-solving processes. Give yourself about a half-hour to do this exercise.

The reason to do this exercise is that seeing images is an aid to helping us visualize everything about our ideal business, including the lifestyle it will allow us to live and the customers we want to serve. If being able to drive a luxury car is important to you, find a

picture of the car you want to own in a magazine and pin it on your vision board.

Bestselling author Sam Sinclair Baker used this technique to help visualize the audience he was writing for. He would find several pictures in magazines that he felt were representative of who his readers would be. He would then clip these and tape them to the edges of his PC monitor, so he would always be looking at them when he typed. In that way, he was better able to simulate having a conversation with them, and indeed, he was known for his conversational style of writing.

Now, place the images and words you ripped out in front of you. Using a poster board, take the words and images that speak most strongly to you and arrange them on the board. As you move the images around, something will begin to feel right to you. When this happens, you know you have placed the images where they should be.

Step back and look at what you have created. Write down any words, thoughts, and emotions that occur to you as you look at the images you created. Certain words will begin to recur as you work through this process. Include them in your vision statement.

Write your vision statement here:

_____

_____

_____

Remember, it's not etched in stone. You'll review it monthly, and tweak it when it makes sense. Post your vision board someplace where you'll see it daily. As your vision evolves or your goals change, update your vision board.

Let Your Vision Protect You from Making Bad Decisions

How does having a vision statement help you in day-to-day operations? It creates an easy test: Does this action move us closer to our vision of what we're trying to become? Yes? Then do it. No? Then don't.

This applies to decisions about clients; investments in equipment and real estate; whom you network with; organizations you may join; PR and marketing; new services you consider adding; new niches you consider serving; conferences, workshops, and boot camps you

Crafting Your Unique Selling Proposition (USP)

In 1961, Rosser Reeves published his classic book *Reality in Advertising,* in which he introduced the notion of the unique selling proposition, or USP. Today, the book is out of print and difficult to get. As a result, most businesspeople don't know the original definition of a USP. Their lack of knowledge often produces USPs that are weak and ineffective.

According to Reeves, there are three requirements for a USP (and I am quoting, in the italics, from *Reality in Advertising* directly):

1. *Each advertisement must make a proposition to the consumer. Each must say, "Buy this product, and you will get this specific benefit."* Your headline must contain a benefit—a promise to the reader.

2. *The proposition must be one that the competition either cannot, or does not, offer.* Here's where the "unique" in unique selling proposition comes in. It is not enough merely to offer a benefit. You must also *differentiate* your product.

3. *The proposition must be so strong that it can move the mass millions (i.e., pull over new customers to your product).* The differentiation cannot be trivial. It must be a difference that is very important to the reader.

Why do so many small businesses struggle and so many advertisements fail? One reason is that the marketers have not formulated a strong USP for their product and built their advertising upon it. Formulating a USP isn't difficult, but it takes some thinking, and many people don't like to think. When you start creating advertising without first thinking about what your USP is, your marketing is weak because there is nothing in it to compel the reader to respond. It looks and sounds like everyone else's, and what it says isn't important to the reader.

In general, big companies achieve differentiation by building a strong brand at a cost of millions or even billions of dollars. Coca-Cola has an advantage because of its brand: If you want a cola, you can get it from a dozen soda makers, but if you want a Coke, you can only get it from Coca-Cola. Intel has achieved a similar brand dominance, at an extraordinary cost, with its line of semiconductors.

Most entrepreneurs are too small—and have too strong a need to generate an immediate positive ROI from their marketing—to engage in this kind of expensive brand building. So we use other means to achieve the differentiation in our USP.

One popular method is to differentiate your product or service from the competition based on a feature that your product or service has that they don't. Here is an example: "M&M's melt in your mouth, not in your hand." Once M&M's established this claim as their USP, what could the competition do? Run an ad that said, "We *also* melt in your mouth, not in your hand"?

As small businesses, we are compelled to create advertising that generates net revenues in excess of its cost. Reeves believed all advertising had to do this. He defined advertising as "the art of getting a USP into the heads of the most people at the lowest possible cost." If I were to modify his definition, I would change it to "getting a USP into the heads of the people *most likely to buy the product,* at the lowest possible advertising cost." But who am I to quibble with the master?

may attend; business books you may read; courses you might take; degrees or certifications you could pursue; and new skills you want to develop—literally, every aspect of the business. Let your vision guide you.

Action . . .

Write Your Vision Statement

It's time to create your own vision statement. Don't worry about trying to make it perfect. What's important at this point is to begin the conversation with yourself about the business you're trying to create. Do this no matter how long you've been in business.

Begin with a clean sheet of paper. Imagine your business three to five years in the future, and answer the following questions.

- ◆ What service(s) do you perform? What products do you sell?

- ◆ For whom? (What types of clients? If you have specific clients in mind, list them.)

- ◆ Where is your business located? Do you work at home or in an office? Describe everything.

- ◆ You've just met yourself on the job. What do you do in the business? Are you an owner or a hands-on employee? Do you render the actual service clients buy or hire employees to do that while you manage and master-mind your business? What is your life like? What about your life makes you happy?

- ◆ How much do you and the business earn? (The amounts won't be the same.)

- ◆ Do you have employees? If so, how many? What do they do? What value do they add to the business? What skills and training do they have? Be as specific as possible.

Action . . ., continued

- What does this business look like when you sell it or turn it over to relatives?

- What does this business do better than any other? What are you known for? What makes you unique or different from your competitors? What is your unique selling proposition (see the sidebar on page 9)?

- How do you feel about this business? What inspires you about this business?

- What are the four or five keywords you use when describing your business to others? What are the words your clients use when describing what you do for them to others?

Now, pull out the strongest words in your descriptions. Look for those words that trigger emotions for you. What jumps out for you? What words generate anticipation and passion when you read them on the paper? These words inspire you, and they belong in your vision statement. Your words should reference the type of client you serve, the service you provide, and the geographic coverage of your service.

Chapter 2
DECIDE WHAT BUSINESS YOU'RE IN

Now that you've painted a vision for your business, it's time to clarify what business you're in. But what does that really mean? It means defining exactly who you are, what you do for people, your primary product or service, and your business's key streams of income. The first thing you need to do is solidify your elevator pitch.

Crafting Your Elevator Pitch

An elevator pitch is a 30-second answer to the question, "What do you do?" You need an elevator pitch because the question "What do you do?" is usually asked by complete strangers in casual circumstances. In these situations, you do not have a captive audience watching you go through your PowerPoint sales presentation, so your answer must be pithy and to the point.

Why does it matter how you answer the question "What do you do?" when speaking to someone you don't know? Because you never know when the person you're speaking to is a potential customer or referral source.

> Most elevator pitches, unfortunately, don't work because they are straightforward descriptions of job functions and titles.

Most elevator pitches, unfortunately, don't work because they are straightforward descriptions of job functions and titles, generating not much else aside from disinterest and a few yawns. For example, a fellow I met at a party told me, "I am a certified financial planner with more than 20 years' experience working." OK. But who cares?

My friend, sales trainer Paul Karasik, has an antidote to the deadly dull elevator pitch. Karasik's three-part formula can enable you to quickly construct the perfect elevator pitch. By "perfect," I mean an elevator pitch that concisely communicates the value your product or service offers in a manner that engages, rather than bores, the other person.

What is the formula? The first part is to ask a question beginning with the words "Do you know?" The question identifies the pain or need that your product or service addresses. For a financial planner who, say, works mostly with middle-aged women who are separated, divorced, or widowed, and possibly re-entering the workplace, this question might be, "Do you know how when women get divorced or re-enter the workforce after many years of depending on a spouse, they are overwhelmed by all the financial decisions they have to make?"

The second part of the formula is a statement that begins with the words "What I do" or "What we do," followed by a clear description of the service you deliver. Continuing with our financial planner, she might say, "What we do is help women gain control of their finances and achieve their personal financial and investment goals."

The third part of the formula presents a big benefit and begins "so that." Here's what the whole thing sounds like: "Do you know how when women get divorced or re-enter the workforce after many years of depending on a spouse, they are overwhelmed by all the financial decisions they have to make? What we do is help women gain control of their finances and achieve their personal financial and investment goals, *so that* they can stay in the house they have lived in all their lives, have enough income to enjoy a comfortable lifestyle, and be free of money worries."

You can construct your elevator pitch today using Paul Karasik's three-part formula:

1. *First part.* Ask a question beginning with the words "Do you know?" that identifies the pain or need that your product or service addresses.
2. *Second part.* Describe your service, beginning with the words "What I do" or "What we do."
3. *Third part.* Explain why your service is valuable by describing the benefits it delivers, beginning with the words "so that."

Choosing Your Niche

Customers today want to hire specialists, not generalists. And specialists are people who serve a narrow, targeted niche that is a segment of a larger field. If you do not already have a niche within the broader market you serve, ask yourself these questions:

> Customers today want to hire specialists, not generalists.

- ◆ What do I like?
- ◆ What am I interested in?
- ◆ What am I good at?
- ◆ What do I have an aptitude for?
- ◆ What is my education?
- ◆ What do I know?
- ◆ What is my experience?
- ◆ What have I accomplished?
- ◆ Which of the above areas had the least competition?
- ◆ Which of the above areas pays high rates?

Your answers will help you identify either a niche market you want to service or a niche skill you want to offer.

Another way to select a niche is to start as a generalist. After 6 or 12 months, look at the work you have done and your customer base.

Was there any area in which you had a lot of sales? For instance, one photographer I knew started as a generalist, but after a year, opened his portfolio and realized he had done a huge amount of industrial photography, which he decided to make his main niche. It worked because when he called on potential clients in manufacturing companies, he had a portfolio full of beautiful industrial shots to show them.

One question that comes up is, "Must I stick to only one niche, or can I have multiple niches?" Author Dan Poynter suggests three or four niches is probably the maximum. His niches are parachuting, self-publishing, how to make money as an expert witness, and taking care of older cats.

More than three or four niches and you begin to spread yourself too thin; you can't be all things to all people. I recommend, for most service professionals, three niches, plus taking on other work outside them if it is offered (but not pursuing it).

Creating a Business to Fulfill Your Vision

Your *vision* might include helping everyone in your town who has back pain feel better, but then you have to decide whether you will open a chiropractic center, teach courses on managing pain, or invent a back brace to do it. You still have to define your business.

> Unless your product is money, realize only a limited number of people will want to purchase what you offer, no matter what it is.

Who are your clients and prospects? Who will buy from you? Who is the right match for the particular expertise that you and your company offer? Everyone? Think again. Unless your product is money, realize only a limited number of people will want to purchase what you offer, no matter what it is. To prosper, you must figure out who those people are, what their need is, and whether you can offer a clear advantage to them while meeting that need. Many small businesses thrive by serving profitable market segments that larger companies ignore. This is known as *niche marketing.*

Defining and Fine-Tuning Your Niche

Your niche describes the service you perform, for whom you perform it, and the results they can expect.

For example, our fictional company, Chiropractic Marketing Plans Inc. (CMP) serves the following niche:

"We develop marketing plans for chiropractors located in our state so they know how to refocus their actions and resources on the clients most likely to help them achieve their vision for their business."

Why is it advantageous to find a niche rather than be a generalist? It's simple. Today, there is more competition in almost everything. That means consumers have more choices than ever, which is good for them, but bad for you. With more suppliers offering similar products and services, the consumer is in control. In addition, the internet makes it easier for consumers to price shop, as well as giving companies the ability to outsource to India or other nations where cheap labor makes it impossible for American vendors to match their price. Bidding sites such as Elance and Fiverr put further downward pressure on prices for writing, graphic design, voice-overs, and related work.

> The more products or service providers available in your category, the more of a commodity your product or service becomes.

The more products or service providers available in your category, the more of a commodity your product or service becomes. When you are selling a commodity, competition is mainly on price, which is a terrible position to be in. Lowering your price means lowering your profit margin until it is no longer worth your while to continue providing the product or service.

The solution is either to offer a product or service that is not widely available (difficult) or to specialize in providing a more common product or service tailored to a specific niche market (easier).

Grow Rich in Your Niche

Why is it important to have a niche?

◆ It's easier to specialize.

◆ You'll have less competition.

◆ You can perfect your expertise.

◆ You can more easily become recognized as the expert in your field.

◆ You'll have loyal clients because your service is tailored to their needs.

◆ You can focus your time and resources on the area where you're most likely to succeed.

As a small business, you don't have the kinds of resources the big players can rely on. They tend to ignore niche markets because they see the returns as too low, but the same $10 million market that's not worth their while can be gold for you. Equally important, once you decide what niche you'll serve, you can stop wasting your resources pursuing clients that don't make sense for your focus.

The groups you target can be consumers, businesses, nonprofits, affinity groups (groups of consumers with shared interests), or governments, but a good niche market has a few basic qualities:

◆ It's easily defined and accessible.

◆ There are good lists, media, exhibitions, and other channels for contacting prospects.

◆ Its members can afford your product or service.

◆ It's being ignored by most of your competitors.

◆ It has a need you can meet while offering a clear advantage.

◆ Its members are passionate about the service you provide.

For example, if you want to make money in advertising as an entrepreneur, an obvious way is to open a small ad agency. And because the startup costs are small, many marketing-minded entrepreneurs of decades past did just that. Some of them made nice livings. A few got rich. Many others scraped by. As time went on, there were too many tiny ad agencies competing for the same clients, with none offering a distinct advantage or having a clear USP.

When one ad agency competes against another, they typically say they are more creative or their advertising gets better results. But rarely can they document and prove the "better results" claim. And "more creative" is subjective. Worse, since every small ad agency made these same claims, it gave them no competitive advantage in selling their services, and in fact made them all look alike.

As the ad agency industry evolved, specialized ad agencies began to evolve as well. One ad agency would specialize in medical advertising. Another would handle only high-tech clients. For a time, this gave these specialized ad agencies a strong competitive position. After all, if you were a medical device manufacturer, all else being equal, would you pick a general ad agency or a medical ad agency with a huge portfolio of successful ad campaigns for medical devices?

> Niche marketing, or market segmentation, divides markets into groups based on similar buying habits or a geographic area.

What happens, of course, is that competitors see your success in the niche you have picked and decide to move in. The number of medical ad agencies grows, and your competitive advantage begins to evaporate. A solution is to "micro-niche." That means specializing in a small area within a niche market. Niche marketing, or market segmentation, divides markets into groups based on similar buying habits or a geographic area. It means focusing on a group of clients who buy similar services to meet similar needs in similar ways. For example, in defining a niche for your medical billing services, you could begin narrowing your focus in this manner:

◆ Doctors are a market.
◆ Doctors who take care of babies—pediatricians—are a niche market.

- ◆ Pediatricians in Southern California are a smaller, more narrowly focused niche.
- ◆ Pediatricians practicing in Los Angeles County are an even smaller, more focused niche.

You might further define the pediatricians you want to focus on by a few zip codes within Los Angeles County, the size of their practice, hospitals they're affiliated with, the insurance they accept, or other factors.

Let's say you're trying to identify a niche for your service that helps women with children start their own businesses:

- ◆ Women 18 to 35 with children are a market.
- ◆ Women 18 to 35 with children under age 6 are a niche market.
- ◆ Women 18 to 35 with children under age 6 and earn $50,000 or more per year are a smaller niche market.

Similarly, depending on the needs you have identified and how well your service meets them, you might want to refine this niche further.

Why Is This a Good Niche for Us?

How do you know what niche is right for you? A great niche matches your knowledge, skills, and passion with the needs or wants of a narrowly defined group. How can you find a niche that is right for you?

1. *Start at the beginning—with your mission.* Your mission statement answers the question, "Why does my company exist?" The best niches are consistent with your mission and your values. Ask yourself, "What do I do well?" and "What do I really enjoy?" There's no sense in growing a business you're not going to enjoy. Then consider your vision. Your vision statement answers the question, "What do I want my company to become?" Now you can begin the search for the type of clients who can use your expertise.

2. *Research.* Where do you begin? Here are some questions to help you narrow your focus:

- Do I have expertise in a particular industry?
- Do I have specialized knowledge or education?
- What is my professional experience?
- Am I an expert in performing a specific task?
- What interests me?
- What do I have an aptitude for?
- What do I enjoy doing and learning?
- What is the most common problem the people I usually work with (or want to work with) have? Is any business addressing this problem well? Is there some expertise I can bring to it that others are not?
- If their most common problem is being addressed well by others, what other challenges or opportunities do they have that no one seems to be addressing well?

The internet offers several great tools for researching niches. Remember, you want people who are interested in what you want to offer. Keyword selection services, such as the Google keyword research tool or WordTracker, that let you get search totals for topics you type in. If you're clueless about what you want to focus on, go to any of these sites and, one at a time, type in the words "learn," "teach," "guide," "how to," "tutorial," "want," "buy," "purchase," and "problem." You'll gain lots of insight into what people want to buy or learn more about.

You can also go to www.meetup.com, where you'll find a group for people with just about any interest under the sun. The topics page breaks down the meetups by categories, popularity, and growing popularity You can attend the meetups and learn more as a member. Most of these meetups are either free or cost a nominal sum to attend.

Yahoo! Groups and Google Groups also have scores of online groups meeting and sharing information with one another. Focus on groups that are active—they have activity level ratings—to get the best insights. One is sure to provide knowledge about the challenges facing members in the niche you're considering.

Here's one more niche research tip: Look at the niche businesses and niche markets that are successful in your field. Is there an adjacent area of interest or related niche that is close but not identical to theirs? You can pick that niche as your own, then emulate the business model they use. If it works in their niche, most likely some modified version will work in yours.

3. *Identify the largest and most profitable of the underserved segments.* For a market to become a viable niche for you, you must be able to make a profit while serving it. Decide which of the segments you identified appeals to you based on your stated mission and vision. Find out how much competition you would face serving this market. If there are too many competitors, you might have a difficult time breaking in unless you offer something that prospects will identify as a *valuable* advantage. Study the niche to determine whether it's potentially profitable.

Ask yourself:

◆ What's the size of the market?
◆ Do these people spend money on the products or services I offer?
◆ What is their biggest problem I could help them with?
◆ Is there an urgency to solving this problem?
◆ What's our potential? (Do you have a realistic chance to generate enough sales in this niche to meet your financial goals?)
◆ What are the trends in this industry or niche? (Is this a growing or a shrinking market? Is this a niche you'll be able to succeed in for several years, or is this likely to be a short-lived but profitable trend?)
◆ What are the keys to succeeding in this niche? (Can you master these?)
◆ Is this niche growing, shrinking, or static?
◆ Are there trends or technologies that could eliminate the need for your product or service among these prospects?

Before starting her business, Chandra Martin Perez, the owner of our model company Chiropractic Marketing Plans Inc. (CMP), knew she wanted to specialize in marketing plans for health-care professionals. But that focus would have created tens of thousands of businesses she could market to. She knew her time and resources would be best served by limiting the business's scope. This is how she narrowed it:

Niche	Establishments	Payroll
Health care establishments	746,000	$590 billion
Health care establishments in California	104,640	$94.77 billion
Health care establishments in Los Angeles County	26,853	$17.5 billion
Chiropractors in Los Angeles County (621310 NAICS code)	1,091	$74 million
Chiropractic Very Small Businesses—VSBs (one- to four-person offices) in Los Angeles County	882	~ $59 million
Chiropractors within 10 miles of her office	169	N/A
Chiropractic VSBs (one- to four-person offices) within 10 miles of her office	143	~$9 million

Source: American FactFinder, 2013 County Business (NAICS)

As you can see, you can get very specific with your niche. Perez chose to focus the first four years of CMP's efforts on one- to four-person chiropractic offices located within 10 miles of her office. Marketing to less than 150 businesses, she still surpassed her revenue and profit goals.

Now it's time to identify your own niche.

Action . . .

Describe Your Niche

Write a description of your niche. The following formula can help:

I (We) _____ for _____

         (describe the service you perform)   (describe the group you perform your services for)

so they _____.

                     (describe the results they can expect)

Describe your niche here:

_____

_____

_____

_____

_____

_____

_____

_____

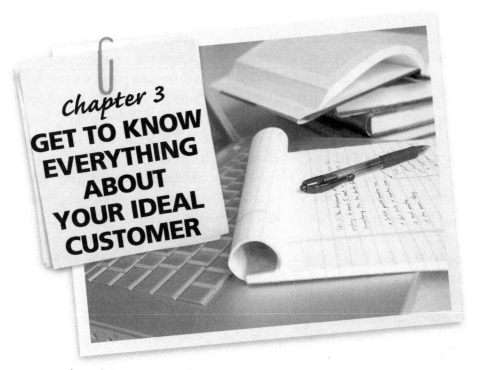

chapter 3
GET TO KNOW EVERYTHING ABOUT YOUR IDEAL CUSTOMER

In the last chapter, you identified your most promising niche. The people and businesses in that niche are your ideal prospects and clients. But how much do you know about your ideal client? And why does this matter? It matters because meeting your clients' needs better than your competitors do will always be your first job as a business—if you intend to be a successful business.

The closer you are to your market, and the more you understand them, the easier it is to quickly build a stronger relationship with them. Prospects are people who have identified themselves as potential customers through some action (e.g., subscribing to your enewsletter or requesting your catalog), but have not actually made a purchase. These prospects are obtained by marketing to audiences, through various media and mailing lists, who fit the description of your target market, but who don't know you yet. We can call the people in this vast prospecting universe "suspects."

For example, if you are a chiropractor specializing in relieving back pain, everyone in your town may be a potential patient, but you don't know whom to target, since you don't know who has back pain and who does not. These are your suspects. Now, you run an ad in the local weekly newspaper advertising a free seminar for Tuesday evening on relieving back pain. That Tuesday, 32 people show up. Unless you are serving a free lobster dinner, only people who have back pain or know someone who has it will come. Therefore, your marketing has successfully completed the first step in the sales process: converting suspects to prospects.

A customer is someone who buys the product now from you. Some business writers separate these buyers into two groups. Users are people who buy the product but are not passionate about it; they are often impulse buyers. Customers are those who buy the product after a deliberate consideration of its benefits; they make what are called "considered purchases," meaning they have considered the buying decision carefully. Beyond customers are buyers so satisfied with your product or service that they proactively recommend it to others; these are called "advocates." Figure 3–1 illustrates this hierarchy of customers.

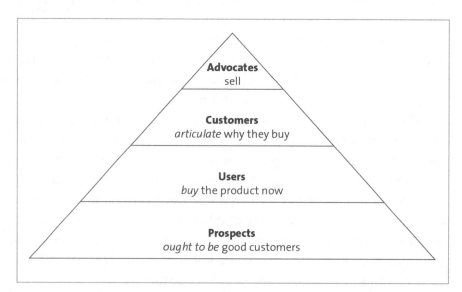

FIGURE 3–1. **Hierarchy of Customers**

Qualifying Prospects

What's the number-one selling mistake that causes entrepreneurs, executives, salespeople, and professionals to spin their wheels, waste their time chasing after people who don't want to buy, and experience enormous frustration when following up leads?

It's failure to determine whether the person or "suspect" making the inquiry is a genuine, qualified prospect or just someone who likes collecting brochures and wasting salespeople's time. But how can you quickly, easily, and accurately determine whether a lead is a qualified prospect? By using my "MAD FU" formula.

The MAD FU formula has nothing to do with anger, or any other emotion, or the "F" word. Rather, MAD FU stands for the five qualities that differentiate a qualified prospect from a time-waster or tire-kicker: *money, authority, desire, fit,* and *urgency.*

> MAD FU stands for the five qualities that differentiate a qualified prospect from a time-waster or tire-kicker: *money, authority, desire, fit,* and *urgency.*

MAD FU says that to qualify a lead, you have to ask them questions. These questions determine whether they have the money to afford what you are selling, the authority to buy it, and a strong desire to own it. In addition, are they a good fit for your business, and do they have a sense of urgency?

Let's look at how to quickly assess all five factors. First, money: Can the prospect afford what you are selling? The easiest way to determine this is to ask, "Do you have a budget for this?" Without a budget, how can they possibly buy your product or service? If they say they do have a budget, ask, "Would you mind sharing with me what your budget is?" Their answer tells you whether they can afford you or not.

Second, authority: Can the person you are talking to write a check or purchase order?

You can determine this by asking, "Who else in your organization is responsible for making this purchase decision?"

The third factor is desire. How intense is their desire to own your product or get your service? How important is it for them to take care of the problem your product would solve for them (e.g., reduce energy costs, control inventory, etc.)? You can gauge their desire through the content of your conversation with them as well as tone and body language. The best prospects have a burning desire to own your product or have you solve their problem.

The fourth factor for qualifying prospects is fit. Is this person a good fit for your business? Is there good personal chemistry between you and them? Does your product or service best meet their needs, or would they be better off using another vendor?

The fifth and final factor is urgency: What is the prospect's time frame for taking possession of this product or having this service performed? The more the prospect is in a hurry, the easier the deal will be to close. But if the prospect has no sense of urgency, you may spin your wheels for months—even years—chasing after her.

The lesson? When your marketing generates a phone call or email inquiry from a potential customer, don't get too excited. Instead,

Seven Questions to Ask about Your Target Market

1. How much income do your customers make?

2. Where are they located?

3. Are they male or female, or a mix?

4. How old are they?

5. What is their level of education?

6. What jobs do they hold?

7. What do they physically look like?

Source: Talon Newsletter, 5/15, p. 3

immediately qualify the lead with MAD FU. Does the person have the money, authority, and desire to buy? Are they a good fit? Is their need immediate? The more "yes" answers you get to the MAD FU questions, the better your chances of making the sale.

Create a Customer Database

One of the marketing tasks you face is to create a list or database of your customers. A database stores all your customer and prospect records on your computer. Each record contains basic information, including customer name, address, city, state, zip, phone number, and email address.

The more information you have in each record, the more useful your database is as a marketing tool. For example, say you sell gourmet condiments. In the customer file, you can indicate which type of condiment each customer has bought (e.g., relish, hot sauce), the dollar amount of the purchase, and the date. Now, when you get a new brand of hot sauce you think is terrific, you can send a postcard

> One of the marketing tasks you face is to create a list or database of your customers.

announcing the new hot sauce just to customers who bought hot sauce from you within, say, the past 24 months.

Why do we want customers who have previously bought hot sauce instead of all customers? After all, someone who buys other condiments may buy hot sauce in the future. And why only customers who have made a recent purchase of hot sauce? The answer is contained in a direct marketing principle called RFM, which stands for *recency, frequency,* and *monetary.*

The first element, recency, refers to how recently the person made a purchase through direct response. According to RFM, those who purchased the most recently are most likely to buy.

This is why it's usually worth paying a premium to rent the "hotline" names on any mailing list—the names of customers who have bought via mail order within the last 12 months or so. The hotline names invariably outperform the other names on the list, because of recency.

The "F" in RFM is frequency—how often the customer buys. Here, we know that the more often someone buys, the more responsive they are to additional offers. This is why some mailing lists offer a selection called "multibuyers" for customers who have bought more than once. Invariably, multibuyers outperform one-time buyers on the list.

The "M" in RFM is monetary—how much money the customer spends, or the size of their average order. Here, you want to look for mailing lists where the average order is in the same range as your product's price.

Let's say you are selling a video program called *Overcoming Infertility: How to Have a Child When You've Been Trying Without Success*. The price is $79. You rent a list of people who have subscribed to an infertility magazine for $12. You mail to the list, and the mailing doesn't pull. Why not?

The problem is this: While the people on the list have demonstrated: a) an interest in infertility and b) that they buy information by mail, they have *not* demonstrated that they will spend $79 to buy something by mail. Twelve dollars, yes; 79 dollars, no. The solution? Find a list of people who have, say, attended a workshop on infertility or bought a test kit via mail order for $50 or $100. This might work, because you know not only that the people on the list are mail-order buyers and interested in infertility, but they will shell out a large amount of money for the right offer.

Monetary and frequency make sense, but the principle of recency is counterintuitive. When I first got into direct marketing, I took a course in direct mail copywriting with legendary copywriter Milt Pierce at New York University. One day another student asked, "Professor Pierce, why is it that, as soon as I give a donation to a charity, they immediately send me another letter asking for more money?"

Milt replied, "Because they know, from experience, that the person who just made a donation is the one most likely to give again."

The student said, "But Professor Pierce, if I just gave money to a charity, then I would feel I'd fulfilled my obligation for at least a while. And I might even be annoyed that they are coming back to me asking for more."

"Nonetheless," Milt replied, "experience proves that the person who just gave is the most likely to give again." He explained that this phenomenon was called recency, that it held for commercial direct response as well as nonprofit, and that it was part of a formula called RFM.

Database Elements

To track RFM and other customer activity, you need to build a database. You can hire a programmer to write a custom database manager for your business, or choose from a variety of off-the-shelf programs (see Appendix D for a list). The data you minimally want in each customer record includes:

- Name
- Address
- City, state, zip
- Phone number
- Email address
- Gender (male/female)
- Birth date
- Recency: date of last purchase
- What they have bought
- Frequency: how often they buy
- Monetary: size of average order
- Source of order or inquiry: web, email, print ad, billboard, etc.
- Method of inquiry or payment: phone, email, PayPal, credit card

> You can hire a programmer to write a custom database manager for your business, or choose from a variety of off-the-shelf programs.

Your database can be stored and managed on either a stand-alone database management program or, more preferable, on an integrated online marketing software system, such as lshoppingcart.com or Infusionsoft.com. If you use a subscription-based web application, such as 1shoppingcart.com, you pay by the month to use the software but do not own it. Therefore, technically, if they went out of business tomorrow (unlikely), your database might be gone.

Climbing the Loyalty Ladder

When you build your database, you will input as much of this data as you have for your customers and prospects.

Murray Raphel has created a device called the "loyalty ladder" to separate the universe of potential buyers into levels. Let's look at this customer universe. A "suspect" is anyone on the planet who could conceivably buy your product, but they are so unqualified and also such a large group that they are excluded from the database (see Figure 3–2).

The next level is "prospects." These are suspects who have passed the MAD FU test and are good potential customers for your product. Once a prospect buys one of your products, he moves up the loyalty ladder into the customer category. A "customer" is someone who

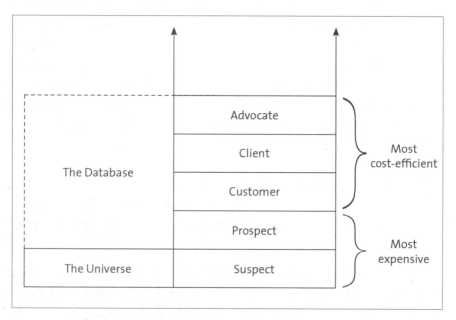

FIGURE 3–2. **The Loyalty Ladder**

may buy every now and then and likes you, but is not a raving fan of your products.

The "client" is the next step up the ladder from the customer. Not only do clients buy, but they are really loyal to your company and will go out of their way to buy from you rather than elsewhere.

At the top of the ladder is the "advocate." The advocate is a client who loves you and your business so much that she goes out of her way to recommend you to others as often as she can because she is a raving fan!

As a rule, the higher up someone is on your loyalty ladder, the more responsive they are to your marketing.

Data Modeling

In data modeling, you create a model of your ideal prospect or customer, then use that model to select similar prospects from the entire pool of available names. That way, you reduce costs and improve results by targeting only those prospects who are the most likely to respond.

The first step in data modeling is to take your customer file—those prospects that have bought from you—and add *firmographic* elements to them. Just as a demographic is a piece of data about a consumer (e.g., age), a firmographic is a piece of data about a business customer (e.g., number of employees). You can add firmographics by running your "house file" against a master database of B2B prospects, such as the ReachBase—see www.reachmarketing.com/b2b-prospecting-database.

> The first step in data modeling is to take your customer file—those prospects that have bought from you—and add *firmographic* elements to them.

Some of the firmographic elements you can add to your house file include:

- ◆ Total number of employees
- ◆ Employees at a given site

- ◆ Company revenues
- ◆ Year founded
- ◆ Industry
- ◆ Business size
- ◆ Zip code
- ◆ State
- ◆ Area code
- ◆ Whether the company is publicly traded

The second step is to analyze your house file by each of the firmographic elements and determine the firmographics of your best customers. Then you target your marketing at prospects who fit that firmographic profile. For example, if you are selling industrial equipment, you may discover that your best customers all have 100 or more employees or $50 million or more in revenues per location. You can then pull the records of all prospects that match these firmographics from commercially available databases of U.S. businesses.

With data modeling, you avoid wasting money on marketing to rented names who are not a good fit. You also increase response rates by mailing, emailing, or telemarketing only to those prospects who most closely fit your ideal customer profile.

The type of customer who buys from you may shift over time. Therefore, data models should be updated every 12 to 18 months to ensure continued accuracy.

Know Your Customers' "Core Buying Complex": The BDF Formula

Big corporations as well as many small and midsize businesses routinely spend thousands of dollars on expensive and elaborate market research studies designed to help them get inside the minds of their customers. These can include mail and online surveys, telephone interviews, and focus groups (see Table 3–1 on page 35).

Entrepreneurs running small businesses worry that if they don't do this kind of expensive market research, they won't know how

Type	Uses and Benefits
Telephone survey	Survey projectable sample to get a feel of where consumer attitudes currently stand.
Mail survey	Survey projectable sample by receiving large numbers of responses while holding down costs. Have 50+ respondents see ad prototypes or sample products to measure interest.
Online survey	Good for surveying your own opt-in house list of customers and prospects fairly quickly and inexpensively; I use www.surveymonkey.com.
Tracking study	Measures attitudes and awareness over time. Provides gradation of interest and readings on trends. Can be done by mail or phone.
Email survey	Used when speed is crucial.
Focus groups	Used when ideas and creative solutions are needed. Gives ability to observe and ask questions. Captures the language in which consumers discuss the product and application.
In-depth one-on-one interviews	Outreach for senior executives, doctors, and other hard-to-reach, high-level consumer audiences. Can uncover their personalities, motivations, and outside buying influences.
Ethnographies	Slides or videos of decision makers in their work or home environment.
Library and online secondary research	Get background information at minimal expense. Provides a foundation for new learning.

TABLE 3–1. **Key Market Research Methodologies** Source: Pranses Research

to reach their prospects and will fail miserably. But for many small companies, the cost of even one study from one of the big market research companies would wipe out their entire marketing budget for the year. Fortunately, there's a low-cost alternative to focus groups and other formal market research studies: the BDF formula. BDF stands for *beliefs, desires,* and *feelings.* The BDF formula says that you can understand your prospect by asking yourself three simple questions:

1. "What do my prospects believe? What are their attitudes?"
2. "What do my prospects desire? What do they want?"
3. "What do my prospects feel? What are their emotions?"

There's no market research required, because you already know these things about your prospects, or else you wouldn't have chosen to start a business that caters to them. Or to quote Dr. Benjamin Spock, "Trust yourself. You know more than you think you do."

For instance, a company that provides "soft skills" training to information technology (IT) professionals was promoting a new on-site seminar. They sent out a flier where the headline was the title of the program: "Interpersonal Skills for IT Professionals." It generated less than half a percent response. So the marketing manager and the owner brainstormed and asked themselves the BDF questions.

Here's part of what they came up with:

◆ IT professionals *believe* that technology is all important, and they are smarter than the nontechies they serve.
◆ IT professionals *desire* recognition, respect, continuing opportunities to update their skill sets in new technologies and platforms, job security, and more money.
◆ IT professionals *feel* an adversarial relationship with end users: They are constantly arguing with them, and they resent having to explain their technology to us ignoramuses.

Based on this BDF analysis, the company rewrote the letter and tested it. This time, it generated a 3 percent response, outperforming the old mailing 6 to 1. And one-third of those who responded purchased an on-site one-day training seminar for $3,000. That means for every 100 pieces mailed, at a total cost of about $100, they got three leads and one order for $3,000—a 30-to-1 return on their marketing investment.

The headline they came up with based on the BDF analysis: "Important News for Any IT Professional Who Has Ever Felt Like Telling an End User, 'Go to Hell.' " Says the company owner, "The BDF formula forced us to focus on the prospect instead of the product (our seminar), and the result was a winning promotion." Amount of money spent on market research before the mailing? Not a dime.

The great sales expert and motivational speaker, the late Zig Ziglar, said, "You can have anything in the world you want if you'll just help enough other people get what they want." But how can you help your clients and prospects get what they want if you don't know their needs and wants? Knowing your ideal client will help you determine what services to offer, when to offer them, how often, and how to price them. Who are the people that characterize your niche, and how will you find and recognize them? To answer this question, you need to develop demographic and psychographic profiles of the group.

> Who are the people that characterize your niche, and how will you find and recognize them?

What Do I Want to Know about My Ideal Client?

For most businesses, selling is a multistage process. You:

- ◆ Get leads on people or businesses that might be interested in your service.
- ◆ After qualifying those leads, nurture a connection with those prospects in which you learn more about their challenges and generate interest in your ability to solve them.
- ◆ Follow up. Follow up. Follow up.
- ◆ Make a presentation with an offer.
- ◆ Close the sale.
- ◆ Grow your relationship in an attempt to serve and sell to them again.

Ask yourself, "How do I appeal to my ideal client at each stage of the selling process?" (see the Selling Stages form in Appendix A). At every stage of the sales process, there's a dance going on between you and your prospect. Selling requires getting and staying in step with your client. To do that, you need to know your ideal client.

Demographic data answer the question, "Who are they?" You'll want to know information such as age, race, or ethnicity (because ethnic marketing might be profitable for your business), gender, education, marital status, occupation, and income.

Psychographic data answer the question, "What do they want?" Psychographics are psychological elements that might impact customers' purchasing decisions, such as personality, values, lifestyle, attitudes, interests, and opinions. Taken together, demographics and psychographics offer insight into your clients' hopes, fears, needs, desires and aspirations, and how they might govern their purchasing behavior.

Questions that might affect how you sell to your niche clients include:

- Are the clients you want to serve international, national, regional, or local in scope?
- What percentage of the decision makers are male? Female?
- What's their average age? Generally, what generation do they belong to? Are they Seniors, Boomers, Gen-Xers, Gen-Yers (see Table 3–2 on page 39)?
- What's their average educational attainment?
- What do they have in common?
- How do they differ?
- How do they get their information?
- To what social class do they belong? To what social class do they want to belong?
- Are they conservative, liberal, or independent thinkers?
- Are they environmentalists?
- Are they healthy, active, sports-minded people?
- What are their purchasing habits? How do they decide what to buy? Who decides? How many people influence the decision?
- How large are their expenditures? How often do they buy?
- Have they used a service similar to yours before, or will you need to educate them?

Generation and Years of Birth	Primary Behavioral Traits
Traditionalists or Matures (1922–1945)	Extremely loyal
	Expects respect and gives respect to those in power and authority
	Follows leaders and conforms to tradition
	Believes that rewards should be given based on length of service
	Believes a person's word is his or her bond
Baby Boomers (1946–1964)	Expects loyalty
	Hard-working and willing to go the extra mile
	Wants customized products and services
	Does not like conflict
	Personal growth and individuality are priorities
Generation X (1965–1980)	Skeptical, detached, and cynical
	Seeks work-life balance
	Independent minded
	Casual and laid-back
	Strong dislike for corporate politics
Millennials or Generation Y (1981–2000)	Values relationships and teams over the organization
	Desires open, authentic, constant, and timely information
	Seeks mentors who will guide and appreciate them
	Technology savvy
	Financially astute and saves money

TABLE 3–2. **Behavioral Characteristics of Consumers by Generation**
Source: Deanne DeMarco, Generation Gaps, Parkside Publishing, 2014.

The guidelines in Table 3–2 can help inform your marketing efforts, telling you what your prospects value, what is important to them, and their patterns of behavior.

If your clients are businesses, you'll also want to know details about their companies:

- What business are they in?
- How large is the business? Is it homebased?
- Who are their best clients?
- What is the company's niche, or what is it known for?
- What are its sales?
- Where is it located?
- How many locations does it have?
- How many employees?
- What are its NAICS codes (replaced SIC codes as government classification of what businesses specialize in)?
- How stable is the business financially?
- Does the business spend on advertising and promotion? How much? Where?
- Why do they buy? To increase revenue? To reduce expenses? To maintain the status quo?
- What criteria do they use to evaluate the service they purchase?

Marketing to the Government

Most small-business owners concentrate on selling to either consumers or business customers. But there is an alternative market that may be applicable to you, depending on your type of business: government sales.

Federal, state, and local governments represent about one-third of the annual gross domestic spending in the United States, spending about $2.5 trillion for goods and services. Though much of this is spent through specific contracts, tens of billions are also spent at the "micro-purchase" level (for federal buyers, anything under $3,000; for state and local government buyers, somewhat less). These purchases are made via government credit cards. The federal card is the SmartPay card; there are currently about 300,000 in use, and in fiscal year 2009 almost $20 billion was spent using SmartPay. No reliable statistics are available for state and local government credit card usage, as there are so many state and local governments.

Government customers are loyal. Once they like you, they will continue to buy from you whenever possible. Mailing to the government is similar to mailing to businesses, but there are nuances you need to be aware of. The following are a few quick tips to get you started. These tips also apply to your website, space ads, and other advertising material.

- *Know your audience.* Who are the users of your product or service, and who are the buyers? These are not always the same people. Is the purchase a team decision? Develop a profile of the person who uses your product, and where possible include the position function, office mission or function, and agency mission. For commodity products where there is broad usage, you need only figure out who the buyer is for each office.
- *Like all direct marketing, the list is the key factor.* Work with a mailing list broker who has experience in business-to-government as well as your product or service niche. Many B2B publications have small segments of government readers, so do not overlook these if the list works for you in your business mailings.
- *The marketing material needs to be well suited to the audience.* Catalogs and line cards (a simple 8½ x 11-inch document listing a company's full product line) go to procurement offices and end users. Procurement offices only care about price, source, and what contracts you are on. Collateral material with success stories, features, and benefits go to end users and decision makers.
- *The message is critical.* Government decision makers still receive lots of mail every day, so you need to get their attention quickly. The key messages are features and benefits for users and others on the decision-making team, and price and contracts for procurement offices.
- *If you have a GSA Schedule contract, clearly say so.* This allows customers to buy from you (up to a certain dollar

amount shown in the schedule) directly without issuing a request for proposal (RFP).

♦ *Make it as easy as possible for people to respond to your offer.* Business reply cards and business reply envelopes still work, so use them in your mailings. Boldface your 800 number and your website address. If you have dedicated government reps, give the direct line(s). Always offer multiple response options.

♦ *Government mailing addresses often have internal routing codes.* Ask for these whenever people are responding to your offer.

♦ *Avoid overmailing to military bases.* All military base mailrooms strictly limit the amount of incoming promotional mail from the same mailer. If you have lots of people on military bases, stagger the mailings by a week.

♦ *Use the SmartPay logo everywhere you use the Visa and MasterCard logos.* If you have a special cover for catalogs going into government offices, include the SmartPay logo on the cover.

♦ *Survey your active customer base to better understand how they gather information during the buying process.* Ask them what they read, what they attend, what they belong to, and what their favorite business-related websites are.

♦ *Be in front of your buyers during the end of their fiscal year (FY).* For feds, September 30 is the last day of the FY; for most state and local governments, it is June 30. Government agencies are not rewarded for thrift. If they do not use their budget, it does not roll over for them to the next FY—it goes back to the general fund. So they spend whatever is left. It is good to remind them 60, 30, and 10 days out that you are available to help them spend those last dollars.

Know the Lifetime Value of Your Ideal Client

Think about it. You have only three ways to increase your sales:

1. Increase the number of clients you have.

2. Increase the frequency of their purchases.

3. Increase the amount of their purchases.

Strategies for growing your business must focus on how to do one or more of these things while keeping costs down. So, to meet the goals you set for your business, you need to understand how much money your average ideal client is going to spend with you throughout the course of your relationship. This will also tell you how much you can afford to spend to acquire a client.

To compute the lifetime value of a client:

1. Determine, on average, how much your ideal client will spend with you each year.

2. Determine, on average, how many years this client will buy from you.

3. Determine, on average, how much additional income you'll make from the referrals this client makes to your business.

For example, if your ideal client spends $2,000 a year with you and buys from you for three years, that client has spent $6,000 with you. If that client refers two others to you, who repeat that pattern, that's an additional $12,000. So, your ideal client has a lifetime value of $18,000. If 50 percent of that were profit, would you spend $1,000 to acquire that client? Yes. Would you spend $5,000?

Obviously, the longer you've been in business, the more data you'll have to determine a client's long-term value and a reasonable investment for acquiring that client. If you're just starting out or don't have a track record yet, make sure this is one of the measurements you use to evaluate your business success. A monthly client report, such as the one shown in Table 3–3 on page 44, can help you collect the information you need to summarize the value of each client to your business.

Know Why Your Client Buys

Look for clues to how your clients' behavior might lead them to use more of your service. Specifically, why would this client buy this type

Client Report (Month/Year)								
	Services Purchased	Problem Solved	Date	Amount	YTD $	Last Purchase Date	Client Since (m/d/y)	Lifetime Value to Date
Client 1								
Client 2								
Client 3								
Totals				$	$			$
Comments:								

TABLE 3–3. **Monthly Client Report**

Consumers	Businesses
Improve the family or home	Become a market leader
Advance in their jobs	Increase productivity
Pursue hobbies	Save money
Feel safe/security	Maximize cash flow
Increase their knowledge	Increase quality
Participate in community activities	Cut overhead
Feel good about achievements	Be perceived as innovative
Enjoy entertainment/recreation	Increase employees' satisfaction
Increase their fitness	Be community-oriented
Enjoy a vacation	

TABLE 3–4. **Why Consumers and Businesses Buy**

of service? What need or want is he or she trying to satisfy? Consumers and businesses buy for different reasons, summarized in Table 3–4.

The more you understand the reasons for buyers in your niche to purchase, the more successfully you can speak to their values as you market to them.

Know What Benefits Mean the Most to Your Client

The more your service appears to be what customers want, the more likely they are to purchase it, but you can't know what that looks like unless you ask them. You have multiple ways to uncover what clients want:

◆ Call and ask them.
◆ Survey them.
◆ Use focus groups.
◆ Do face-to-face interviews.
◆ Survey your employees.
◆ Invite comments from clients.
◆ Have a regular group of client advisors.
◆ Review feedback forms from salespeople, who often have new insights about what the market needs.
◆ Attend events and conferences your client group attends.
◆ Get input from clients on new programs, prospects, and services.

Know the Steps in Your Clients' Buying Process

Why is it important to understand your prospects' buying process? Because you want to appeal to buyers at every stage of the process so that by the time they make their decision, it's clear that you offer the best response to their needs or wants. As a marketer, you want to influence prospects the moment they start thinking about solving their problem or buying your type of service. You want to know:

◆ Who makes the decisions?
◆ Is the decision impulsive or deliberate?

- Do consumers view my product or service as a value-added purchase or a commodity?
- How price sensitive is this market? How can I win business without being the low bid? Must I service what I sell? Can I sell my customer an extended warranty or service plan?
- Will my prospects research this purchase online before coming to my store or showroom?
- Are prospects in my industry mainly generated through referrals from their neighbors, relatives, and friends?
- Do consumers feel knowledgeable about my product, or are they looking for an expert to guide and advise them?
- Do decision makers shop around before purchasing?
- Are products and services like mine readily available, and do my customers know about them? Or do I have the market to myself?
- Are my competitors as busy or as hungry as I am? How far are they willing to go to take business away from me?
- How do they pay? Can they purchase outright, or do they require financing?
- How much is it worth to them to solve their problem?
- When and how do they purchase? Seasonally? Locally?
- Are they loyal to their current supplier? If I get them to buy, how long will they remain my customer, and on average what will they spend with me during that time?
- What warranty or guarantee is standard in my industry? Can I afford to offer a stronger one, and would it make any difference to my prospect?

Know What You Can Learn from Your Current Clients

Once you determine who your ideal client is, take a second look at your current clients. Have you been pursuing the types of clients that are best for you? Take some time and review your client roster with the intention of profiling them demographically and psychographically to learn as much as you can about them. Do you know what they value? What benefits are important to them? What is their buying process? Where do they go for information?

Start with what you already know about them. Learning your clients' needs and tastes is something you'll do throughout the duration of your business—if you're wise. So don't wait to know everything about your client. This is a recipe for analysis paralysis. Get started with what you know, and use every opportunity to learn more.

Create a client profile for each of your clients, and add to it any time you have contact with that client. A profile you might build in Access or another database is shown in Table 3–5. Link this to your client report to keep both updated. Remember, knowing and understanding your clients' wants and needs better than your competitors do is one of the keys to successful niche marketing. (See Appendix A for a blank "Client Profile Form.")

CLIENT PROFILE	
Contact Information	
Client Name	
Title	
Company	
Phone Number	
Fax Number	
Address, City, State, Zip	
Purchasing History	
Client Since	
Services Purchased (Dates and Amounts)	
Biggest Challenges	
Perceived Value of Solving Their Challenges	

TABLE 3–5. **Client Profile Form**

Purchasing History	
Client's Competitors	
Their Main Clients	
Year-to-Date Purchases	
Referrals Given	
Lifetime Value	
Client Preferences	
Preferred Method of Contact	
Frequency	
Birthday	
Anniversaries	
Favorite Restaurant(s)	
Spouse	
Children	
Hobbies	
Likes/Dislikes	
World News	
Issues Affecting Them	
Marketing Efforts	
Type/Dates/Results	
Next Action (Schedule It)	

TABLE 3–5. **Client Profile Form,** continued

Action . . .

Describe Your Ideal Client

Write a description of your ideal client. Add as much detail as you need to be clear about who this client is. What is your client's most pressing problem? What aspirations does he or she have that might drive buying habits? What influences your ideal client's purchasing decisions?

_____

_____

_____

_____

Describe your current clients: _____

_____

_____

_____

Comment on how closely your actual and ideal clients match. Describe what they have in common. Describe how they differ. If there is a wide disparity between the two, describe the changes you intend to make to bring them closer together. _____

_____

_____

_____

_____

_____

Action . . .

Describe Your Ideal Client, continued

What does your ideal client want to experience when doing business with you?
Is it the same as what your current clients want? _____

_____

_____

_____

What do you need to do to find more of your ideal clients? _____

_____

_____

_____

Chapter 4
WHO IS THE COMPETITION?

It's tough to do a better job than the competition if you don't know anything about them. That should seem obvious, but too often service businesses launch without asking, "Who else does what we do?" and "What can we bring to the game that they don't?" Deciding who your competitors are, what they offer, and whom they serve will help you position your business at a more competitive advantage.

Some businesspeople, either through pride or ignorance, believe they genuinely have no competition. This is seldom, if ever, truly the case. Since the prospect is not on his deathbed and does not yet own your product, he has at least one alternative: to not buy it and carry on as he has been doing all these years. So one alternative to your offer is inaction, and it is the easiest alternative for the consumer to take: People like doing nothing and enjoy not spending money or dealing with salespeople even more.

Other entrepreneurs tell me their product or service is truly superior, and therefore they have no real competition. The problem is the consumer does not share the view that your product is unique and superior, and is not inclined to believe you. You may genuinely offer advantages your competitors don't. But their marketing campaigns and salespeople are out there telling prospects that, in fact, they can offer everything you can and more. Lying? Maybe. But the consumer can't tell.

In other product categories, the opposite situation is true: Marketers are surrounded by swarms of competitors, which both they and their prospects are acutely aware of. In these situations, you obviously need to know how the top competitors are positioning themselves, the products and services they offer, and even what they say about you.

The Three Sources of Competition

The prospect has a problem. You know your product is the ideal solution. Yet he doesn't buy. Why not? In a word, competition.

> You do not have a monopoly on solving the customer's problem.

You do not have a monopoly on solving the customer's problem. He has many options. Therefore, he does not have to buy from you. And many will turn to one of the other options instead of you. The purpose of marketing is to get more prospects to buy your product or service, instead of the competitor's.

You face three primary categories of competition. First, nothing. Rather than go to the expense and headache of solving their problem, they decide to just live with it. For example, despite bad breath, cavities, loose teeth, and pain, 1 out of 3 Americans did not visit a dentist within the past year. So a big competitor for dentists is patients doing nothing.

Second, do it yourself. If you are a painter, you will lose jobs to people who want to save your fee and just paint their home themselves. Do it yourself is a primary competitor for home repair services, from gutter cleaning to lawn care.

Third, you face competition from other companies in your market who offer the same or similar products and services as you do. Again, the goal of marketing is to get people to buy from you instead of your competitors.

SWOT Analysis

A SWOT analysis is a useful tool, in which you examine the competition from four vantage points:

1. *Strengths.* What are they really good at? In what way is their offering superior to yours?
2. *Weaknesses.* What does the competition do poorly? What is inferior about their product or service that you can exploit?
3. *Opportunities.* What applications, regions, or markets need solutions and are not getting them? What ripe opportunities for new sales are your competitors neglecting?
4. *Threats.* What market conditions, disruptive technologies, or other changes in the marketplace endanger your business and threaten to halt your ongoing success?

For instance, a high-tech manufacturer introduced a new entry in a crowded niche: devices that measure color on physical objects. Instead of designing their product in a vacuum, they studied all the competitors and made a comprehensive list of the flaws and weaknesses of the competing products. They then designed and build a spectrophotometer in which all these defects and weaknesses were corrected. The launch of the new system was incredibly successful.

Monitoring the Competition

You want to keep current with what your competitors are up to. Here are a few ideas for doing so:

◆ Hire secret shoppers to anonymously shop at the competitor's stores or purchase the product by phone or online.

◆ Subscribe to the competitor's free enewsletter to be kept abreast of all their latest developments.

◆ Mine their website for detailed information. Look at their HTML code to see what key words they optimize their site for.

◆ Order their product online so you will be placed on a list to get all their future email promotions.

◆ Go to industry trade shows, grab a plastic bag, and fill it with your competitors' sales brochures and catalogs.

◆ Do an online survey using www.surveymonkey.com to get consumer opinions regarding both your product and the competition.

◆ Hire top salespeople, product managers, and designers away from your competitors. Despite nondisclosure agreements, you may learn some of their trade secrets.

Who Is Your Top Competitor?

Do you know who your top competitor is? And if so, is it because you think so or because your ideal clients see the business that way? How does this company stack up on the things that matter to your ideal client?

Clients perceive differences among competitors, and you need to know what your clients' perceptions are of you and your competition. That way, you can highlight the positives in your marketing, and look for ways to overcome both perceived and real negatives.

Look for the Gaps in Service to Your Niche

You want a clear snapshot of your competitors as they are today. But you'll also need to stay on top of your competitors' activities in the future. So start building files on them now. Look for changes that pose an opportunity for you or a threat to your business.

First, categorize your competition. Who is comparable to you in their service offerings, quality of service, and price? These are your most direct competitors. Identify the top five or ten.

Don't forget about your indirect competitors. These companies don't offer the same service you do, but your ideal clients see their offerings as an alternative to yours. For example, two movie theaters showing the same movies are direct competitors. However, for consumers looking for entertainment, indirect competitors might be live theater, sporting events, theme parks, and nightclubs. They're all vying for entertainment dollars.

Here are some questions to consider when analyzing your competition:

- ◆ What service(s) do they offer?
- ◆ What is their chief focus?
- ◆ If your niche can be divided into categories (beginner, intermediate, and expert, for example), which group do they focus on? Can you profitably target the ones they do not?
- ◆ What advantage do they offer? Don't try to duplicate your competitors' advantages unless you can do it better.
- ◆ What is the main message they communicate in their marketing materials? How do they position themselves?
- ◆ What is their reputation or image in the industry? Can you own a position differentiated from theirs? For instance, if they are the 800-pound gorilla with vast resources and experience, can you be the nimble spider monkey willing and able to do more? Think Avis vs. Hertz.

> Make a list of your favorite businesses. Ask yourself why you choose to shop with them over their competitors.

Make a list of your favorite businesses. Ask yourself why you choose to shop with them over their competitors. Is it their offerings? Quality of service? Reliability? Courtesy? Prices? What else? How are they positioned in the market vs. their competitors? What can you learn from these businesses and apply to your own?

Now, think of businesses that you'll never do business with again. Why? What made you *feel* this way? What can you learn from these experiences and apply to your business?

You're trying to find a window for your business in your clients' and prospects' minds. Examine your competitors' websites, press releases, case studies, articles, and other promotional presentations to identify how they position their business with clients.

Questions to ask about your competitors:

- What do your competitors do well?
- What strengths do they have? Do they offer guarantees? Strong offers? Are they financially stronger?
- What segments, needs, or opportunities within your niche do they ignore?
- What do they do poorly or less than well?
- Why do clients like doing business with them?
- What criticisms do naysayers make about them?
- Why don't former clients do business with them any longer?
- What can you learn from them?
- What can you do better than they do?
- What do you do that your competition can't copy or improve?
- What do you do that they can do better?
- Are they doing anything that could take business away from you?
- What trends or changes might create an opportunity for you?
- How do they price their services? How do your prices compare? If you charge more for the same services, can you demonstrate the added value you bring? If you charge less, can you demonstrate that you bring as much value as those charging more?
- How do they package their service to make it most attractive to clients? (With special offers, bonuses, guarantees, payment plans, longer service hours, more service providers?)
- What weaknesses do they have?
- Do their business practices present any opportunities for you?

Here's an example: Dave, an insurance agent, carried a line of auto insurance for teens. He advertised a deep discount on auto insurance for new drivers who got good grades in school. Unfortunately, all his competitors offer the same good-student discount. So parents asked him why they should have their teen insured with him rather than other agents in town.

One day he wrote his home phone number on the back of his business card, handed it to the prospective customer, and said, "Your child may be out one night, drink, and be unable to drive. Give him this card with my home phone number on it. He can call me at any time of the day or night. If he should not be driving, I will pick him up and drive him home safely." No other agents in the area were willing to go this extra mile, giving Dave a unique selling offer he could use to close more sales.

Action...

Write Your Description of the Competition

Use the table to identify strengths and weaknesses of both you and your competitors. Think back to the things you identified as important to your ideal client in the last step. How well are competitors addressing those issues? Do you see any gaps? Opportunities?

Feature	Your Business	Competitor 1	Competitor 2	Competitor 3	Competitor 4	Competitor 5
What service(s) do they offer?						
Primary focus						
Perceived advantage						
Message						

Feature	Your Business	Competitor 1	Competitor 2	Competitor 3	Competitor 4	Competitor 5
How do they position themselves?						
What do they do well?						
Strengths						
Segments of your niche they ignore						
Things they don't do well						
Reason clients like them						
Reason former clients don't like them						
Things you can learn from them						
Things you do better than they do						

Feature	Your Business	Competitor 1	Competitor 2	Competitor 3	Competitor 4	Competitor 5
Things you do they can't copy or improve						
Things they do that can take business away from you						
How do they price their services?						
How do they package their service? (With special offers, bonuses, guarantees, payment plans, longer service hours, more service providers, etc.?)						
Weaknesses						
Opportunities for you						

Write a summary of what you found in analyzing your competitors. Where are the opportunities for you?

_____

_____

_____

_____

_____

_____

_____

chapter 5
STRATEGIZE: POSITION YOUR BUSINESS

Let's summarize where we are now. We have a clear, powerful *vision* of where we intend to take our business. We've defined our *niche*, so we know whom we're focusing on. We've analyzed our *client* base and prospects to understand why and how they buy our services and how this benefits them. We've scrutinized the *competition* to learn how they position their businesses to gain trust and attention from prospects.

Now it's time to *position* our business to gain a "window in the minds" of prospects, define our goals for the next year, and begin building a *strategy* that will implement our vision.

Bull's-Eye: Position Your Business

As discussed in the previous chapter, a positioning statement (see Table 5–1 on page 62) tells your clients and prospects how you want to be perceived in the marketplace. It tells them the benefits of doing business with you and why the value you'll provide them is unique.

Core Value Proposition	The Core Value Proposition is the highest-level selling point—the ultimate advantage—that a product or company offers. In business, it usually includes an implied or explicit reference to ROI.
Unique Selling Proposition(s)	A USP is a specific, strongly communicated benefit to the customer that the competition ether cannot, or does not, offer. A USP is a unique advantage that strongly differentiates you from your competition.
Positioning	Determines what kind of customers your product will appeal to vs. what segment of your market your competitors are targeting; compares your product to the competition in terms of quality, features, design, price, and service.
Benefits	A benefit is what the product does for the customer (e.g., saves time or money, helps him lose weight; makes money; improves health, etc.)

TABLE 5–1. **Positioning**
Source: David Fideler, "Unlocking Your Core Message," Core Message Analysis, p. 5.

You'll use your positioning statement as the basis for all the messages you send your prospects about your business. It will be reflected in your website content, in every press release, in speeches you give, in articles you write, your blog posts, and even in your PowerPoint presentations. It's how you'll "brand" your business. It's what you'll be known for. However, just making a positioning statement means little if you don't integrate the unique value it identifies into every aspect of your business.

Here's how to develop your positioning statement:

◆ Remind yourself of what's important to your prospects. What value or criteria do they use most to choose their vendor?
◆ Review the comparisons you made between your business and your top competitors in Chapter 4.
◆ Choose the one thing that makes you distinctive from your competitors that your prospects will value most.

◆ Tell your prospects how this distinction will benefit them (also called your unique selling proposition, or USP; again see Table 5-1).

FedEx's positioning statement, for instance, was for many years "FedEx: When it absolutely, positively has to be there overnight." As a business owner whose ability to win contracts has from time to time depended on my bid absolutely, positively getting there overnight, I liked this positioning statement. Since the advent of email, of course, FedEx has become much less critical to information workers, because our product (documents) can be transmitted instantly to customers over the internet at virtually no cost.

A general format for writing a positioning statement includes the following:

We sell [your service type] for [Your ideal client type] that need/want to [the problem you solve and why your solution is different]

Now you try it. Remember, your positioning statement should focus on what you do, whom you do it for, and the unique benefit for your clients. Focus on just one promise.

Write your positioning statement:

_____

_____

_____

How to Build a Stronger USP

Here's a trick question: What's better, chopped liver or filet mignon? Most people answer "filet mignon." But that's the wrong answer. The correct answer is that filet mignon isn't better than chopped liver, nor is chopped liver better than filet mignon. If you picked "filet mignon," you should have said, "I like filet mignon better," and not "filet mignon *is* better." One is not inherently superior to the other. It's a matter of taste. I like chopped liver, so to me, filet mignon is not better.

What does this have to do with your positioning USP? Plenty! Every business needs to have a USP, a reason why customers should buy from you instead of from your competitors.

Do you know what the most common USP is—the one business owners give most frequently when customers ask why they should buy your product instead of the competition's? It is also, strangely enough, the weakest USP: It's "we're better." Why is "we're better" such a weak and ineffective USP? Because better is nonspecific and difficult to prove. You say you're better. I say I'm better. It's difficult to prove—and just saying it causes prospects to disbelieve you. Also, better is such a general term, that it has little meaning. Same thing with the overused "quality."

How do you create a USP that gets people to want to buy your product instead of the competition? There are many methods, but I will describe just three of them here.

The first is to focus on a feature of your product—one that is different or unique, and delivers an important benefit to the user. Consider Crispix cereal. The manufacturer didn't say it "tasted better." They said Crispix "stays crisp in milk"—a benefit consumers wanted.

The second way to create a USP with selling power is to narrow the target market—focus on a specific market niche. For example, there are thousands of business consultants out there, all fighting for clients. But not my old high school chum, Gary Gerber. He has all he can handle, with potential clients waiting in line to hire him. Why? Because he is not just a business development consultant—Gary is a business development consultant specializing in eye doctors.

It doesn't hurt that, before becoming a business development consultant to eye doctors, he owned the largest and most successful optometry practice in New Jersey. If you were an eye doctor looking to build your practice, who would you want to work with—Gary or a consultant who says he can help you but has never worked with an eye doctor before?

The third way to create a winning USP is with branding. The branding approach usually takes a massive, costly advertising campaign that small businesses cannot afford, although there are ways to shortcut this, such as with a celebrity spokesperson. A great example is the George Foreman grill: This is clearly not the world's best grill, nor do I recall the manufacturer making this claim in their commercials. But it is the only grill you can buy with the name "George Foreman" on it. So if you want a grill that cooks good food, you can get it lots of places. But if you want a "George Foreman" grill, you can only get it from the George Foreman grill company.

A good place to start when formulating your USP is by asking yourself these questions:

- ◆ What is different about my product that delivers an important benefit to the user?
- ◆ Is there an industry, application, or other niche I can specialize in?
- ◆ Is there a way to brand my company or product in a unique fashion with appeal to consumers?

The more your positioning statement differentiates you from your competitors, the easier it will be for you to promote and sell your product. Conversely, a positioning statement that does not reflect a strong USP is a handicap. After all, the USP is the reason prospects should buy from you instead of other vendors. If you cannot articulate why they should hire you instead of your competitor across the street, how can you answer the question "Why should we buy from you?" when prospects ask it? And they ask it all the time.

> The more your positioning statement differentiates you from your competitors, the easier it will be for you to promote and sell your product.

Let's take a closer look at the USP and how to find one that powerfully differentiates you from your competitors while giving consumers a compelling reason to prefer your service, offer, or brand. Here are the three components of a successful USP:

1. Each advertisement must make a proposition to the consumer. It must say: "Buy this product, and you will get this specific

benefit." So to begin with, there must be a compelling benefit. For instance, "The CryoQuad Quiet-Cool air conditioner reduces your summer electric bills by 25 percent while keeping your house cool and comfortable."

2. The proposition must be one that the competition either cannot, or does not, offer. It must be unique—either in brand or a claim not otherwise made in that particular field. This is the "unique" in "unique selling proposition." You must clearly differentiate yourself from the competition. For example, "The CryoQuad Quiet-Cool air conditioner features our patented energy-saving TwinStar freon pump that spreads the cool air evenly throughout the room vs. other units that only cool the air in their immediate area."

3. The proposition must be so strong that it can move the mass millions (i.e., pull in new customers to your product). This means the USP cannot be a trivial difference; it has to be something important, something the customer really cares about. Consider our a/c example again: "The energy savings you get by cooling your home with a CryoQuad Quiet-Cool can pay back the cost of the unit by the end of the summer if you get it now . . . and save you hundreds of dollars more in energy costs over the lifetime of the unit."

To sum it up, you only need three criteria for effective advertising with a USP:

1. Does the ad project a proposition?
2. Is it unique?
3. Does it sell?

The old ad campaigns for Wonder Bread are a classic example of a USP stated clearly, simply, and lucidly. "Wonder Bread helps build strong bodies 12 ways." What's interesting is that if you associate your product with a strong USP in the consumer's mind, it's difficult for competitors to take it away from you. After all, could you imagine another brand of bread saying, "We also build strong bodies 12 ways?" Every time they said it, the buyer would think of Wonder Bread—and nothing else.

Here's another example: A software company sold an "application development tool" that computer programmers used to develop web-based applications. They needed a USP, but the applications built with their tool weren't really better than applications developed using other methods. But their tool saved time: Tests showed that it took one-third the time to develop web applications using their software than other methods. The company combined this with their money-back guarantee to come up with the following USP: "Develop web-based applications three times faster or your money back!" Does this meet our criteria for a strong USP? Yes:

1. It has a strong benefit: develop applications faster.
2. It is unique: They are the only application tool developer not merely claiming but promising (with a money-back guarantee) to help the buyer develop applications three times faster.
3. Since programmers are always swamped and productivity is a major issue, a tool that helps them produce their work in one-third the time is a strong enough benefit to get them to try the product.

Pick Your Place on the Positioning Spectrum

No one can be all things to all people. The "positioning spectrum" refers to how you want to position your product in the marketplace. For instance, BMW and Mercedes-Benz are positioned on the high end of the car spectrum as luxury cars. The Saturn is a low-end car that seems to be positioned as an affordable automobile for young men and women who are early in their careers and with limited funds.

On an episode of *Shark Tank*, judge Robert Herjavec had invested in a company that made designer sweaters selling for $65 each. At a meeting, the owners showed Robert designs for $40 sweaters, which they figured would help expand their sales to consumers who do not want to pay $65 for a sweater. Robert felt the cheaper sweaters conflicted with the company's core value proposition of providing unique sweaters, which naturally cost more. He advised the owners to forget $40 sweater buyers and concentrate on selling to people who can afford to and are willing to pay $65 for a sweater.

One dentist I know of positions himself as a high-end cosmetic dentist for patients who can pay cash for $10,000-plus dental implants without blinking. A friend from high school, who is also a dentist, has his offices in a poorer neighborhood and hired bilingual staff so they can communicate with their many Hispanic patients. They both make good money as dentists. But they do it in a completely different way.

Offer Proof for Your Positioning Statement and USP

Nowhere do some marketers think less like consumers than when it comes to proving the claims they make in their promotions. And there is nothing that sticks out like a sore thumb more to the reader than an outrageous claim that is not backed by a single iota of proof.

> Nowhere do some marketers think less like consumers than when it comes to proving the claims they make in their promotions.

For instance, I was writing a sales letter to sell subscriptions to a magazine covering the defense industry. When I asked the subscription manager what made their product different, she said,

"We aren't usually the first to report on a story. TV, newspapers, and the internet all beat us to the punch, since we are a monthly. But we analyze and interpret the news so our readers can make better decisions based on what the facts really mean."

"That's fascinating," I replied, scribbling eagerly. "Can you give me an example?" Her reply: dead silence. Their USP was that this publication analyzed military events more accurately and in-depth so military people could make better strategic decisions based on this analysis. Yet no one at the publication could give me a single example to prove it!

Can you imagine claiming that you could help a general plan victory in battle, or help people get better jobs, or help companies reduce their insurance costs—without producing one good story or example to prove it? Sounds absurd, but dozens of promotions I see do just that! Often, these promotions have no proof for their major claim because the marketer has never bothered to ask for it. If you're going to aggressively market your product through the mail or online, collecting such proof from satisfied customers should be your number-one priority.

People are skeptical that your product can deliver the benefits you promise, because everyone is promising those same benefits. When you show how a particular feature delivers the benefit, it becomes more believable to the prospect. For instance, if you tell the buyer your computer system never loses data, he thinks, "How can that be?" But when you describe the feature—that it automatically backs data up to the cloud, and the system automatically backs up to that tape drive daily—then your claim becomes more believable.

Fortunately, it's easy to come up with strong proof for product claims, though it will involve a bit of time and effort up front. First, figure out the claim you want to prove or demonstrate; for example, "XYZ is the only product that does [Benefit] for [Audience] by [Method]." Then, send a simple letter or form to your customers. Ask them: "Has our product [XYZ] helped you achieve [Benefit] by [Method]? We are looking for success stories from customers like you. If you have a success story to share with us, please summarize it below and send this form back to us. If we use your story in our marketing, you will receive a free [NAME OF GIFT]."

Offer a nice gift in the $50 to $100 price range to anyone whose story you use. This will be sufficient to motivate people to take the time to think about your product and relay the story of how it helped them. Do this until you have, ideally, 12 great stories you can use. Then use them as follows:

◆ In an ad, lead-generating letter, or email, in which you can build your copy around a single compelling story

◆ In a traditional direct-mail package, with a multipage letter packed with proof; tell three of the stories in detail, and summarize three to six more

◆ Reprinted as a group of testimonials on a single printed sheet you mail in your sales literature or post on a testimonials page on your website

The bottom line: The more thoroughly you demonstrate how your product delivers a particular benefit in a unique fashion, and prove it has done so through user success stories, the more effective your marketing will be.

Testimonials: The Quickest, Most Powerful Way to Support Your USP

Using testimonials—quotations from satisfied customers and clients—is one of the simplest and easiest ways to add instant credibility to your promotions.

Always use real testimonials instead of made-up ones. Even the most skilled copywriter can rarely make up a testimonial that can match the sincerity and credibility of genuine words of praise from a real customer or client.

> Always use real testimonials instead of made-up ones.

Prefer specific, detailed testimonials to general or superlative ones. Upon receiving a letter of praise from a customer, our initial reaction is to read the letter and find the single sentence that directly praises our company or our product. With a blue pencil, we extract the words we think are kindest about us, producing a bland bit of puffery such as: "We are very pleased with your product." But most testimonials would be stronger if we included more of the specific, detailed comments our client has made about how our product or service helped him. After all, the prospects we are trying to sell to may have problems similar to the one our current customer solved using our product. If we let

Mr. Customer tell Mr. Prospect how our company came to his rescue, he'll be helping us make the sale.

Don't try to polish the customer's words so it sounds like professional ad copy. Testimonials are usually much more convincing when they are not edited for style. They're also more believable when you use a full attribution. We've all opened direct-mail packages that contained testimonials from "J.B. in Arizona" or "Jim S., Self-Made Millionaire." Include the person's name, city and state, and (if a business customer) their job title and company.

There are two basic ways to present testimonials: You can group them together in one area of your brochure or landing page, or you can scatter them throughout the copy. A third alternative is to combine the two techniques, placing many testimonials in a box or insert sheet and a smattering of other testimonials throughout the rest of your copy.

I've seen both approaches work well, and the success of the presentation depends, in part, on the skill of the writer and the nature of the piece. But, all else being equal, I prefer the first approach: Group all your testimonials and present them as a single block of copy. This can be done in a box, on a separate page, or on a separate sheet.

My feeling is that when the prospect reads a half dozen or so testimonials, one right after another, they have more impact and power than when they are separated and scattered throughout the piece. On my site, all the testimonials are on one long page. I have seen other sites where one or two testimonials appear randomly throughout, which to me dilutes their effectiveness and impressiveness.

Finally, get the customer's permission to reprint his words before including his testimonial in your marketing campaign. Send a letter quoting the lines you want to reprint. Ask permission to include them in ads, direct mail, brochures, and other materials used to promote your firm. This way, you can use the testimonials again and again.

Describe What You Want to Accomplish this Year

Now that you've staked out your position with a strong USP, how do you become that company to your prospects? And how long will it take to brand you as the company in your positioning statement? It starts now. Go back to your vision for your business, and think of where you want to be three years from now. Write a list of what you want to accomplish. Be specific about revenues, earnings, the clients you have, services you offer, employees, locations, and anything major that will help define your goals for the next three years.

Ask yourself where you need to be one year from now to accomplish these goals. How will your business be different one year from now? What are your goals for the next year?

A goal is a statement of a result you want to achieve. Goals have been defined as "ends toward which efforts are directed." Goals tell us what we need to spend our time on today if we're going to accomplish what we say we intend to accomplish by our deadline. Your goals should further your vision.

A goal has several attributes, commonly referred to as SMART:

◆ Specific
◆ Measurable
◆ Action-oriented
◆ Realistic: Make your goals big (shoot for the moon) but also reachable, to create excitement and a challenge.
◆ Timely: Give them a deadline.

And if they're going to be met successfully, goals are almost always *written*. The very act of writing a goal sends a set of instructions to our subconscious, releasing it to go to work on accomplishing the goal for us.

Research tells us that those who set goals increase their motivation to achieve, are more self-confident, and are more likely to eliminate habits that hold them back. Pretty strong reasons for wanting to set goals.

So what are your goals for your business this year?

Chiropractic Marketing Plans has one main goal for this year: Increase revenues 33 percent, from $150,000 to $200,000. Currently, CMP averages 29 clients per year throughout Southern California, with a growth of two to three new clients each month. Perez charges

$5,000 to create a plan for a new client and $500 to review the plan in subsequent years. The company has a retention rate of 35 percent; these clients pay CMP to review their plans every year.

CMP's ideal clients are chiropractic practices that focus on services to families. Most have a well-defined service to offer families nonprescription, noninvasive treatment for pain and other common health ailments. This is appealing to families who want to stay away from taking medications or giving them to their children whenever feasible.

The problem is, CMP's clients need help educating families about the benefits chiropractic treatment can offer, and they don't know how to organize their efforts to accomplish this. Competitors offer telephone coaching services to assist the practices, but they skip or skimp on a well-thought-out marketing plan before jumping into implementation. Many practices are dissatisfied with their coaching results; without a plan to focus their efforts, they don't see the growth they expect.

CMP's solution is to focus practices first on a plan, then work with coaches who can lead them through the implementation steps. CMP has successfully completed action plans for more than 150 clients. Although the feedback from clients has been positive, CMP hasn't tracked their clients' results as carefully as they should. One of their implementation tactics will be to institute a tracking program.

Chiropractors in their target market obtain information from four main sources: *Chiropractic Economics* magazine, the California Chiropractic Association, ChiroWeb online, and *American Chiropractor* magazine. Word of mouth is also strong among local chiropractors.

CMP's message is "Grow with a Plan for All Seasons," because family practice can remain a profitable niche, even during economic downturns for those chiropractors who have a growth plan. CMP will lean heavily on low-cost tactics, such as email and article marketing, speaking, networking, and direct mail to reach its target market. Perez estimates expenditures of $5,000 in marketing costs for the year.

Your Business at a Glance: The Capabilities Brochure

In the pre-internet era, businesses did not have websites to tell prospects all about the company and its services. Therefore, all businesses created what was called a "capabilities brochure," summarizing the business, including its position, mission, vision, capabilities, products, services, benefits, USP, and advantages.

Even in the internet era, it may be a good idea to create such a brochure. Going through the exercise can help you and your prospects get a clearer picture of your business and what it offers. Although you don't have to actually print it—you can post it in HTML or as a PDF on your website—I recommend you create a print version. When you get an inquiry, you can immediately email a PDF of the brochure or a link to the HTML version so the prospect's questions are answered instantly. However, people tend to forget the HTML version after they starting clicking away, and many won't print or save your PDF. Therefore, a good strategy is to put a print version in the snail mail at the same time. A few days after your phone conversation, the brochure arrives on the prospect's desk, reinforcing your message and reminding him of what you offer. Use the form shown in Figure 5–1 to plan and create an effective capabilities brochure.

---

1. **Objectives of the brochure (check all that are appropriate):**

   ❑ Provide product information to customers

   ❑ Educate new prospects

   ❑ Build corporate image

   ❑ Establish credibility of your organization or product

   ❑ Sell the product directly through the mail

   ❑ Help salespeople get appointments

   ❑ Help salespeople make presentations

FIGURE 5–1. **Literature Specification Sheet**

❏ Help close the sale

❏ Support dealers, distributors, agents, and sales reps

❏ Add value to the product

❏ Enhance the effectiveness of direct-mail promotions

❏ Leave behind with customers as a reminder

❏ Respond to inquiries

❏ Hand out at trade shows, fairs, conventions

❏ Display at point of purchase

❏ Serve as reference material for employees, vendors, the press, investors

❏ Disseminate news

❏ Announce new products and product improvements

❏ Highlight new applications for existing products

❏ Train and educate new employees

❏ Recruit new employees

❏ Provide useful information to the public

❏ Answer the prospect's questions

❏ Generate new business leads

❏ Qualify your company to be on a customer's approved vendor list

❏ Other (describe): _____

2. **The type of literature needed (check one):**

❏ Annual report

❏ Booklet

❏ Brochure

❏ Case history

❏ Catalog

FIGURE 5–1. **Literature Specification Sheet,** continued

❏ Circular

❏ Data sheet

❏ Flier

❏ Invoice stuffer

❏ Newsletter

❏ PDF brochure for email delivery

❏ Poster

❏ Other (describe): _____

3. Topic

◆ What is the subject matter of the brochure? (Describe the product, service, program, or organization being promoted.) _____

_____

◆ What is the theme or central message (if any)? _____

_____

4. Content

◆ Is there an outline of the main points and secondary points that must be included in the brochure and the order in which they should be presented? _____

_____

◆ Is the outline thorough and complete? Does it cover all points?

_____

_____

◆ What is the source of the information? Have you provided the copywriter with the necessary background documents? _____

_____

FIGURE 5–1. **Literature Specification Sheet,** continued

◆ What facts are missing? What additional research (if any) is required? _____

_____

5. Audience

◆ Geographic location _____

◆ Income level _____

◆ Family status (Married? Single? Children? Divorced or widowed?)

_____

◆ Industry _____

◆ Job title/function _____

◆ Education _____

◆ Politics _____

◆ Religion/ethnic background _____

◆ Age _____

◆ Concerns (reasons why they might be interested in your product or
service or organization) _____

◆ Buying habits/purchasing authority _____

◆ General description of the target audience (in your own words)

_____

_____

6. Sales appeals

◆ What is the key sales appeal of the product? _____

◆ What are the supporting or secondary sales points? _____

_____

FIGURE 5–1. **Literature Specification Sheet,** continued

7. Image

◆ What image do you want your literature to convey to the reader?

_____

8. Sales cycles

How does the brochure fit into your sales cycle? Check all that apply:

❑ Generate leads

❑ Answer initial inquiries

❑ Provide more detailed information to qualified buyers

❑ Establish confidence in the company and its products

❑ Provide detailed product information

❑ Answer questions frequently asked by prospects

❑ Reinforce sales message for prospect ready to buy

❑ Support salespeople during presentation

❑ Close the sale

❑ Other (describe): _____

_____

9. Competition

What images and sales appeals do competitors' brochures stress?

Competitor	Image	Key Sales Appeal

FIGURE 5–1. **Literature Specification Sheet,** continued

10. **Format**

   ◆ Approximate number of words _____

   ◆ Number of color photos _____

   ◆ Number of black-and-white photos _____

   ◆ Number and types of illustrations and other visuals (describe)

   _____

   ◆ Number of pages _____

   ◆ Page size:

   ❑ 8½ x 11" ❑ 7 x 10" ❑ 6 x 9" ❑ 5½ x 8½" ❑ 4 x 9" ❑ Other

   ◆ Method of folding or binding _____

   ◆ Number of colors used in printing:

   ❑ 1-color ❑ 2-color ❑ 4-color process ❑ Other

   ◆ Type of paper (weight, finish, texture, color) _____

11. **Budget**

   Use the worksheet below to estimate costs.

Task	Cost
Copywriting	
Photography	
Illustration	
Design and layout	
Typesetting	
Mechanicals (paste-up)	
Printing	
TOTAL	$
Number of copies to be printed	
Cost per copy	

FIGURE 5–1. **Literature Specification Sheet,** continued

12. Schedule

How long will it take to produce?

Task	Number of Days to Complete
Copy	
Copy review	
Copy rewrite	
Design	
Design review	
Design revision	
Typesetting	
Photography and illustration	
Mechanicals	
Delays, mistakes	
TOTAL	

FIGURE 5–1. **Literature Specification Sheet,** continued

Action . . .

Write Your Goals for Your Business for the Next Year

Try to focus on no more than three to five major goals. You don't want to be overwhelmed.

_____

_____

_____

Describe Your Strategy for Achieving Your Goals

Next, lay out your strategy, or approach, to meeting your goals. You want a strategy that will bring in a steady stream of clients. Make sure your strategy includes the following details:

- ◆ Your target or ideal client

- ◆ Your target's primary problem that makes them an ideal client for you

- ◆ Your solution

- ◆ Your proof that you can do what you say you can do

- ◆ How you can differentiate your business in ways that matter to your ideal client

- ◆ The best places to promote your solutions to your ideal client (this is information you identified when doing your client profiles)

- ◆ Your message, which should get your ideal client interested in learning more about your services (whatever you say, it has to be all about them, not about you)

- ◆ How much you plan to spend to implement your strategy (expect to spend 2 to 4 percent of expected sales on your marketing budget)

CMP has one main goal for this year: Increase revenues from $150,000 to $200,000. To reach their goal, CMP's strategy is to:

- Become well known for writing marketing plans for chiropractors, because no one else in their coverage area is doing this

- Dominate their field within a 10-mile radius of their office

- Add 15 net new clients

- Increase their client retention rate to 40 percent

- Earn income by matching clients with coaches to implement the plan

- Add a midyear review service to increase the usage frequency of their services

Write Your Strategy for Meeting Your One-Year Goals:

_____

_____

_____

_____

_____

_____

_____

_____

Chapter 6
BUILD OUT YOUR PRODUCT LINE

To be in business, you have to have a product or service to sell. But to succeed in business, you have to have multiple products and services to sell. If you only have one product or service, your business is almost certainly not a viable business, but more like a hobby or avocation: You may make sales and get paid, but you will never grow very large or become very profitable, much less make a living. Exceptions? Of course.

Why do you need additional products and services to sell people who have bought one product from you? Recall our earlier discussion of lifetime customer value (LCV). LCV is the amount of money a customer spends with you over the period for which she remains an active customer. Say you have a grocery store. The average customer spends $100 a week, or $5,000 a year. If the average customer stays with you five years before moving away or switching to another grocery store (because it's closer, has a better selection, offers lower prices, or the customer grows unhappy with your store), that customer has an LCV of $25,000.

The money in most businesses is not made in the initial sale, but in repeat orders from the same customers. The first product you buy from a company is known as the "front-end" product or "front-end" sale. The process of getting a new customer to make their first purchase from you is called "acquisition," because you are acquiring that person as a customer. The additional products the person buys from you once they become a customer are known as the "back-end." And for most businesses, the back-end is where the profit is made.

Why is the back-end so much more profitable than the front-end? One obvious reason is that the front-end is a one-time sale, where the back-end is many sales over an extended period. In addition, the back-end sales are easier and less costly to make.

Customer acquisition through a front-end product offer is challenging and expensive. You are attempting to get a stranger who has never done business with you before to do so, and it takes a lot of sales and marketing effort to overcome their skepticism and get them to risk spending money with you. It is much easier and less costly to sell additional back-end offers to existing customers than to acquire new customers. On average, making sales to an existing customer is five times less expensive than making a first sale to a new customer.

Therefore, you need a back-end of additional products and services to sell to customers who have already purchased their first product or service. (*Note:* For the rest of this discussion, let's use the word "product" to mean "product or service," and "product line" to mean "line of products or menu of services offered.")

One of my clients is a large marketer of self-help audio learning systems, sold mainly through direct mail. This client does not make a profit on the first order he gets from you. However, he has a back-end of dozens of other programs, which he aggressively sells to existing customers to turn each customer from a loss into a handsome profit.

Often, marketers will sell the first product at cost or even at a loss to gain as many new customers as they can as swiftly as they can because they know from the LCV the enormous value of each new customer they add to their list.

A product sold at or below cost to acquire new customers is called a "loss leader." An example is the mail order magazine ads you see from coin and precious metals companies offering silver or gold coins "at cost." The company makes no money selling the coins at cost, but it wins new customers, which has enormous LCV.

In the service sector, "buying the business" is a derogatory term used to describe the practice of "lowballing" (underbidding) to win a contract. Those who frown upon the practice say that if you lowball to get the first contract, you can never charge that client your regular rates—and you have just acquired a highly unprofitable piece of business. But there are two flaws in their thinking.

First, it's simply not true. Just call your lowball price quote an "introductory special." Make it clear that the product or service usually costs more—and will in the future—but that customers can get a great deal when they act now. Second, "buying the business" often turns out to be a smart move—especially when you take into account the LCV of the customer you are trying to win.

To determine how much they can afford to spend to get a new customer, many service firms make the mistake of basing that figure on the average size of the first order. Therefore, if the front-end product or service is $500, they won't spend anywhere near that to acquire the customer, for fear of operating at break-even or even a loss. If they want to double their money on the promotion, the most they'll spend to make the sale is $250.

But smarter marketers know that the amount of money you can spend to acquire a new customer should be based on LCV, not just the revenue from the first order. For instance, if the average unit of sale is $500, the average number of purchases per year is two, and the average customer remains a customer for five years, the lifetime customer value is $500 x 2 x 5 = $5,000.

Based on the average lifetime value, you can see where it would, in fact, be worth spending $500 to acquire a new customer. The business owner who understands LCV as it relates to customer acquisition has a tremendous advantage: He is willing to spend more to acquire new business, because he knows its true value.

Based on an understanding of this principle, marketing guru Jay Abraham frequently advises clients to give salespeople a 100 percent commission on the first sale, instead of their regular 10 percent or whatever. The 100 percent commission gives the salesperson much greater incentive to go out and get new business. And the company gets their usual profit on all the repeat sales.

A company selling books to corporate librarians asked me to devise a marketing campaign to get new corporate accounts to start ordering books from them. I asked the owner what he would be willing to spend to get a new account. He said about $300. Forget advertising, I advised. Just open up an account for every company you want as a customer—and put $300 in it! Send each prospect a personal letter telling them they already have an account with you—and that it contains $300 they can use at any time this year. Instead of a sales or marketing campaign, my client gave the money he would have spent to generate leads and makes sales calls directly to his key prospects, so they could try the service at no cost. It worked like a charm!

Today online trading services use the same tactic. They send you a letter telling you they have opened an account for you with $75 or so in it. You get the money when you do your first trade.

Need to stimulate business? Calculate LCV, decide what percentage of that amount you want to spend on acquiring new customers (10 percent is a common figure), and just give potential customers the money in exchange for trying your product or service.

Creating New Products

When designing products for your line, keep in mind that a product is not just a physical object made of such-and-such material, weighing so many pounds, and having particular dimensions and colors. A product is much more than that. Marketing writers are fond of noting that consumers don't buy products—they buy the benefits the product offers.

Books are a good example. If you think of a book as a physical product, it is essentially paper and ink. The value of the paper and ink that went into manufacturing this book is much less than the price you paid for it. But you are paying not for paper and ink, or words on a page, or even the information and ideas. You are paying for the value of that information and those ideas, which is their ability to help you improve your business and make you more money. How-to writer Jerry Buchanan once said, "When you sell a man a how-to book, you are not selling him paper and ink; you are selling him a whole new life."

So in planning a new product, you have to determine what features to build into it. But you should also think about how these features can deliver the benefits your buyers want. Other aspects of a physical product you must consider in the design stage include models available, sizes, colors, options, accessories, weight, dimensions, and packaging.

Virtually all products are defined not just by their physical features, but also by the company and service behind them. What kind of warranty or guarantee will you offer? What kind of service and support comes with the product? Does the seller or the consumer pay for shipping and handling?

One technique for planning new products that has been successful in the past but is mostly overlooked today is this: Write the strongest ad or sales letter you can for the product you want to introduce before you actually design and build the product. Then test the ad or letter. You can show it to potential buyers and get their reaction. Or you can test and produce the product only if there is interest.

Use the worksheet in Figure 6–1 on page 88 to make sure you cover all the important points in your ad or letter when describing the new product you want to create. In the left column, fill in the important facts about the new product; e.g., features, colors, options, pricing, and so on.

Then for each product fact in your ad or letter, rate it in terms of consumer appeal and whether it is a strong selling feature or not. For instance, if the variety of colors in which you are producing the product is a real plus to buyers, rate it a 4 or 5.

Any product fact or description in your ad or letter copy rating a 3, 4, or 5 should strongly be considered for inclusion in the actual

1 = weak; don't stress this aspect in promotion
5 = strong; stress in advertising
NA = not applicable

Name of product: _____

Category	Comment	Ranking
Packaging		
Description		
Benefits	1.	
	2.	
	3.	
Features	1.	
	2.	
	3.	
Perceived Value		
Models, Colors, and Special Features Available		
Options/Accessories		
Warranty/Guarantee Policy		
Price		
Ease and Method of Purchase		
Method of Delivery or Distribution		
Speed of Delivery		
Service and Support		
Reputation of the Seller		

FIGURE 6–1. **Product Definition and Description Ranking Sheet**

product. Any item rated 1 or 2 probably isn't worth developing and can safely be omitted.

Features and Benefits

You've heard it said before that when advertising your product, you should stress features instead of benefits. But it's a little more complicated than that. To be accurate, product attributes aren't just divided into one of two categories—features or benefits. Experienced marketers know that there are four levels of production description. These are *features, advantages, benefits*, and *ultimate benefits*, the hierarchy of which is illustrated in the FAB (feature/advantage/benefit) Pyramid (Figure 6–2). The more you understand and use all four levels in your advertising—not just benefits—the more effective your advertising will be.

The lowest level of the pyramid is features. A feature is what a product is or has—the literal physical description of the product. For

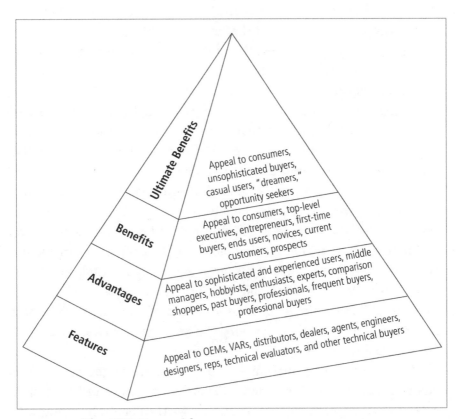

FIGURE 6–2. **The FAB Pyramid**

instance, one feature of a tire is that it is steel-belted. Another might be that it is double-ply. Although experts tell you to "stress benefits, not features," a feature can be a selling point even if the prospect doesn't know what it is. For instance, when I was a kid, brochures for the new car models coming out would boast about "rack and pinion" steering. The car makers hyped it so much, everyone asked dealers, "Does the car have rack-and-pinion steering?" Yet I bet not one buyer in a hundred really knew what rack and pinion steering was. I still don't.

Next, there are advantages. An advantage is a feature your product has that competitive products do not have. You know that to get consumers interested in your product, you must show how your product is different than competing products. The advantage is that point of differentiation. For our tire example, it might be that our tire is the only steel-belted radial that is also double-ply.

Moving up the hierarchy, the next level of product description is benefits. A benefit is what the product does and how the consumer comes out ahead as a result of this capability.

Going back to our tire example, the benefit of a steel-belted double-ply radial might be that the tire grips the road tighter and increases safety while driving, or that it can drive for another 100 miles after being punctured before you have to change it.

At the top of the product description hierarchy are what I call ultimate benefits. An ultimate benefit is "the benefit of the benefit"— the most important way in which the product improves the user's life. Ultimate benefits include saving money, saving time, making money, success, self-esteem, security, safety, joy, pleasure, and happiness. Remember the TV commercial for the tire showing a baby sitting in the middle of a tire? That's an example of showing the ultimate benefit: Simply put, they're saying, "If you buy our tires, you won't kill your baby."

In business-to-business marketing, a benefit might be "reduces energy costs." The ultimate benefit is often "makes you a hero within your company," meaning that if you achieve the benefit by purchasing the product, senior management will look upon you favorably.

To make your copy richer, deeper, and more credible, don't just talk about benefits. Instead, use all four levels of product description: features, advantages, benefits, and ultimate benefits.

Why not just focus on the highest level—ultimate benefits? Well, although ultimate benefits are powerful, they are too generic and not specific enough. To give your advertising specificity, state the specific benefit (e.g., "reduces energy costs 50 percent") that delivers the ultimate benefit ("you'll be the hero of your company").

To differentiate your product from others that deliver a similar benefit, you need to explain the advantages—how your product is different from or better than the competition. Lots of marketing seminars urge you to stress benefits instead of features, but you should use both.

Reason: Prospects are skeptical that your product can deliver the benefits you promise, because everyone is promising those same benefits. When you show how a particular feature delivers the benefit, it becomes more believable to the prospect. For instance, if you tell the buyer your computer system never loses data, he thinks, "How can that be?" But when you describe the feature—that the material is automatically backed up to the cloud—then your claim becomes more believable.

Turn Product Flaws into Selling Points

No matter how well you plan your product or how meticulously you fabricate it, no product is perfect. Your product will have strengths competitors do not have, but also be weaker in other areas. The trick is to highlight your strengths, of course. But rather than hide your weaknesses, which almost never works (your competitors will be sure to point them out for you), you can gain leverage by turning them into an advantage or selling point.

Here's an example: Legendary adman James Webb Young, who started selling fruit by mail around the same time that Harry & David did, tells the story of an apple-growing season where he was nearly ruined. Violent hail storms bombarded his apple trees with ice pellets, causing bruising and pock marks.

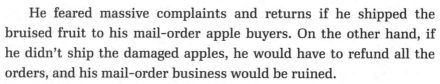

He feared massive complaints and returns if he shipped the bruised fruit to his mail-order apple buyers. On the other hand, if he didn't ship the damaged apples, he would have to refund all the orders, and his mail-order business would be ruined.

However, the apples were damaged only cosmetically. The hail had pockmarked the skin, but it did not affect the flavor or freshness. Young went ahead and filled his orders with the pockmarked apples, and in each box shipped, enclosed a preprinted card that read as follows (I am paraphrasing):

"Note the pockmarks on some of these apples. This is proof that they are grown at a high mountain altitude, where the same extreme cold that causes sudden hailstorms also firms the flesh and increases the natural sugars, making the apples even sweeter."

According to Young, not a single order was returned. In fact, when orders came in for next year, many order forms had handwritten notes that said, "Pockmarked apples if available; otherwise, the regular kind."

Young's story proves what experienced marketers know: Often, by being truthful about your weaknesses and flaws, you can gain substantial credibility with your buyer, increasing loyalty, sales, and customer satisfaction.

How to use this technique: Pick one weakness of your product or company. Talk about it frankly in your marketing. Show why either: a) the weakness is not really important, or b) how you have designed your product or service to either overcome, solve, or compensate for the weakness.

Buying Motivations

Which elements of the FAB Pyramid—features, advantages, benefits, or ultimate benefits—should you stress in your marketing communications? Which will motivate the consumer to buy your product most effectively?

One way to determine this is with a tool called the FCB Grid (see Figure 6–3 on page 93), named after the ad agency that developed it: Foote, Cone & Belding. The grid helps pinpoint consumer buying motivation based on two factors.

The first factor is involvement: Is this a purchase decision you devote much thought and time to? In the figure, you can see that the purchase of a new camera is a high-involvement activity. You might go to several stores to research it, review digital camera pricing online, ask friends for recommendations, and so on. An example of a low-involvement purchase decision would be buying paper for your laser printer: Whenever you run out, you go to Staples and buy more reams of whatever they happen to have in stock.

The second factor determining consumer buying motivation is emotion: Is the buying decision based on cold logic (thinking), or is there a strong emotional component to it (feeling)? An example of a feeling-based purchase decision might be when a bride-to-be shops

	Emotion	
	Think	Feel
High Involvement	Computer	Diamond engagement ring
Low Involvement	Paper clips	Birthday card

FIGURE 6–3. **The FCB Grid**

for her wedding gown, while a thinking-based purchase decision might be buying blank CDs for your PC.

Determining the degree of involvement and emotion places the purchase decision in one of four quadrants on the FCB grid, which, in turn, tells us what elements of FAB to stress in our marketing copy. For a high-involvement, feeling-based purchase like buying a new car, we would be in the upper right quadrant. That would mean marketing copy should stress ultimate benefits and benefits, plus some advantages, with features being a minor part of the copy.

On the other hand, a digital camera would be a high-involvement purchase, but thinking-based, so it would fall in the upper-left quadrant. Here our marketing messages would stress features and advantages (e.g., a larger memory for storing more images), but also hit benefits (e.g., you can store more photos of your grandkids to show off to friends).

Pricing

What should you charge for your product? That, too, is a component of product development. Are you looking to create a low-priced item you can sell as a loss leader to bring in new customers (remember, a loss leader is a low-priced product, often sold at or below cost, to acquire new customers)? Or are you looking to create a high-priced back-end product to sell to your existing customers?

As a business owner and marketing advisor, I have a prejudice against the discount business model or any business operating on a tiny profit margin. To me, it's more rewarding to command a higher price, charge premium fees, and get paid very, very well for what I sell. Especially if you are in a service business, competing on price means you work harder to earn less. Who wants that?

But in a competitive world where many other businesses seemingly offer products and services similar to yours, how do you command a premium price? There are five factors you can control or exploit to enable you to charge a much higher price than your competitors in virtually any field—and have more customers than you can handle waiting in line, cash in hand, to pay it.

The first factor is supply and demand. According to simple economics, the greater the demand for something and the more limited the supply, the more the seller can charge and get paid for it. Since you're not OPEC, you probably can't control the supply of your product or service. So what you have to do is create an overwhelming demand for you, your product, or your service. Perhaps the easiest way to do this is to position yourself as the pre-eminent expert or authority in your field. If people view you as *the* guru in property taxes, hazardous waste cleanup, or whatever your field is, they will come to you first, knocking each other over to hire you instead of your lesser-known competitors.

The second factor you can control is your market niche. As a rule of thumb, the narrower your market niche, the more you can charge. Specialists can always charge more than generalists. If you are a marketing consultant handling any small-business clients you can get, you have lots of competition and great difficulty commanding a premium fee. On the other hand, if you specialize in the marketing of accounting practices, accountants will pay a premium to get your advice because it applies to their own situation.

The third factor you can control is value. If your competitors all sell audiobooks with six CDs for $79, and you want to charge $300 for six CDs on similar topics, why should the buyer pay it? You could include a CD with related software programs (e.g., if the album is about time management, the CD could contain a personal day planner). The material cost is only a dollar or so per CD, but the perceived value of software is easily $100 or more, enabling you to charge a premium price for your package. And that's the trick: to add extras that have high-perceived value but don't cost you much.

Free is one of the most powerful words in sales. In the late '70s, when I took my first marketing job in Baltimore with Westinghouse, we had a secret marketing weapon we referred to as the "junk cabinet." It was filled with all sorts of advertising specialties—favorites were golf balls and golf tees—all imprinted with the Westinghouse logo.

My first thought was, "Who would want this cheap crap?" Turns out, everybody.

Whenever a salesman was giving a high-ranking general a tour of the plant (our biggest customer was the military), he'd invariably ask us for golf balls and tees. I was fascinated to see that the presentation of these items—which only cost a few bucks—thrilled the customers to no end.

Once, we sent Westinghouse customers a single cufflink with an invitation promising they would get the matching link when they came to our exhibit at a major trade show. We barely had enough room in our giant booth to accommodate those who came—almost all asking for their free cufflink.

The conclusion: People love to get free stuff. By offering a small free gift to your prospects, you can significantly boost the response to your marketing efforts at minimal cost. If your prospect is an information seeker, then a free information premium—a booklet, a white paper, a special report—can perform well.

If your prospect is not a reader, then use a merchandise premium. The possibilities are almost limitless: coffee mugs, golf balls, T-shirts, golf caps, tape measures, mini-tool sets, pens, key chains, luggage tags, and calculators, just for starters. The cost of the premium depends on what you can afford to spend to acquire a new customer. But in most instances, we're looking for premiums that cost $10 or less.

You can improve your response rates by offering a premium that has a perceived value much higher than its cost. A CD can be a great premium, because the value of its content—whether images, video, audio, or software—can be extremely high (software sells from $19 to $500 or more per program), but the duplication cost is a few bucks apiece. You can also offer this on a 1GB flash drive, which has a high-perceived value, can include a lot of content, and can be reused by the client.

On the other hand, a publisher did a promo that bombed when it offered a deck of playing cards with a famous editor's photo on them. Perceived value is low: Everybody knows a deck of cards costs about 99 cents in CVS.

Advertising Age magazine had a spectacular success offering a personalized coffee mug with the subscriber's name on it. What made it work was that the name was incorporated into a headline—"Bob Bly Wins Marketing Genius Award"—that was laser-printed on a facsimile of the front page of an *Ad Age* issue.

In addition to high-perceived value, look for premiums that are unique. The Sovereign Society, a newsletter on offshore investing, had great success offering new subscribers an unusual premium: their own Swiss bank account.

I advise every direct marketer to offer a premium, whether you're generating sales leads or selling a mail-order product. Offering a gift with an inquiry or order adds perceived value to your offer. It also allows you to legitimately work the word *free* into your headline or envelope teaser—and in doing so increase your chances of catching the prospect's attention and getting an inquiry or order.

Years ago, when I was selling business writing seminars to Fortune 500 corporations, I charged $3,500 a day. Many other trainers charged $1,500 to $2,500 a day for similar programs. To add value so I could get my fee, I offered unlimited free 30-day follow-up, where the attendees could call me for advice and ask questions without charge for a full month after the seminar date. While this follow-up service had a high-perceived value (I described it as a $1,000 value in my sales literature), and training directors loved the idea, in reality very few seminar attendees took advantage, so it cost me almost nothing to deliver.

The fourth factor you can control is ROI. If you design your product or service so it generates a large ROI that is easy to see and measure, it will be much easier to sell at the price you want to get. As consultant Jay Abraham says, "Will you give me a quarter if I give you a dollar?" If you can prove a 4:1 ROI from your product or service, it's like selling a dollar for a quarter—an easy sale to make. For example, $200 for a high-tech thermostat may seem like a lot of money, but not if the manufacturer can prove that installing the thermostat will save the homeowner $300 to $1,000 a year in heating and air conditioning costs.

The fifth factor you can control is customers' concern about whether they will be satisfied with your product. You can control this by offering a money-back guarantee. Guarantees overcome sales resistance. If you guarantee customers will be happy and you will refund their money if they are not, they will be more willing to pay your price, no matter what it is.

We all know that a strong money-back guarantee is a powerful weapon for overcoming buyer resistance and boosting your sales. But you can run into problems when your guarantee has flaws. The best guarantees are:

◆ Fair
◆ Generous
◆ Long term
◆ Unconditional

When any of these four elements is missing, sales are likely to suffer. For example, many of my clients are newsletter and magazine publishers. A number of these publishers offer lifetime guarantees. They permit the subscriber to cancel at any time and receive a prorated refund on "unmailed issues."

But if you offer both a bill-me option as well as payment with order—as I often come across—such a lifetime guarantee actually gives the customer an incentive *not* to pay upfront. Think about it: Say the customer checks the "bill-me" option for a monthly magazine, gets his first issue, and then writes "cancel" on his invoice. The publisher doesn't send him a bill for one issue, nor does the publisher ask for the magazine back. So the customer gets a free issue.

But if the customer pays in advance, then cancels after the first issue, he gets a refund for 11/12th of the subscription price (the 11 unmailed issues) and, therefore, ends up paying for the issue received. Why should the bill-me customer get a free issue, but not the payment-with-order customer? It isn't fair and doesn't make sense, considering a cash-with-order customer is more desirable than a bill-me order. Solution: Offer a full money-back guarantee within the first 30 days, then prorated refund thereafter.

Remember, you benefit enormously from offering a guarantee, because it gets more people to trust you and buy from you. But the customer benefits too: He gets a chance to try the product risk-free.

Most people won't take unfair advantage of your guarantee. If you sell a quality product, accurately described in your marketing, at a price that's fair in relationship to its value, your return rate will be low—probably less than 5 percent.

That still means 1 in 20 will ask for a refund. Give them back their money promptly and with good cheer. Few things will cause more customer dissatisfaction and ruin your reputation faster than being difficult, adversarial, and uncooperative when people believe what you said in your guarantee and take you up on it. Don't get angry with these folks. Returning the product is their right—and part of your cost of doing business.

> Remember, you benefit enormously from offering a guarantee, because it gets more people to trust you and buy from you.

And there you have it. Increase demand for your product or service, target a vertical market niche, add value, generate a good ROI, and guarantee satisfaction, and customers will gladly pay your price, even if it's 50 to 100 percent or more above what your competitors charge.

One risk of charging high prices is that it may induce "sticker shock" in your prospects when you tell them. "Sticker shock" refers to a price so high that when you reveal it to the customer, he or she is flabbergasted and immediately protests that "your price is too high" or "I could never afford this." If your customers experience sticker shock, it means you have not convinced them that the price of the product is a drop in the bucket compared to the value of the product. Even if you've done a good job of communicating value, the prospect may experience sticker shock if the price is extremely high or beyond their means.

Sticker shock reduces your chances of closing the sale: If customers gasp when they learn the price, they're probably not ready to pay it. If, as a marketer or salesperson, you can head off sticker shock before it happens, your odds of closing the sale increase tremendously.

How do you prevent sticker shock? One way is to show the customer products in your line with higher prices before showing him the product you want him to buy. In his book *Influence*, Robert Cialdini describes how this is done in a retail setting. Say you want to sell $100 sweaters in your store, but are afraid your customers will faint at the price. You put a table in the aisle near the front door and place three stacks of sweaters on it. As a customer walks into the room, she sees the first stack. All the sweaters in this pile cost $300. "What a rip-off!" she thinks. "No way would I pay that." Then she examines the second pile, which contains $200 sweaters. "Phew," she thinks. "That's a little better." She continues to go down the table until she comes to the third stack—your $100 sweaters. By that time, she is so relieved that a sweater won't cost her $300 or even $200 that the $100 you are asking seems like an incredible bargain.

Breaking the price into monthly installments is another effective way to minimize sticker shock. For instance, the Franklin Mint was selling a collectible chess set. The pieces were each hand-painted pewter miniatures of Civil War figures, sent to you one per month. For these hand-painted collectible figurines, the price was only $17.50. Seems like a bargain for a collectible item, right? But if you multiply $17.50 times the number of pieces (32), the entire chess set cost a hefty $560 (the board was yours free once you bought all 32 pieces). If the Mint's ad had said, "Civil War Chess Set—$560," how many do you think they'd have sold? Not many, right?

> Another way to avoid sticker shock is to present the price at the beginning and get any price objections out of the way upfront.

Another way to avoid sticker shock is to present the price at the beginning and get any price objections out of the way upfront. Most advertising for expensive products builds desire and perceived value, then reveals the price once the customer is sold. An opposite approach is to state the price upfront and use the exclusivity of a big number to weed out nonprospects. This is illustrated by an old cartoon showing a salesman in an auto showroom saying to a customer, "If you have to ask how much it costs, you can't afford one."

For example, say you are selling a financial service for $2,500 a year. That's on the high end for financial advisories, so you risk inducing sticker shock when you introduce the price at the end of the copy. The solution is to introduce the price at the very beginning. The idea is to deal with it upfront and get it out of the way (e.g., "This service is for serious investors only. It costs $2,500 a year. If that price scares you, this is not for you."). If the prospect continues reading your promotion after seeing that on page one, you know that they are willing to pay the high price provided they perceive high value.

An element of exclusivity and snob appeal is at work here: The more you tell someone they do not qualify, the more they will insist they do and want your offer. The classic example is Hank Burnett's famous letter for the Admiral Bird Society's fundraising expedition. The second paragraph states: "It will cost you $10,000 and about 26 days of your time. Frankly, you will endure some discomfort, and may even face some danger." Once readers have seen the price and decided to continue reading, the possibility of sticker shock is eliminated because they already know what the product costs. Surprise is eliminated, and sticker shock is all about surprise.

Recurring Revenues

Most businesses focus on the one-shot, upfront sales model. The customer buys the product, gives the vendor the payment, and that's it.

But your cash flow as well as your financial security can be improved with recurring revenues. That means instead of buying just once, the customer for one reason or another has to continue to give you money on a regular basis, usually monthly or annually. Here are a few of the recurring revenue streams:

 ◆ *Subscriptions*. Magazines are a good example. Although the buyer has no contract to do so, 40 percent to 80 percent will renew their subscriptions annually.

- *Insurance.* You have to pay the premium on your policy monthly, quarterly, or annually.

- *Investment advisors.* They manage an account holding your money for which they get an annual fee, typically around 1 percent of the funds in the account. On a million-dollar account, that's $10,000 a year.

- *Continual usage.* Cable television, website hosting, long-distance phone service, and other services the customer needs on a continual basis give you a recurring income stream, often monthly but sometimes annually.

- *Locked-in services.* These are services you buy where you could switch to another service provider, but it is decidedly inconvenient to do so. Example: your accountant. He has all your tax records and knows your business or personal financial situation well. Therefore, you pay him to do your tax returns once a year like clockwork.

- *Internet marketing.* You can have recurring revenue with a membership site for which members pay a monthly fee in exchange for access to content and maybe services provided by the site.

- *Club or association memberships.* Memberships typically have a 10 percent higher renewal rate than magazines and newsletters.

- *Service contracts.* Certain equipment like central air conditioning systems and full-house standby generators must be serviced at minimum annually. Consumers buy service contracts that they pay for annually or quarterly. The contracts usually cover an annual routine inspection and maintenance, plus periodic repairs and emergencies as needed.

- *Home services.* This includes services like weekly house-cleaning maid service or annual termite inspection and treatment.

The advantage of recurring income is it helps you avoid the feast or famine, crisis-lull-crisis work and revenue flow that many businesses without ongoing revenue streams are vulnerable to.

Chapter 7
ASSESS YOUR TACTICS

Now that you've mapped out your strategy for achieving your goals, it's time to identify the tactics you'll use to implement your strategy. First, you'll need to define your outcomes. What do you want your prospects and clients to do in response to your tactics? Next, what message do you need to give them to motivate them to take the actions you want? Only then can you decide which tactics are most likely to give you the desired responses.

In marketing, rarely will employing only one type of tactic result in everything you want to accomplish. So, first, evaluate the range of tactics available to you. Then choose the best three to five, so you won't be overwhelmed. Last, you'll write a description of the tactics you've decided to use. Trial and error will let you identify which tactics are working.

Determine the Response You Want from Your Prospect

Tactics are the actions you take to implement your strategy. Think about these carefully so you can determine what response you're trying to generate from your target audience. For example, you might want them to:

- Go to your website to get more information.
- Fill out an online survey.
- Call to speak with a salesperson.
- Request that a salesperson call them.
- Attend a free webinar.
- Download a free white paper.
- Call for more information.
- Agree to a sales meeting or presentation.
- Attend a free seminar or workshop.
- Request a free product demo.
- Take a 30-day free trial of the product.
- Refer your services to others in your target market.
- Become an affiliate and sell your products and services.
- Buy the product with a credit card.

Decide What Message Will Stimulate This Behavior

Next, ask, "What message(s), if properly conveyed and believed by my audience, will stimulate this behavior?" "Can I support the message with evidence?" "Do I have testimonials, case studies, thank-you letters or notes, or other support?"

Here are some tips on crafting a message to generate the desired action on the part of the prospect:

- *The "so what" test.* After you write your copy, read it and ask whether it passes the "so what" test. Copywriter Joan Damico explains, "If after reviewing your copy, you think the target audience would just respond with 'so what,' then keep rewriting until they'll say something like, 'That's exactly what I'm looking for. How do I get it?'"

  Copywriters' agent Kevin Finn adds, "When copy is being critiqued, you should ask after each and every sentence, 'So what?' It's a technique that can assist in changing copy to be more powerful."

◆ *Use the key copy drivers.* Make sure your copy hits one of the key copy drivers as defined by direct marketing experts Bob Hacker and Axel Andersson: fear, greed, guilt, exclusivity, anger, salvation, or flattery.

"If your copy is not dripping with one or more of these, tear it up and start over," says copywriter Denny Hatch.

◆ *The drop-in-the-bucket technique.* "You have to show that the price you are asking for your product is a 'drop in the bucket' compared to the value it delivers," says copywriter Mike Pavlish.

Information marketer Fred Gleeck says this is a function of product quality, not just copywriting. "Produce a product that you could charge ten times as much for," says Gleeck. "If you really have a product that is so much more valuable than the price you're charging, it becomes much easier to sell it hard."

◆ *Know your audience.* Understand your target market—their fears, needs, concerns, beliefs, attitudes, desires. "My way to be persuasive is to get in touch with the target group by inviting one or two to dinner for in-depth conversation," says Christian Boucke, a copywriter for Verlag Rentrop in Germany. "I also call 15 to 40 by phone to get a multitude of testimonials and facts, and go to meetings or exhibitions where I can find them to get a first impression of their typical characteristics. Ideally, I accompany some of them in their private lives for years. By this, I understand better their true underlying key motivations."

◆ *Write like people talk.* Use a conversational, natural style. "Write like you talk," says Barnaby Kalan of Reliance Direct Marketing. "Speak in language that's simple and easy to understand. Write the way your prospects talk."

◆ *Be timely.* "Pay close attention to goings-on in the news that you can and should link to," suggests Dan Kennedy in his *No B.S. Marketing E-Letter* (June 2002). "Jump on a timely topic and link to it in useful communication with present clients, in advertising for new clients, and in seeking media publicity."

- *Lead with your strongest point.* "When I review my writing, or especially others', I find they almost always leave the most potent point to the last line," says copywriter John Shoemaker. "So I simply move it to the first line. Instant improvement."

- *Use the tremendous whack theory.* "I employ Winston Churchill's 'tremendous whack' theory, which says that if you have an important point to make, don't try to be subtle or clever," says marketing professional Richard Perry. "Use a pile driver. Hit the point once. Then come back and hit it again. Then hit it a third time—a tremendous whack."

- *Build credibility with your reader.* "In my experience, the number-one key to persuasion is this: Communicate trust," says copywriter Steve Slaunwhite. "If you do this well, you at least have a chance at engaging and persuading the reader. If you don't do this well, however, no amount of fancy copywriting techniques will save you."

- *Don't use an "obvious lead."* Instead of writing your lead as if you are just starting to talk to the customer, says marketer Bryan Honesty, write as if you were already engaged in a conversation with the customer and are simply responding to her last statement. Examples: "You have the gift. You just don't know it yet." "You can't quit on your dreams now." "So why is it so hard for you to lose weight?"

Decide Which Marketing Tactics Will Best Support Your Strategy

Choose only those tactics that support your strategy and positioning statement. Remember, everything should work toward the same outcome. Tactics take many forms, and there are several types. Table 7–1 highlights some of the most common tactics.

Product/Service Tactics
Add value-added features: alterations, overnight delivery, consultants to assist with specialized problems, installation, free repairs.
Introduce a new service to add depth.
Introduce new packages to fit specific markets and applications.
Create exclusive distribution channels.
Package services or products together to make the package more attractive.
Package a product with its accessories.

Pricing Tactics
Introductory pricing (low fees to capture new clients willing to try out your service at a low-risk fee)
Image pricing (low prices to appeal to fee-conscious prospects; higher prices to appeal to value-conscious prospects)
Tier pricing (quantity breaks)
Bundling pricing (if you purchase this item also, you'll pay only $ for both items)
Value-added pricing (free installation, free training, free ebook, etc.)
Pay one price (membership club fees that open up the entire inventory to members)
Non-negotiating price (e.g., Saturn cars—lowest price guaranteed)
Free shipping

Packaging Tactics
Image—how you communicate your positioning and brand with business cards, letterhead, product packaging, logos, etc.
Demonstrations (lunch 'n' learn sample trainings; food tables at Sam's Club and Costco; clothing sellers do fashion shows)
Displays—point of purchase, interactive kiosks
Customer service tactics
Technical support
Flexible hours of operation
Refund guarantees

TABLE 7–1. **Common Tactics to Support Your Strategy**

Packaging Tactics
Guarantee your estimates (e.g., the maximum bill will be 110 percent of the estimate)
Flexible delivery times
No/low minimum order
Installment payments
Credit
More payment methods

Communication Tactics
Website(s) for every service you offer
Your website URL on all your promotions
Articles written by you
Press releases
Public speaking
Direct mail
Postcards
Telephone calls
Internet advertising
Classified ads
Yellow Pages
Trade shows
Viral, word-of-mouth, referrals
Social media (YouTube, LinkedIn, Facebook, Twitter)
Business cards
Networking
Salespeople
Joint ventures, cross promotions
Affiliate programs
Podcasting
Webinars
Blogs
Teleseminars

TABLE 7–1. **Common Tactics to Support Your Strategy,** continued

Communication Tactics
Seminars
Workshops
Lunch 'n' learns
Surveys
Online courses
Newsletters
Ezines
Gift certificates
Contests
Publicity events
Signs
Banners
Pay-per-click (PPC) advertising
Google AdSense
Sponsorship
Sales letters
Case studies
Email marketing

TABLE 7–1. **Common Tactics to Support Your Strategy,** continued

Tactics that Reach Your Target Market

As you evaluate each tactic, ask yourself whether it will appeal to your target audience. Specifically, how will it help move forward your strategy for meeting your goals? Table 7–2 on page 110 shows a variety of marketing channels and their relative effectiveness when targeting narrow niche markets. They are rated on a scale of 1 to 5 based on whether they are best at reaching broad audiences or narrow niche markets. In fact, your very ability to conduct a targeted marketing campaign aimed at a narrow niche group of buyers depends on whether there are media available that enable you to reach your potential prospects cost-effectively.

KEY
1 = broadly targeted, horizontal media, aimed at a mass market
5 = highly focused, vertical media, aimed at a narrow audience with specialized interests

Marketing Tool	Degree of Targeting
Newspaper advertising	1
Magazine advertising	4
Broadcast advertising	1
Cable TV advertising	4
Network radio	2
Spot (local) radio	3
Billboards	1
Transit advertising	1
Catalogs	5
Direct mail	5
Postcard decks	4
Publicity and public relations	3
Telemarketing	4
Trade shows	4
Websites	3
Email marketing	5
Pay-per-click advertising	4
Banner advertising	3
Organic search	4
Email marketing	4
Social networking	2

TABLE 7–2. **Degree of Targeting by Industry or Specialization**

Years ago, I worked with a company that sold business services to medical group practices. They targeted radiologists, and doctor lists are easy to get. However, they discovered their target prospect was not the doctor, but the radiology practice's business manager. Their mailing list broker did not have a medical list targeting the radiology manager. They found out that, as is often the case, there was a small trade association serving the marketplace they wanted to reach. In this case, it was the Radiology Business Managers Association (RBMA). The RBMA had a monthly newsletter, and the company had good success with full-page ads in this publication, because they could target the radiology practices' business managers directly and write an ad to their needs and concerns.

Inbound vs. Outbound Marketing Tactics

Which works best—inbound or outbound marketing? By *inbound*, we mean prospects contact us "out of the blue," as it were, because they somehow know about us or find us. *Outbound* marketing requires us to actively reach out and touch prospects proactively (e.g., with a postcard, telemarketing call, email, or magazine advertisement).

The question of which marketing—inbound or outbound— generates the best leads can't really be answered authoritatively, because it's too broad. If we say the winner is inbound, does that mean *every* type of inbound communication produces better leads than every type of outbound communication? No, it doesn't.

A better way to approach the question is to examine each inbound and outbound marketing channel and evaluate the quality of leads produced on a case-by-case basis. In Table 7–3 on page 115, I list the major marketing promotions used for lead generation, indicate which I consider inbound vs. outbound, and rate them on a scale of 1 to 5 (1 = low, 5 = high) for quality of leads and ROI (you may disagree with some of my choices and ratings). *Quality of leads* mainly measures whether the marketing communication attracts prospects who fit your customer profile, have a need for your product or service, and are predisposed to buy from you instead of your competitors.

ROI measures whether the leads turn into orders, generating revenues far in excess of the time and money spent to obtain them. (*Note:* These ratings are my own and are to a degree subjective, based on three decades of experience; they are not based on statistically valid research.)

The biggest controversy in lead generation is traffic generated by organic search (when you search for information on Google or another search engine). Some marketing writers erroneously tell us that organic search brings you the best leads. They reason that prospects would not be searching your keyword unless they were researching a product purchase. Therefore, organic search brings you good prospects—those in shopping mode.

> The biggest controversy in lead generation is traffic generated by organic search.

The quality of organic search leads depends, however, on the keywords being searched. We find that searches performed on broad keyword terms (e.g., limousines) attract visitors who are in the early stages of product research, and therefore not hot leads. When a search is performed on highly specific keywords (e.g., used Lincoln Continental limousine for sale in New York area), the prospect is most likely farther along in the research process and closer to making a buying decision.

The reason I do not rate organic search leads higher in Table 7–3 is that, while these prospects may be predisposed to buying, they are in no way predisposed to buying from *you*. Indeed, the very fact that they are doing a Google search on a generic keyword probably means they have little brand loyalty. As a freelance copywriter, some of the worst leads I get are people searching for freelance copywriters on Google. These prospects often view copywriting as a commodity service and are likely to choose low price over experience and quality, as many internet shoppers do in numerous categories.

Conversely, the best leads service professionals get are typically people who call or email us because they know us by reputation and may even be fans of our work. By far, the most qualified leads I get are prospects who have read my books and articles, or have heard me speak at a seminar, conference, or workshop.

Creating and disseminating content related to your product or industry is a proven technique for establishing yourself as a thought leader in your field or niche. Therefore, a prospect who is an avid reader or student of your writings and talks is predisposed to doing business with you, because they consider you a guru or expert.

I rated social networking a 4 in lead quality. Networking has always produced good leads, and social networks are basically networking moved online. So far, however, most B2B marketers have been unsuccessful in establishing hard metrics to measure social media ROI. Some argue that the ROI has to be high because social networking is virtually free. But they neglect ROTI, return on time invested. A survey by Michael Stelzner of *Social Media Examiner*, the largest online magazine covering social marketing, found that experienced social media users spend two to four hours per day on social networking, which means an investment of up to half their workweek.

Direct mail has long been considered the "work horse" of lead-generating marketing communications. Ten years ago, I would have rated the lead quality a 4, because postal lists enable narrow targeting, so you can mail only to prospects who fit your ideal customer's profile. I downgraded direct mail lead quality from a 4 to a 3, because, lately, I find prospects with more urgent needs respond to electronic or phone marketing, while those whose need is not as immediate are more likely to mail back a business reply card requesting your catalog, brochure, or white paper. The ROI of direct-mail-generated leads is a 4, because the leads you do close often make significant purchases in the multiple thousands of dollars. You can, as a rule, get from 10 to 25 percent or more of direct mail leads to take the next step in your buying cycle, whether agreeing to see your rep or sending you a purchase order. Direct mail that's working usually generates a positive and significant ROI, producing revenues many times greater than the campaign cost.

Email gets a 3 in lead quality. You can target the right prospects. But internet users have an element of distrust for email, so a single email isn't going to move prospects very far forward in the buying cycle. ROI is a 5. That's because email marketing is so cheap, even a few orders can give us an ROI equal to many multiples of the promotion cost. When you are renting opt-in e-lists, your cost per thousand can be $200 or more. Emailing your own list, depending on what service you use, is a fraction of a cent per name.

I also gave public relations an ROI rating of 5 because the cost is so minimal that any business generated usually pays for the PR campaign many times over. Lead quality of PR is a 4, because people believe and trust editorial content more so than marketing copy.

The point is that in the debate of outbound versus inbound marketing, you simply cannot make a sweeping generalization about which is better. You must evaluate the lead quality and ROI of each marketing channel individually. Table 7–3 on page 115 is a starting point. But the quality and ROI for each medium can vary greatly from industry to industry, even from company to company. My recommendation: Test them, track results, do not repeat those that fail, and do more of the ones that do work.

> The question boils down to not whether inbound vs. outbound marketing is better, but which one is better for you.

The question boils down to not whether inbound vs. outbound marketing is better, but which one is better for you. I feel that, for small businesses selling technical, trade, and professional services as opposed to physical products, inbound offers the advantage of producing more qualified leads that are easier to close.

The most obvious type of outbound promotion for selling services is cold calling. Can cold calling work? Absolutely. I know for a fact that cold calling can work. How? Because I've tested it. Not in my freelance copywriting, but for another venture—with pretty good results. Also, I personally know a number of people who are very successful with cold calling. Despite this, I dislike cold calling—and I rarely recommend it.

One drawback of cold calling is that it's labor-intensive. Unless you can outsource your cold calling—a viable option, by the way— then it requires you to spend hours dialing the phone. And for every hour you're cold calling, you're losing an hour of billable time.

A second drawback of cold calling is that it's not exactly fun. You're calling perfect strangers and interrupting busy people. If you

Marketing Channel	Category	Lead Quality	ROI
Articles	Inbound	4	4
Blogs	Inbound	4	3
Books	Inbound	5	4
Direct mail	Outbound	3	4
Email marketing	Outbound	3	5
Organic search	Inbound	3	3
Pay-per-click advertising	Outbound	4	3
PR	Inbound	4	5
Print advertising	Outbound	4	2
Seminars, live	Outbound	5	3
Social networking	Inbound	4	2
Telemarketing, inbound	Inbound	5	4
Telemarketing, outbound	Outbound	2	3
Teleseminars	Outbound	4	4
Trade show exhibits	Outbound	2	2
Yellow Pages	Outbound	5	3
Webinars	Outbound	4	4
Websites	Inbound	3	3
White papers	Inbound	4	3

TABLE 7–3. **Marketing Channel Lead Quality and ROI**

get a 10 percent response, then for every ten calls you make, nine people will reject you—right over the phone. Some will be nice about it. A few may be downright mean or abusive. And because you called them unsolicited, and interrupted whatever they were doing, you have to take it. Politely.

But in addition to these drawbacks, there are two bigger problems with cold calling and other outbound marketing methods. First, it violates the *busy doctor syndrome*. This term was coined by the late Howard Shenson, who wrote many books on consulting and seminar promotion. The busy doctor syndrome says that people would rather hire those they perceive as busy and successful. They do not want to hire those who seem desperate and in need of work.

If you're sitting at a phone cold calling potential clients, how busy and successful do you think you seem to them?

The second reason I dislike cold calling is that it puts you in a weak position for negotiating anything about your service—terms, scope of work, fee, payments, delivery dates. The three reasons prospects agree to pay premium prices are:

1. They want or need what you are selling.
2. They perceive it as exclusive and difficult to get.
3. They believe that if they do not act quickly, it will be snapped up by others and therefore not available.

When you cold call, reasons 2 and 3 disappear. After all, when you call strangers on the telephone, then obviously you have a surplus of what you are selling. I urge you to practice what I call the *Silver Rule* of marketing and selling. I call it the Silver Rule because I first heard it from my old friend, marketing consultant Pete Silver, although I don't think he actually called it the Silver Rule. Peter said: "It is better to get *them* (prospects) to come to *you*, than to have *you* go to *them*."

> The Silver Rule:
> "It is better to get them (prospects) to come to you, than to have you go to them."

Cold calling and other outbound marketing doesn't do this. So what type of marketing follows the Silver Rule? Inbound marketing, including advertising, direct mail, enewsletters, and email marketing. So do things like establishing yourself as a recognized expert by giving seminars and speeches, or writing articles for publications read by your potential clients, or writing books.

When you get an inquiry from someone who subscribes to your enewsletter, you are negotiating from a position of strength—because *they* came to *you*, rather than *you* calling *them*. When someone approaches you at a conference, says they loved your speech, and asks about engaging your firm's services, you are in a position of strength. After all, they see you as the expert.

Why does Tom Peters get $30,000 or so to give a one-hour speech on business—and have more business than he can handle—while other speakers struggle to get bookings for $3,000 or less? It is largely because, as a best-selling author, he is perceived as an expert. He has become a wealthy entrepreneur simply by practicing the Silver Rule. And so can you.

The Rebirth of Direct Mail

One tactic I include in virtually all my marketing plans is direct mail. This surprises many of my colleagues and readers. "Isn't email much cheaper?" they ask. "Isn't direct mail an obsolete marketing method?"

You would think so, but on the contrary, within the last few years, direct mail has undergone a rebirth. Response rates, for those of us who use it, are on the rise, where previously they were getting smaller and smaller.

Why is direct mail working so well once again? One big reason for the resurgence is that the prominence of digital over print has caused a decline in direct mail usage, so there is less competition in the mailbox. From 2008 to 2012, the average number of direct-mail packages received in U.S. households per week declined almost 36 percent. As the late direct-mail copywriter Paul Bringe observed, "When the feed is scarce, the chickens will peck at anything."

According to an article in *Target Marketing* magazine, 79 percent of consumers say they act on direct mail immediately, and 56 percent say print marketing is the most trustworthy of all media channels.

The myth of digital killing print is simply not true. In 2014, more than 8 out of 10 American adults said they would rather read a magazine in print than online. Two thirds prefer paperbound books to ebooks. Young people are no exception to the widespread preference for print over digital: In a report by ad agency JWT (J. Walter Thompson), almost 8 out of 10 millennials said print makes them feel more connected than digital.

"You're thinking print is dead, while digital is growing more and more every day," says digital strategist Channon McCoy. "This is not the case. With more and more companies abandoning traditional forms of mass communication, it is easier to stand out and reach your target, whether young or old, with tangible promotions like direct mail."

According to a survey by Greenhat, a marketing strategy company, B2B marketers on average spend 28 percent of their budget on digital marketing and 21 percent on traditional offline marketing. So print is hardly dead, accounting for one dollar out of every five spent on marketing. Here's more proof: According to management consulting firm Kurt Salmon, 11.9 billion print catalogs were mailed in the U.S. in 2014. While many consumers order online for convenience or go to a retail location to get the product right away, they also enjoy thumbing through catalogs to look at products and get ideas. In addition, receiving a catalog reminds them of the availability of a product or the existence of a merchant they otherwise would have never remembered.

The Direct Marketing Association (DMA) notes that, based on lifetime customer value, direct mail generates $12 in revenues for every dollar spent on paper, printing, postage, list rentals, and mailing fees. That makes it an extremely profitable marketing tactic, even for companies that are moving toward digital.

Direct-Mail Design

A traditional direct-mail package has multiple components, including an outer envelope, sales letter, brochure, lift note, and reply element.

When you are selling a high-end professional service to a sophisticated audience and want to convey an image of professionalism, all components should be printed on the same color paper stock: cream, ivory, and white are the top three choices. When you are selling mail-order merchandise to consumers, especially middle America, make each package element a different color; for example, a kraft-brown envelope, white letter, four-color brochure, lift note on robin's egg blue stock, order form on canary yellow. This makes each element pop visually, compelling the recipient to handle and look at all of them.

One characteristic of printed direct mail is that when you are attempting to generate an order and not just a lead, long copy often works better than short copy. For instance, a financial advisor was mailing a two-page flier to invite people to his free investment workshops, which he uses to find prospects, a percentage of which become his clients after follow up. He hired a freelance copywriter to write a new mailer. But when the copy was put into a layout, it was four pages instead of two. When the financial advisor showed the four-page mailer to a marketing expert in the investment niche, the guru told him it would not work because it was too long and people are in a hurry. The advisor mailed the copy anyway—and it generated twice as many enrollments in his workshop as the shorter copy. His conclusion: "When you are deciding what to do with the million dollars you plan to invest, you will find the time to read good long copy."

A Word about Branding

The tactics we've been discussing are direct-response tactics designed to generate either an order or an inquiry. Most small businesses use some variation of classic direct response in their marketing, with the goal to get the prospect into the store or showroom, or onto the website, or to call for an appointment. We call this lead generation.

> Most small businesses use some variation of classic direct response in their marketing.

Small businesses favor direct-response and lead-generation marketing because they produce a tangible, measurable result with a positive ROI: You spend $1,000 to mail out a few hundred mailers. You get 30 people to inquire about your product or service. Ten become customers, spending an average of $1,000 on their first order. Your revenue from the campaign is $10,000, giving you a tenfold ROI.

"Branding" is a different animal and the tactic favored by SMBs (small- to medium-size businesses) and giant corporations. Branding doesn't seek an immediate order or lead. Rather, it is designed to get consumers to remember and think favorably about a product, so when they have a need, they buy the product. Most national brands—Coke, United Airlines, Toyota, and Nike—are brand advertisers.

Should you be a brand advertiser? In a word, no. For two reasons. First, it costs too much and can quickly exhaust a small business's marketing budget without causing the cash register to ring. Second, even if you can afford brand advertising, to be effective, it requires massive repetition in multiple media. A big corporation has the resources to indulge in brand marketing without seeing an ROI. A small business does not.

This is why some products should advertise using Google AdWords. Let's say you publish a $20 book on how to overcome insomnia. You calculate that to be effective, you cannot pay more than a dollar a slick for "insomnia" and keywords related to it (e.g., sleep, trouble sleeping). But when you go to bid, you find the price for these keywords is outrageous and well beyond your budget. Why? Multibillion-dollar pharmaceutical companies selling over-the-counter and prescription sleeping pills are competing with you for those same keywords. They have much deeper pockets. Worse, you are a direct marketer who wants to make a profit on your pay-per-click (PPC) ad campaign. The pharmaceutical companies don't measure ROI for PPC advertising, and don't hesitate to spend $10 or even $20 per keyword.

Marketing in Larger Companies

Larger companies have an additional challenge: how to allocate resources among different levels of marketing. Should an ad in *Fortune* magazine talk about the corporation as a whole, a new technology, or a specific product?

	Mission	To This Audience	Through These Media	To Sell
Corporate	Sell the corporation as a corporation	Business leaders, Financial influentials, Government opinion leaders, Community, Academia, Press	Television, Business publications, Major newspapers	Basic strengths of the corporation
Business Units	Present capabilities for markets/ industries	High-level decision makers, Planners/ engineers, Financiers	General business and horizontal industry publications	Systems capabilities, Broad product and service capabilities
Divisions	Inform prospects of available products and services	Specifiers, Designers, Purchasers, Purchasing influences	Vertical publications, Functional publications	Specific products and services

TABLE 7–4. **Marketing Communications Responsibilities**

Table 7–4 provides some guidance. As you can see, in larger companies, marketing resources must be allocated across three levels. At the top is corporate communications. These are marketing programs that promote the company as a brand name. Microsoft TV commercials often promote Microsoft as an entity and the Microsoft brand, rather than specific software or services.

The second tier is to promote the individual business units or companies operating under the corporate umbrella. When I worked at Westinghouse, I was responsible for marketing the division of Westinghouse that manufactured defense and aerospace products. I had no involvement in refrigerators, transportation systems, or any other area.

The third tier is marketing resources devoted to particular divisions, each of which is responsible for a different product line. While at Westinghouse Defense & Aerospace, I worked for the business unit that manufactured radar systems for airports and military applications. While the company made many other products, such as fire control systems for F–16 fighters, ships, and tanks, others in my department handled those divisions, while I was responsible for the radar division.

Action . . .

Identify the Tactics You'll Use

Let's review the progress of our example company, Chiropractic Marketing Plans, based on the tactics discussed in this chapter.

Goal for this year: Increase revenues from $150,000 to $200,000.

To reach their goal, CMP's strategy is to:

1. Become well-known for writing marketing plans for chiropractors because no one else in their area is doing this.

2. Dominate their field within a 10-mile radius of their office.

3. Add 15 net new clients.

4. Increase their client retention rate to 40 percent.

5. Earn income by matching clients with implementation specialists.

6. Add a midyear review service to increase the frequency of usage of their services.

After careful analysis, CMP decided the initial tactics most likely to be effective for them are:

1. Form joint ventures with coaches who specialize in building chiropractic practices.

2. Write articles for both online and offline magazines.

3. Institute a strong referral program.

4. Use direct mail.

5. Speak to chiropractic groups.

Now, it's your turn.

Identify the three to five tactics you'll begin with and why you think they're your best choice given your goals and strategies.

_____

_____

_____

_____

_____

_____

_____

_____

_____

_____

_____

_____

_____

_____

Chapter 8
INTEGRATE ONLINE AND OFFLINE MARKETING

Earlier in the book, we discussed how we live in a world of multichannel marketing, in which campaigns use not a single medium, like print ads or radio commercials, but use a mix of online and offline tactics to multiply effectiveness, impact, and results. Now let's look at some of the internet marketing methods you can use in combination with offline marketing. The main online marketing techniques we will look at include email marketing, enewsletters, websites, blogging, and social networking.

Sequences

The biggest advantage of multichannel marketing and the advent of low-cost online channels, such as email and landing pages, is it allows us to execute extended sequences of marketing messages to the same audience rather than hit them only once or twice, like with a single sales letter or a telemarketing call.

The first step in doing a marketing sequence is strategy—determining what will be the core messages in each sequence. Often the sequence is as follows:

- ◆ The early efforts establish a relationship with the audience, perhaps providing useful free content as an incentive.
- ◆ The next batch of communications introduce the products and make special offers, such as discounts or free bonus gifts with purchase.
- ◆ The third batch of communications have a tone of increased urgency, often providing reasons why the recipient should take action now instead of later.
- ◆ The final few efforts inform readers that the special offers will soon expire and now is the last chance to take advantage of them.

Often the results are better when marketers integrate different channels into the sequence. Some of the marketing tactics that can be used in the sequence include:

- ◆ Sales letters
- ◆ Postcards
- ◆ Self-mailers
- ◆ Email marketing
- ◆ Enewsletters
- ◆ Telemarketing calls

The temptation when sending a direct-mail sequence is to make them all look the same in size and design. Branding marketers (see Chapter 7) like this approach because they feel it helps build image and awareness, but actually what happens is the prospect begins to think she has gotten the mail piece before, and, therefore, throws it away without opening it.

Direct marketers that use letter sequences for renewals and billing sequences have found that by changing the outer envelope so it looks like it came from another company, they get a huge spike in response. So much for design consistency and branding.

According to marketing expert Jerry Jones, selling big-ticket items today requires more steps than it used to: "We used to generate a lead, send a response package, and a few follow-ups via mail to get the sale," he says. "Today, if you're not willing to do 15, 20, even 30 or more follow-ups to the initial inquiry, using every media available, you won't make nearly the sales you should."

Brick-and-mortar businesses tend to use a mix of offline and online tactics in their sequences and other marketing initiatives. Many internet businesses stick mostly or solely with online channels. They like the speed and low cost. And they seek to build businesses that operate mainly online without physical locations or even much human contact.

> Brick-and-mortar businesses tend to use a mix of offline and online tactics in their sequences and other marketing initiatives.

Internet marketers brag about the passive income they enjoy: money coming in 24 hours a day from their websites and landing pages, seemingly without effort on their part. But building an internet marketing business—which includes building a large opt-in e-list, creating products, building landing pages, sending out enewsletters and solo email marketing messages, online advertising, article writing, setting up the back-end systems—requires a lot of upfront work. What's nice about an internet business, though, is that once the setup is done, it requires less time and effort to operate than a traditional brick-and-mortar store where things like fulfillment are done manually and you have to be physically present to run the business (as demonstrated in Figure 8–1 on page 128).

Email Marketing

Email marketing can be extremely profitable. I distribute approximately a million email messages a month for my online business, and it generates a handsome six-figure income in return. According to *Newsmax* (5/29/2015), email sent to prospect lists has conversion rates from 5 to 5.9 percent. But email is less effective today than it was a few years ago, and I have grave concerns about its future.

Why has email marketing response declined so dramatically? Spam filters are one reason. But the main reason is probably the glut of email messages each of us receives daily. When you get 100 or

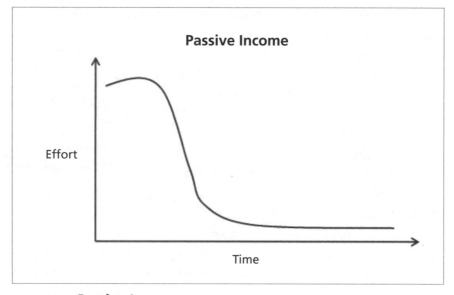

FIGURE 8–1. **Passive Income**
Internet businesses are a lot of work upfront but, once up and running, can throw off multiple streams of passive income.

200 email messages a day, just getting through them becomes a drain on your time and productivity. To protect themselves, many people simply delete emails from anyone they don't know. They assume it is spam or don't want to risk a virus infection, so they click "delete" and your message is gone.

How do you overcome this obstacle and get your prospects to open, read, and respond to your email marketing messages, then buy the products you are selling? By becoming part of the prospect's "email inner circle." Let me explain what the inner circle is and how you can join it. According to a survey by Nielsen/NetRatings, most people regularly open and read emails from a maximum of 16 permission-based sources. The only way for you to break into this inner circle is to displace someone already in that inner circle, according to the survey. An article in *DM News* concludes, "Marketers will have to enter that emerging inner circle of trusted companies from whom people are willing to keep reading emails."

How do you break into this inner circle of email senders whose messages your prospects will open and read? Despite the proliferation of free online newsletters (ezines), the best way to become part of a prospect's inner circle is to write and publish a truly valuable ezine. If you publish your ezine regularly (at least once a month) and provide content of genuine worth, readers will value your publication and establish a relationship with you. You will have entered their inner email circle, because they will view anything with your name in the "from" line as being from a trusted advisor and worth their time to at least open. The ezine is offered free. Your money is made by sending, at virtually no cost, email sales messages to your subscribers. Agora Financial, for example, doesn't charge for a subscription to the *Daily Reckoning*. But by marketing aggressively to the *Daily Reckoning* subscriber list, they generate approximately $275 million in online sales of their newsletters and services each year—at very little cost.

Similar to ezines are short news bulletins, which some marketers send to their subscribers on a regular basis. For instance, *Computerworld* magazine (*CW*) sends a daily online update with short items from the magazine. *CW*'s daily online updates have become part of the inner circle for many IT professionals who must keep up with developments in hardware and software.

If you do not publish your own enewsletter, you can still break into the prospect's inner circle by advertising in one of the newsletters they subscribe to. You can purchase a short online ad in these updates, thereby buying your way into the reader's inner email circle. Another way to break into the prospect's inner circle is with periodic service and upgrade notices. Software users, for example, will read and open emails from the software publisher that contain news about upgrades, technical information, or service policies. If your customers regularly need to receive service and product news from you, get in the habit

> If you do not publish your own enewsletter, you can still break into the prospect's inner circle by advertising in one of the newsletters they subscribe to.

of delivering it via email. Then they will be "trained" to read your emails, so when you send a promotion, it, too, will get opened and read.

Customers also value and read two specific types of emails: transaction confirmations and account status updates. So you can get your promotional message read by embedding it into routine emails that contain transactional or account status information. A good example is Amazon.com, whose customers open and read the emails they send because they might contain news about their orders.

> When a prospect subscribes to your enewsletter, you can send them additional content via email to keep them updated on the topic between regular issues.

You can also break into the customer's inner circle by offering timely news and updates through free email alerts. When a prospect subscribes to your enewsletter, you can send them additional content via email to keep them updated on the topic between regular issues. These alerts must contain useful news and information, not just sales pitches. The most successful marketers keep the information content of the emails high, but also liberally promote products and services to these email alert recipients.

Another idea is to form a club and invite your prospects to join it. They will read emails from clubs, associations, online communities of interest, subscription-based websites, and other organizations of which they are members. Therefore, if you can create a club or have your email distributed by one of these membership organizations, you can easily enter the prospect's email inner circle.

As a rule of thumb, whenever you can send email to your prospect using one of the above methods, your chances of getting opened and read increase exponentially vs. sending a typical promotional email. Remember, people buy from people they know, like, and trust. When you become part of the inner circle, your prospects know, like, and trust the email messages you send, giving you an inside track to getting them to spend their online shopping dollars with you.

Writing and Publishing a Free Marketing Enewsletter

As we discussed in the previous section, an ezine is a powerful marketing piece. If you want to market your product or service over the internet, I strongly urge you to distribute your own ezine free to your customers and prospects, for a couple of reasons. First, an ezine allows you to keep in touch with your best customers—in fact, with all your customers—at virtually no cost. Because it's electronic, there's no printing or postage cost. Second, by offering potential customers a free subscription to your ezine, you can capture their email addresses and add them to your online database. You can then market to your prospects, also at no cost.

Whether you are generating leads or direct sales, there are two ways to sell to your ezine subscribers. You can place small online ads in the regular issues of your ezine; these ads are usually a hundred words or so in length and include a link to a page on your site where the subscriber can read about and order the product. Or you can send standalone email messages to your subscribers, again promoting a specific product and with a link to your site.

There are thousands of ezines published. Examples of successful, moneymaking ezines include John Forde's *Copywriter's Roundtable* (http://copywritersroundtable.com/), Paul Hartunian's Million-Dollar Publicity Strategies (www.hartunian.com), and Agora's *Daily Reckoning* (www.dailyreckoning.com). No two ezines are alike, and there is no single accepted formula for writing and designing ezines. However, my ezine, *Bob Bly's Direct Response Letter*, has been pretty successful for me (www.bly.com), and I do have a formula for producing it.

When you are dealing with a free ezine, people only spend a little time reading it before they delete. I am convinced that most subscribers do not print out the ezine, take it home, and curl up with it on the couch to read later. Therefore, I use a quick-reading format designed to allow the subscriber to read my ezine online right when it opens. In this formula, my ezine always has between five and seven short articles, each just a few paragraphs long. Every article can be read in less than a minute, so it never takes more than seven minutes to read the whole issue, though I doubt most people do.

SEO Your Website

An estimated 80 percent of online purchases begin with prospects using a search engine, such as Google, to find the products they are interested in. Therefore, it makes sense to optimize your website so it ranks higher in Google and other search engines. How do you do this?

"My advice is always to write for people, not search engines," says copywriter Dianna Huff. "Yes, it's good to place the correct keywords in the body copy, and yes, it's correct to place your most important keyword at the beginning of the title tag and in the headline of the page. However, you don't *have* to do this to achieve high rankings. And you certainly should not do it if your copy ends up sounding spammy. If you want a site to rank well, you have to optimize it, but not at the expense of the marketing objectives. Copy should be written for people, not search engines."

"Over the years, the tactic I found that works best is to have the most targeted keywords toward the top of the page and work your way down, like a reverse pyramid," says internet marketing consultant Wendy Montes de Oca. "The entire page should be keyword dense, and there can be some repetition, but from my understanding of search engine spiders, they like more organic content."

Let's say you have a website that has not been optimized, and you want to optimize it now. How do you go about it? First, determine which keywords are best for your industry or traffic you are looking to generate. Keywords are the terms your prospects and visitors will type into the search field when they are looking for your type of product or service. So consider the words and phrases they might use to describe your products or services.

Here are some additional tips for selecting keywords:

◆ Use plurals for your keywords, but avoid excessive repetition.
◆ Misspell keywords if misspellings are common. For example, DIRECTV, a digital satellite television service, is frequently

referred to as "Direct TV." If your name is misspelled regularly, include that spelling in your keywords as well.

◆ Don't always use obvious keywords. Include phrases that may get fewer searches but higher results.

◆ Don't let your combined keywords exceed 1,000 characters. The fewer keywords, the greater impact they will have.

> Don't always use obvious keywords. Include phrases that may get fewer searches but higher results.

Need help coming up with a list of likely keywords? There are tools that can help. Wordtracker helps you find all keyword combinations that bear any relation to your business or service, and they offer a free 30-day money-back guarantee. Wordstream has a free keyword search tool: www.wordstream.com/keywords.

Next, create "meta tags" on all pages of your website, based on the keywords you target. These are descriptive text written in HTML code on your site. They are not visible on your web pages, but search engines can read and find them. Before you create your own meta tags, it's a good idea to take a look at those of your competitors and colleagues. Fortunately, you can easily open a window and view the meta tags of any website you visit. From your browser's toolbar, simply choose the "View" menu. Then click on "Source," and a window will open with HTML text that you can study. The most important meta tags are found near the top of the page in between codes like this: <head> and </head>.

If you are creating your own website, depending on which software you use, all you have to do to add meta tags is type the words you've chosen in the appropriate places. The key meta tags for marketing purposes are title, description, and keywords. These tags control what web surfers see when your site is listed in the search engines, which means they will help people decide whether to visit your site.

The "title" tag is what your visitors see at the top of their browser windows when they are visiting your site, as well as what they will see in their bookmark lists. So make sure each page has a title that makes sense to visitors, not just to you. Be descriptive; failure to put strategic keywords in the page title is often why web pages are poorly ranked. The title tag can be a maximum of 95 characters, including spaces, but ideally no longer than six or seven words.

When your website comes up in search engine results, the meta tag identified as the "description" is often the opening statement people will use to decide whether to access the link. The description should concisely answer the question "What do you do?" For example: "XYZ Design provides client-focused, creative, and effective graphic design, art direction, and project management for marketing communications." The description tag should be a maximum of 220 characters with spaces.

Five Ways to Get Your Website Ranked Higher on Google

Search engine optimization expert Don Kaufmann gives these guidelines for getting your website ranked higher on Google:

◆ Always add new content. Google ranks sites higher when they are frequently updated.

◆ List your site on the top niche directories and subdirectories in your industry.

◆ Use longer copy: a minimum length of 250 words per web page.

◆ Post online videos. Since its acquisition of YouTube, Google places greater ranking emphasis on video.

◆ Add credibility icons. Start with trade association membership icons or the Better Business Bureau logo.

Put your keywords in your meta tags. You also should include your keywords in the first 25 words of your homepage. You can use Good Keywords (https://goodkeywords.com) as a meta tag creation tool. Keep adding the keywords you need into the "Base Keyword" field available within the software. Once you are done, a simple click will get you the required keyword meta tag, ready to be pasted into your HTML file. Now your website is "primed" for optimum search engine placement. Write the best copy you can on every page of your website. Once you've written the strongest copy you can, go back and insert keywords from your keyword list into the copy, wherever and as frequently as you can, without disturbing the style, tone, meaning, and persuasiveness of the copy. If forcing a keyword disrupts the flow, don't do it.

Five Steps to Building Your E-List

Many marketers want to cut marketing costs by shifting more of their marketing budgets from traditional direct mail and paper newsletters to email marketing and enewsletters. But if you want to ramp up your online marketing program, you should start building a large opt-in e-list of customers and prospects now.

Why? Because without a significant online "house file" (list of opt-in subscribers), you can only reach prospects in your niche by renting other marketers' opt-in e-lists, which is hardly cost-effective: Each time you want to send another message to your industry, you have to rent the list again, at a cost that can easily reach into the hundreds of dollars per thousand names.

Some marketers buy databases containing email addresses of business prospects in their niche market. This can work if you are sending highly targeted emails on extremely relevant topics and offers to narrow vertical e-lists. But when you send email messages to non-opt-in lists, you are mostly asking for trouble. The CAN/SPAM Act, a law that defines what is considered illegal spam, does not prohibit emailing people who have not opted in, but people on non-opt-in e-lists are much more likely to register spam complaints than those on legitimate opt-in e-lists—and far less likely to buy from you.

So the best online strategy for marketers is to build your own opt-in e-list of subscribers. Doing so eliminates the cost of renting opt-in lists while preventing the spam complaints and lower response rates typical of non-opt-in purchased or rented lists.

When you own an opt-in e-list covering a sizeable percentage of your target market, you can communicate with your prospects and customers as often as you desire or think is appropriate at minimal cost. Being able to send an email to your target market with a few mouse clicks makes you less dependent on costly direct mail, print newsletters, and other paper promotions.

By using a double opt-in process that requires new subscribers to verify their identity before being added to your e-list, you help minimize spam complaints and bounce-backs. Owning a large opt-in e-list of target prospects also decreases marketing costs and improves lead flow and revenues.

So how do you build a large and profitable opt-in e-list of qualified B2B prospects in your field? Here are five ideas:

1. *Dedicate a portion of your online marketing budget exclusively to list-building.* Most marketers drive traffic either to their website homepage or landing pages relating to specific offers (e.g., free webinar registration, free white paper download, purchase a product). Yet a lot of the traffic they drive to these pages is existing customers and prospects who are already on their e-list.

   You should spend a minimum of 20 percent of your online marketing budget building your house opt-in e-list. That means getting qualified prospects in your industry who have not yet opted into your online subscriber list to do so. There are many online marketing options that work well for e-list building programs. These include pay-per-click advertising, postcard marketing, banner advertising, online ads in other marketers' enewsletters, video marketing, viral marketing, editorial mentions in trade publications, online article marketing, affiliate marketing, and social media, to name just a few.

2. *Calculate your maximum acceptable cost per new subscriber.* When evaluating marketing methods for e-list building, you have to weigh the cost of acquiring the new name vs. the value that new name has for your business. To determine value, divide the total annual revenues generated by your online subscriber list by the number of names on that list. For example, if your 20,000 online subscribers account for $600,000 in annual sales, your subscriber value is $30 per name per year.

   You decide how much you are willing to spend to acquire a subscriber worth $30 per year. If uncertain, use this rule of thumb: List-building campaigns should ideally pay back their cost within three to six months. Therefore, if your names are worth $30 per year each, you can afford to spend up to $15 per subscriber to acquire new names.

3. *Publish a free enewsletter.* As previously discussed, the best way to build and regularly communicate with an opt-in list of prospects is to publish and distribute a free enewsletter on a specialized topic related to your product line and of interest to your target prospects.

   > When evaluating marketing methods for e-list building, you have to weigh the cost of acquiring the new name vs. the value that new name has for your business.

   Publishing a free ezine gives you two important benefits for your online marketing efforts. First, it gives you a standing free offer you can use in your e-list-building efforts—a free subscription to your e-newsletter. Second, having the enewsletter ensures that you communicate with your opt-in subscribers on a regular basis. This regular communication builds your relationship with your online prospects while increasing the frequency of branding messages and online marketing opportunities.

4. *Build a "free-on-free name squeeze page."* With a staggering number of free enewsletters on the internet competing for attention, it's not enough to have a simple sign-up box on

your homepage for your free enewsletter. You should offer a bribe as an incentive for visitors to subscribe. The best bribe is a free special report the visitor can download as a PDF file in exchange for opting in to your e-list. For instance, if you sell supply chain management software and publish an ezine called *The Strategic SCM Partner*, offer a short bonus report called "Seven Steps to Improving Supply Chain Management in Your Enterprise" as a premium for new subscribers.

Drive traffic not to your homepage or standard subscription form but to a special "free-on-free name squeeze page"—a landing page highlighting this offer. We call it a "name squeeze page" because it extracts or "squeezes" new names for your list from web traffic. "Free-on-free" means you are offering free content (the report) as a bribe to get the visitor to accept your free offer (the enewsletter subscription). For an example of a free-on-free name squeeze page, see www.bly.com/reports.

5. *Capture the email addresses of site visitors who do not buy, subscribe, or register.* Put in place one or more mechanisms for capturing the email addresses of site visitors who do not buy a product, download a demo, subscribe to your free online newsletter, or take other actions that opt them into your e-list.

If you are not proactively making an effort to capture email addresses of site visitors who do not otherwise register, you are leaving money on the table. Here are some more methods of increasing email address capture.

Increase Email Address Capture

Did you ever go to a website or landing page to learn more about a product you were interested in and then end up deciding, for whatever reason, against buying it? I'm sure you do this all the time. I know I do. Next time you do it, watch what happens when you click away from the site without making a purchase. If you are allowed to leave without further interaction, then you have just witnessed the most common online marketing mistake: namely, the website failed to capture your email address.

Why bother to capture the email addresses of visitors to your landing pages and other websites? There are two primary benefits: First, you can send these visitors an online conversion series—a sequence of follow-up emails delivered by auto-responder. The conversion series gives you additional opportunities to convince these prospects to buy and can significantly increase your overall conversion rate. A landing page may have only a 1 percent to 5 percent conversion rate, but add an online conversion series of emails, and conversion rates can increase to 10 percent, 20 percent, or more.

> The faster you can build a large e-list, the more profitable your internet marketing ventures will become.

Second, as we've been saying, the best names for your email marketing efforts are in your house e-list. So the faster you can build a large e-list, the more profitable your internet marketing ventures will become. How much more profitable? Internet marketing expert Fred Gleeck estimates online revenues of 10 cents to $1 or more per name per month for small businesses selling information products online (other industries may have different figures). Therefore, a 50,000-name e-list could generate annual online revenues of $600,000 a year or higher. Many businesses do significantly better. Agora Financial has, as near as I can figure, online sales of more than $100 million a year from about half a million names—a hefty $16.70 per name per month. Hewlett-Packard has 4.5 million ezine subscribers, from whom they generate $60 million in monthly sales.

So how do you maximize the capture of email addresses from site visitors? For those who buy something, you require them to give you their email address on the transaction page to complete their order. But what about those who visit but do not buy? Use a "pop-under" window. When you attempt to click away from the landing page without making a purchase, a window appears. The copy in this window says something like, "Wait! Don't leave yet!" and makes a free offer. Typically, this offer is some sort of free content, such as a downloadable PDF report, an e-course delivered via auto-responder, or an ezine subscription, given in exchange for the visitor's email address.

To see how this works, go to one of my sites, www.becomeaninstant guru.com, and leave without buying. Unless you have a pop-up blocker, a pop-under window comes up that offers you a free 50-page special report that normally sells for $29. In exchange, all I require is your email address.

Some marketers ask for the email address and offer the free content within the actual landing page itself—often in a sidebar. The problem with such an approach is that it gives the prospect a choice between a free option and a paid option for two content offers on the same topic, and by giving that choice, you risk having people take the free offer and bypass the paid offer.

The big advantage of the pop-under is that visitors see it only after they have read to the point where they are leaving without ordering. Therefore, the free content offer doesn't compete with or distract visitors from the paid product offer. Any time you create a landing page or website selling a product without a pop-under or other mechanism for capturing email addresses, you are leaving money on the table.

Blogging

A simple, three-step content plan is the key to using a blog to successfully market yourself, your business, your book, or your other information products. The plan doesn't need to be complicated to succeed. Here's an overview of the process Roger C. Parker used to update his *Published & Profitable* writer's daily tips blog (http://blog. publishedandprofitable.com).

Step 1: Identify Posting Frequency

Start by asking yourself, "How many times a week do I want to post?" Everyone has to answer this question for themselves. The right answer depends on your marketing goals, how comfortable you are as a writer, and how much time you have for marketing. If your goal is to immediately gain awareness and search engine visibility, the more you blog, the better.

Some marketers blog once a week. Roger blogs twice a week. More important than the number of posts you add each week, however, are the *consistency* and *predictability* of your posting. You want to create the habit of frequent posting and build it into your weekly schedule so that it becomes a part of your routine. You also want your market to look forward to your new posts.

Step 2: Commit to Specific Days of the Week

It's not enough to say: "I'm going to blog twice a week, without fail!" A general statement like that is an invitation to failure. What it takes to succeed in blogging is to make a commitment like one of the following:

- I am going to post once a week, on *every Thursday.*
- I am going to post twice a week, on *Tuesdays and Fridays.*
- I am going to post *every weekday.*

Making a commitment to post new blog content on specific days adds the *power of intention.* The commitment to post on specific days converts a "goal" into a specific, measurable task. It also provides a deadline. If you have committed to adding blog content on Tuesdays and Thursdays, for example, you know that you have to work on your blog posts Monday and Wednesday. (Working on your blog posts a day ahead of time ensures that they will appear on schedule.)

Step 3: Identify Specific Blog Topics

The final step to success is to identify the recurring topics, or themes, you're going to post about each week. For example, here's the formula Roger uses for posting to his *Published & Profitable* blog (http://blog. publishedandprofitable.com):

- *Mondays:* Post about a planning topic.

- *Tuesdays*: Blog posts are devoted to writing topics, such as shortcuts, techniques, and tips.
- *Wednesdays*: Feature a promoting tip useful for authors or internet marketing professionals.
- *Thursdays*: Blog about a profit tip, such as ideas for recycling and reusing information, or creating new information products.
- *Fridays*: Post announcements about upcoming events.

Your schedule doesn't have to be as aggressive. You can choose to commit to adding new blog posts one, two, three, or four times a week. The important thing is that you make a commitment to post about specific topics on specific days of the week. Knowing what you're going to be blogging about on specific days not only creates the time to prepare the posts, but engages your subconscious brain. As a result, while you are doing other work, driving, or sleeping, your brain is subconsciously processing ideas and looking out for possible topics for upcoming posts. The three-step formula helps you create a platform that paves the way for your occasional "news" post, or promoting your upcoming events, or new products and services.

Social Media

Unless you have been living in a cave for the past couple of years, you've no doubt at least heard of social networking, the practice of connecting online with friends, colleagues, and customers using special websites and tools created for that purpose. These social networking sites include Facebook, LinkedIn, Twitter, and many others. It isn't a fad. It isn't an excuse to get out of work. Social networking is how people do business now.

Social networking (see Chapter 15) is an activity that is only going to grow more common as computers become more sophisticated. According to a study conducted by Jupiter Research, end-user-generated revenues from social networking, dating, and content delivery sites are expected to rise from $527 million in 2007 to over $5.7 billion by the year 2012—and social networking sites alone are expected to account for over half this total.

Chapter 9
PUT YOUR MEASUREMENTS IN PLACE

Now that you've decided which tactics you'll use initially to implement your strategy, you need to put measurements in place that will tell you how well the tactics are working. Table 9–1 on page 144 summarizes some of the major marketing tactics you may need to track and measure.

Building in measurements is the difference between a plan that's a nice read and one that's a true gauge for staying on track with your goals. But what exactly will you measure? That depends on the factors that tell you whether your business is succeeding. You need to identify the key indicators. These key indicators should always align with your goals, be important gauges of success, and be measurable.

You can use Table 9–1 to track and compare the relative effectiveness and utility of the various marketing communications methods in your plan. The first column on the left lists the various media you are using. In the columns to the right, you rank each communications method on a scale of 1 to 5 (1 = bad, 5 = good). In the table, we give an example of a CAST analysis done for an

	Impact or Impression	Audience Size	Cost Per Contact	Sales Lead	Message Control	Flexibility	Timing Control	Repetitive Contact	Reaction Speed	Credibility	Closing the Sale
Sales Rep	5	2	1	3	4	5	5	2	5	5	5
Media Advertising	4	5	4	4	5	1	3	5	2	4	2
Reference Publication	2	4	4	3	5	1	3	3	1	2	1
Public Relations/ Publicity	3	5	5	5	2	1	1	4	2	5	1
Exhibitions/Trade Shows	5	2	2	2	4	5	1	2	5	5	5
Catalogs/Literature	3	3	3	2	5	2	2	3	2	4	3
Direct Mail	4	4	3	5	5	3	3	4	3	3	3
Telemarketing	2	3	2	3	4	5	5	2	5	3	2
Email	2	3	4	4	4	4	4	4	4	2	2
Social Media	3	5	5	1	3	3	3	3	3	3	1
Blog	2	2	3	2	3	3	3	3	3	3	1
Website	3	3	4	3	4	4	3	2	2	3	3
Infographics	4	2	2	3	4	3	2	2	2	4	2
Online Ads	2	4	3	4	4	4	4	4	4	2	2
Landing Pages	2	2	3	5	4	4	3	3	3	3	4
Webinars	4	2	3	4	4	4	4	2	3	4	4

TABLE 9–1. **CAST (Comparative Analysis of Offline Sales Tools)** Key: 1 = Bad, 5 = Great.

industrial manufacturer. As you can see, the criteria they measured marketing tools against included ability to generate sales leads, the cost per contact made, and whether the tool resulted in leads that closed.

Decide which data will tell you how well you're doing. Then, decide what outcomes you're looking for with each. For example, if cost per sales lead is critical, which of the tools in your CAST rank a 5 or a 4 in lead-generating effectiveness? If the best tool you have generates inquiries at a cost of $50 per lead, does your business model allow you to make a profit at that cost? If not, you must continue to test lead-generating methods that generate leads at a cost that lets you make money.

What Metrics Should You Measure?

Measure your outcomes. Choose data that tell you whether you're succeeding with each aspect of your strategy. Common measurements include:

- Revenue
- Number of inquiries
- Number of orders
- Average order size
- Expenses
- Break-even sales
- Cash flow
- Receivables (funds you have billed for and expect to come in)
- Payables (funds you have promised for merchandise or services and must pay)
- Average collection days (tells how long it takes to get paid)
- New clients
- Client retention rate
- Sales revenue growth
- Cost of acquiring a client or making a sale
- Lifetime value of a client
- Promotional costs

- Email open and click-through rates
- Online conversion rate
- Website traffic
- Page views
- List growth
- Changing value of your assets
- Liabilities
- Debt-to-asset ratio
- Net annual revenues
- Gross annual revenues
- Profit margin
- Market share
- Client feedback and ratings of your service

A 2013 McKinsey & Company analysis of more than 250 engagements over five years revealed that companies that put data at the center of their marketing and sales decisions improve their marketing ROI by 15 to 20 percent. That adds up to $150 to $200 billion of additional value based on a global annual marketing spend of an estimated $1 trillion.

Using Google Analytics

Whenever you are selling products and services online through your website, being able to track your potential customers from the arrival point to making a purchase,is the most important part of understanding whether your marketing and customer acquisition strategy is working or not. Use Google Analytics to determine where your customer came from first, such as a link from a general social media advertisement for new customers or a targeted email blast or mobile text message for current customers. Among the data Google Analytics provides:

- The number of visitors, both unique and returning
- Page views
- The links they used to arrive at your site

◆ The average time they spent on your site and how many pages they viewed

What's the Big Deal about Big Data?

A relatively new concept in marketing is *big data*. The technical definition of big data is a collection of data so massive and complex that computers cannot handle it. When applied to marketing, it means analyzing huge volumes of data to understand customers better and make wise marketing decisions. For direct marketers, the critical skill is to translate what your data tells you into actionable marketing ideas that improve results, regardless of how much data is involved.

But in practice, data doesn't have to be petabytes or even terabytes to be "big." Any amount of data that a marketer can't easily analyze and convert into meaningful, actionable insights can be considered big data, at least as far as the owner of the data is concerned.

For instance, Trident Marketing, a direct-response and sales firm, constructed a data warehouse in 2012 to collect thousands of data points from internal databases and external sources. An analytics solution was then used to determine which customers were most likely to buy which products, and when. The company increased sales tenfold over four years while reducing marketing costs 30 percent. And in 2013, T-Mobile pooled data through their IT structures for customer transactions and interactions. By leveraging this data with CRM and billing system transaction data, T-Mobile reportedly cut customer defections in half in a single quarter (http://louisfoong.com/interesting-infographics-whats-big-deal-big-data. The ALEA Group—a marketing group, October 25, 2013: *Interesting Infographics: What's the Big Deal About Big Data?*).

+ The bounce rate, or simply the percentage that landed on just one page and then left immediately
+ The type of device used, such as cell phone, tablet, or PC
+ The specific geographic location they came from, such as zip code, city, state, and country
+ And more

Also important is determining if adding a video to your message is more successful than sending pictures with your text content in getting sales conversions. This can be done with A/B testing, using one message with video and text, and one message with just pictures and text. What platform you use, such as Facebook vs. mobile, and at different times of the day, is also useful strategic information.

Google Analytics tracks your customer from the landing page and tells you whether the customer went straight from the landing page to the shopping cart and made the purchase, or if the customer left instead. If the customer clicked on the shopping cart but did not go through the final purchasing process, then this would be shopping cart abandonment and may indicate that the customer thought the price was too high.

However, as stated previously, you can still capture a new customer at this point by setting an automated pop-under message, offering a free report or newsletter subscription when the customer clicks to leave the empty shopping cart page. The ROI through Google Analytics is balancing what you spent to send out the message to pull in new and current customers and the rate of increased percentage in sales from a previous marketing strategy.

Calculating Return on Marketing Dollars (ROMD)

At least once a week I get an email from someone asking me, "What's considered a good response rate for direct mail?" (I also get asked the same question for response rates to radio commercials, print ads, and online advertising.) In some ways, it's a meaningless, even absurd, question. Why? Because the only logical—and honest—answer can be "it depends." What does it depend on? The product, the marketing, the mailing list, the offer, the price, the economy, the terms, the guarantee, the cost of the mailer—even what happens on the evening news the day your piece is mailed.

My usual response is to ask my email correspondent, "Well, what is your marketing goal?" By that I mean, "Are you hoping your direct mail will make a profit—that is, generate $1,000, $2,000, or $3,000 in sales for every $500 spent on the mailing?" Many small-business owners want that kind of return or better. They want direct mail to generate a return on marketing dollars (ROMD) that's some multiple of its cost. (ROMD is the ratio of sales generated by a promotion to the cost of that promotion.) On the other hand, traditional direct marketers, especially large ones, are often content to have a mailing bring in new customers "at cost."

By "bring in new customers," we mean getting strangers whose names appear on the mailing lists we rent to place their first orders with the company. By "at cost," we mean the company makes no profit on the initial order (e.g., a mailing that costs $10,000 generates $10,000 in sales, as previously stated). Experienced direct marketers are often content to bring in new customers at cost because they know that once they acquire a customer, they can make money on the "back end"—selling additional products to that same customer. So whether your goal is to acquire new customers at cost, double your money on the mailing, or whatever else, you need to know the percentage response required to *break even*. For instance, if your gross profit is $70 per unit sold and mailing a thousand pieces costs you $700, you need ten orders to break even—a 1 percent response.

The gross profit on your product is the selling price minus the cost of goods. If your product sells for $80, and it costs you $10 to make or buy, your gross profit is $70 per unit. Sure, there is the cost of shipping and handling, but for our purposes, I will assume that

> By "bring in new customers," we mean getting strangers whose names appear on the mailing lists we rent to place their first orders with the company.

you charge your customers for shipping and handling and the extra charge just covers the cost.

The cost of the mailing is calculated by adding the cost of its four components: mailing list rental, postage, printing, and *letter shop*— the cost to assemble the components of the direct mailing and bring it to the post office. These four expenses are *recurring costs*, which means you incur them every time you mail.

"What about the fee I paid my copywriter and graphic artist?" I am often asked. These are one-time charges and are typically not incorporated in the break-even calculation. Rather than go through the calculations here, let me send you to a free online tool that can perform this break-even calculation for you: www.dmresponsecalculator.com.

By the way, a lot of people also ask me: "I've heard that the average direct mail response rate is 2 percent. Is that true?" It was never really true and is less so now. The 2 percent figure was, at one time, the average response rate to direct mail packages selling magazine subscriptions. The response rates for other products and offers were different. For instance, seminar promoters often got response rates from 0.25 percent to 0.5 percent, and sometimes as low as a tenth of a percent. And response rates overall today are declining. One fundraising consultant told me that response rates for direct mail in the nonprofit field used to average 3 percent, but today, they are closer to 1 percent. The reason for the decline: Consumers are bombarded by so much mail and so many other competing advertising messages that it's more difficult to grab their attention.

Calculating and Measuring Return on Time Invested (ROTI)

Do you need a lot of money to conduct a marketing campaign? It depends on the media you select. Blogging and social networking cost almost no money. TV advertising and direct mail, by comparison, are rather expensive.

Virtually all effective marketing channels require either time or money. You do not need both. If you have little time but a lot of money, you can buy the advertising exposure you need. On the other hand, if you are on a beer budget but are willing to put in a lot of time and effort, you can market your products and services on a shoestring.

> Virtually all effective marketing channels require either time or money.

With marketing media that cost little money, there is still an investment to implement the tactic, and that investment is your time. That is no small investment. One can argue that time is even more valuable than money, being the one resource you cannot replace: You can always make more money, but once an hour is gone, you can never get it back.

For social media, blogging, public speaking, networking, and other time-intensive marketing methods, I measure a metric called ROTI, or *return on time invested*. To measure the cost of the time invested, you multiply the hours spent on the activity times your hourly rate. You then compare that with the revenues generated from the marketing activity. If the dollar value of the time spent is less than the value of the sales generated, the ROI is negative and the activity is a drain on your resources. On the other hand, if the value of the clients, contracts, and orders you get from the marketing activity is many times greater than the dollar value of your time invested, it has a positive ROI and should likely be continued or even ramped up.

For instance, a colleague told me she spent ten hours writing a major think piece for her blog. She said it was a success because of the buzz it created and the large number of people going to her blog to read the article.

But so far, none of those people has hired her or bought anything from her. If her time is worth $150 an hour, the time invested in this blog marketing effort is worth $1,500, and the revenue produced is zero. That's a zero ROTI, which in my book means the whole effort was of questionable value and the time could have been better spent on more profitable activities.

She would argue that there are other benefits to her blogging not taken into account by the ROTI. These include gaining visibility for her ideas, establishing herself as a thought leader in her field, and increasing the number of subscribers to her blog as well as adding many new Twitter followers.

Those kinds of results are "soft metrics." A soft metric is one that generates a return other than orders, sales, and revenues. I do not dismiss the value of soft metrics; they can be beneficial. I have sought them many times in my marketing. But at the same time, if the ROTI of a time-intensive marketing activity is low, you need to question whether it is worth your time and effort to conduct it.

Measuring Web Metrics

Lord Kelvin, inventor of the Kelvin temperature scale, said, "When you can measure something and can express it in numbers, you know something about it." Web metrics are the numbers that let you know something about your website's performance and ROMD, ROTI, and web analytics, the most popular being Google Analytics, are the software that lets you measure those numbers.

In the early days of the internet, websites were the online equivalent of sales brochures or general advertising: pages posted online to disseminate product information, establish an online presence, and help position the company in the marketplace.

> Today's most successful websites are the online equivalent of direct-response marketing.

Today's most successful websites are the online equivalent of direct-response marketing. They have specific marketing objectives and business goals, and their performance and sales can be precisely measured.

Measuring web metrics is a critical step in determining whether a website is producing a positive ROMD and serving users in the manner intended. Web analytics is the study of user interaction with a website by collecting information about what the visitor does. This data is tabulated and refined into reports and visual presentations to help analysts understand whether a website is achieving a set of desired results.

Today, there is a vast array of metrics, ranging from simple to complex, for measuring web marketing performance. Some of the web metrics measured include click-density analysis, visitor primary purpose, task-completion rates, segmented visitor trends, and multichannel-impact analysis. Other techniques used in web metrics include web traffic data, web transactional data, and web server performance data. Each one serves a purpose for webmasters to keep tabs on traffic to their websites. Following are more details about these techniques and more.

Click-Density Analysis

Click-density analysis is used with site overlay of the web analytics tool. This tool helps you see if your visitors are clicking on what you want or clicking on something else. It is powerful because it allows you to look at your web pages and see what various segments of your customers are doing. In other words, if you segment your traffic, you know what each segment is doing when they get to your web pages. You may find, for example, that traffic that comes from Google is different or takes different actions than traffic that comes from Yahoo!.

> Most webmasters look at page views to show them how many visitors come to their web pages.

Visitor Primary Purpose

Most webmasters look at page views to show them how many visitors come to their web pages. The page views tell how many times the web page or pages were loaded, but not why the visitor showed up to begin with. Why did they come to your website? You can find out by simply placing a survey on the main web page people enter the most, and ask them why they came and what about your website they liked or didn't like.

Asking for this information can help you plan to sell products or provide information that will suit the majority of your visitors. The more you know about your visitors and why they show up, the better you can gear your website toward them. The drawback is if you are trying to sell something on your site, the more questions you ask visitors, the fewer orders you get. Even asking one or two simple questions can cause many visitors to leave without taking the desired action.

Task-Completion Rates

> Page views are common for purposes of data collection, to determine which pages are being seen and which aren't.

Page views are common for purposes of data collection, to determine which pages are being seen and which aren't. But webmasters wanted more. They wanted to know if their visitors actually performed an action to complete a task found on a web page—for example, if someone went to the FAQs page and clicked on a link to see an article. This helps webmasters know if the content placed on each web page actually works. Of particular importance is the shopping cart abandonment rate: how many people who start to use the shopping cart abandon it before the order is placed.

Segmented Visitor Trends

There used to be no way of separating the data when key web metrics were gathered. Sometimes certain data needed to be separated to be analyzed more thoroughly. Now there are vendors such as ClickTracks, now owned by Lyris (www.clicktracks.com/products/pro/index.php) that provide segmentation of data, so the information we want to know can be separated into a readable format.

Multichannel-Impact Analysis

In the past, you may have used other channels to help promote your website, including TV, radio, or print ads. Unfortunately, there was no clear-cut way to measure these channels. With multichannel-impact analysis as part of the web metrics tools, you can measure the traffic generated by channels. This way, you can properly monitor where your traffic is coming from and judge which channel sources are the most productive.

Web Traffic Data

Of all the web metrics tools used, web traffic data may be the most useful and most popular. Web traffic data started out as web server logs, then became JavaScript tags. Traffic data became a goldmine for webmasters, as it contained a lot of valuable information, such as number of visitors to a website, the number of bytes sent and received, the page the visitor came from, what pages were seen, the visitor's IP address, the authenticated user name of the requester, the date and time of the request, and so much more.

> Of all the web metrics tools used, web traffic data may be the most useful and most popular.

Web Transactional Data

Any time a transaction occurs on a web page, especially if it is set up for ecommerce, the data is recorded, then becomes available and viewable as part of the web metrics tools. The data contains the number of customers, number of orders processed, average size of the order, and total daily revenues.

Web Server Performance Data

Since the internet has become so widely used, with millions of people logging in every day (www.internetworldstats.com/stats.htm), there

> Web server performance data also includes information about what parts of a website are viewed, what files are downloaded, and what scripts run.

are many people doing business online. This has its advantages and disadvantages. The advantages are that more people are able to get information they need, shop, and conduct business online. On the other hand, the disadvantage is that this creates a lot of traffic and places a heavy load on web servers. This is why web performance data are critical to webmasters or system administrators, who can view the data logs, see what is happening regarding traffic, and determine the course of action to take to ensure that the web server keeps operating and their clients' websites do not go down. Web server performance data also includes information about what parts of a website are viewed, what files are downloaded, and what scripts run.

Web Logs

The original source of data collection at the dawn of the web was web logs. In the beginning, web logs were primarily used to capture errors generated by web servers. Over time, they were upgraded to capture more data, including server usage trends and browser types. When this occurred, they switched from being technically based to marketing-based. Web logs work like this:

- A customer types your URL into his or her browser.
- Your web server receives the request.
- Your web server accepts the request and creates an entry in the web log for the request, including the page name, the IP address and browser the customer used, and the date and time of access.
- The web server sends the requested web page back to the customer.

The reason web logs are popular is because they are the most easily accessible source of data. Mechanisms are in place that collect the data and create web logs. Web logs are also the only data-capture mechanism that captures and stores the visits and behavior of robots (software applications that run automated tasks over the internet), which are sent from search engines. Furthermore, when using web logs, you own the data. Other web analytic tools use vendors to collect the data.

Web Beacons

Web beacons are 1 x 1 pixel transparent images placed in web pages and used in combination with cookies to help webmasters understand the behavior of their customers. A web beacon allows the site to record every action taken by visitors when they open the page. The beacon is part of the web page, but because it is transparent, it is invisible to the eye. Web beacons came about at the time banner ads were popular on the web. This was the prime way that people caught the attention of consumers when they visited certain sites. When the visitor saw the ad, they would click on it and arrive at the predestined website, where a tool was used to measure or keep count of that click.

Other bits of information that may get recorded include the IP address of the visited web page, the time the page was viewed, the type of browser used to retrieve the image, and any cookies (parcels of text sent by a server to a web browser) used. Cookies are used for authenticating, tracking, and maintaining specific information about users, such as site preferences or the contents of their electronic shopping carts. Web beacons work like this:

> A web beacon allows the site to record every action taken by visitors when they open the page.

- ◆ A customer types your URL into his or her browser.
- ◆ Your web server receives the request.
- ◆ The web server sends back the requested page, along with the request for the 1 x 1 pixel image, which is then sent to a third-party server.

- As the page loads on the customer's browser, it executes the call for the 1 x 1 pixel image, which sends the data about the page view back to the third-party server.
- The third-party server sends the image back to the requester's browser along with code that can read cookies and capture anonymous visitor information, including the page viewed, the IP address, the time the page was viewed, the cookies that were set, and a lot more.

You may find web beacons used in emails, including enewsletters or promotional emails, as a way to track open and response rates. One advantage to using web beacons is they are easy to implement: They consist of only a couple of lines of code. Web beacons can be optimized to collect only the data you want and can collect data from multiple websites at the same time.

JavaScript Tags

JavaScript tagging happens to be a favorite for webmasters. Many vendors and web analytics rely on JavaScript tagging to collect the data they want. JavaScript allows more data to be collected, which helps lessen the load on the web server.

With JavaScript tagging, each web page requested can be sent out with no need to worry about capturing data. The data are captured on other servers, processed, and made available to webmasters. Here's how JavaScript tagging works:

- A customer types your URL into his or her browser.
- Your web server receives the request.
- The web server sends back the requested page along with a snippet of JavaScript code that was appended to the page.
- As the page loads, it executes the JavaScript code. This, in turn, captures the page view, visitor session, and cookies, and sends it back to the server that is collecting the data.

JavaScript tags are easy to implement because they involve only a line of code placed in a web page. If you don't have your own web server, a third-party vendor can provide the code for you.

With JavaScript tagging, you have control of what data you want to capture.

Packet Sniffing

From a technical perspective, packet sniffing is one of the most sophisticated tools for data collection. Examples of data it collects include server errors, bandwidth usage, all technical as well as page-related business data, passwords, names, addresses, and credit card numbers. In a nutshell, it collects every possible bit of data that can be recorded, which creates security risks.

> From a technical perspective, packet sniffing is one of the most sophisticated tools for data collection.

Packet sniffing has been around for quite some time, but despite its longevity, not too many people use it, considering IT would have to install additional software on their already taxed web servers. Packet sniffing uses six steps to collect data:

1. A customer types your URL into his or her browser.
2. The customer's request is sent to the web server. Before it gets to their server, it passes through a packet sniffer that collects attributes of the request, which are sent back to the packet sniffer.
3. The packet sniffer sends the request to the web server.
4. When the web server receives the request, the requested web page is sent back to the customer by way of the packet sniffer.
5. The packet sniffer takes the requested web page, captures necessary information about the web page, and stores the data.
6. The packet sniffer then sends the page on to the customer.

A packet sniffer can be software that is installed on a web server, or a piece of hardware installed in the data center, which reroutes all traffic to the web server.

Key Metrics Measured

There are dozens of different ways to measure website performance by tracking metrics. Here are just a few of the key metrics marketers and webmasters routinely measure using analytics tools:

♦ *Unique visits:* How many people total visit the website per month, rather than the total number of hits or clicks

♦ *Page views:* What pages on a site were seen the most

♦ *Pages:* Which pages cause visitors to abandon the site

♦ *Bounce rate:* How many people driven to the site from an external traffic source (organic search, pay-per-click, banner ads) viewed just one page of the site and then left—an indication of poor search optimization and lack of compelling content

♦ *Stickiness:* How long people stay on a particular page or website when they arrive; the longer they stay, the greater your chance of making a brand impression or sale

♦ *Site entry points:* How do people get into your site and the pathway they travel to reach your landing or transaction pages

♦ *Keywords and phrases:* Which keywords and phrases people searched to find your site

♦ *Conversion rate:* Percentage of visitors to a transaction page who take the indicated action, whether it's downloading a white paper or purchasing merchandise

♦ *Click density:* Measures the amount of clicks on each area or "zone" of the web page (including links, images, text, and white space) to show which spots users are viewing and clicking, and which zones they ignore

Marketing Performance Reporting

Ultimately, you want to quantify the outcomes of your tactics. Then, you want to compare how your actual results stack up against your expected results. You don't just want to know whether you completed the proposed activities; you want to measure the results of those activities.

In other words, rather than just measuring whether the two articles per month you'll use as a tactic for generating leads were published, you need to measure the number of qualified leads you received as a result, and then measure whether the leads led to sales. Remember, you're trying to quantify which tactics will give you bottom-line, dollars-and-cents results.

Just remember that, ultimately, you want to measure your *outcomes:* revenues, new clients, commissions from joint ventures, lower client acquisition costs, and so on. Table 9-2 on page 162 shows a form you can use to keep track of inquiries and sales generated by almost any type of promotion imaginable.

You can start tracking results by creating a simple system. Remember, the point is to be able to tell whether you're nailing your expected results. First, list everything you'll track. Decide when and how often it will be tracked, then list the expected result for each item. Also list the source of the information you'll use to get the actual result.

Keep score easily using Table 9–3 on page 163. The beauty of this table is that it's easy to revise, add, or delete columns as your needs change. You can create it in Excel or Word. At the end of each month, add the printout to a three-ring binder. Create tables to summarize quarterly results. If you need a system more detailed than this one, get input from your accountant or bookkeeper on how to design it.

Determine How Often to Review the Data

Decide what makes sense for your business. At the very least, every week, you should track your progress in meeting your monthly goals. For some businesses, it makes sense to tabulate everything daily. This may become especially important when cash flow is tight and bills are due.

The software that runs my internet marketing business tracks my key metrics—including orders, units sold, and gross revenues—in real time. You could look at it every five minutes, but you'd never get anything else done. What I do is look at just the week's gross

Month _____ Year _____

Ad or Mailing _____ Key Code _____

Product_____ Offer_____

Total Cost _____ Total Sales _____

Day	Number of Inquiries	Total Inquiries to Date	Day's Sales	Total Sales to Date
1.				
2.				
3.				
4.				
5.				
6.				
7.				
8.				
9.				
10.				
11.				
12.				
13.				
14.				
15.				
16.				
17.				
18.				
19.				
20.				
21.				
22.				
23.				
24.				

TABLE 9–2. **Inquiries and Sales Form**

Tracking Results for Month/Year								
Goal	Strategy	Tactic	Data	Cost		Outcome		Source Used
				Expected	Actual	Expected	Actual	
	Strategy 1	Tactic 1						
	Strategy 2	Tactic 2						
		Tactic 3						

TABLE 9–3. **Tracking Results for Month/Year**

revenue to date at the end of each day. That way, I know whether I am on track to meet my revenue goal. If not, I can take actions to increase sales activity. At the end of each week, I look at a detailed report with all my metrics, including click-through rates, conversion rates, open rates, opt-outs, and new names added, and plan for the next week accordingly. The point is, you should set a regular period for entering and reviewing your results. It will soon become apparent whether you need to adjust your tactics. You can find out about the integrated ecommerce software I use in my online business at http://www.webmarketingmagic.com.

Chapter 10
WRITE YOUR PLAN

At this point, you've collected most of the information you need to write your plan. What remains is to sit down and write it.

In addition to providing you with a roadmap for your marketing efforts for the next 12 months, the plan can save you time communicating your business vision and objectives with others. You may want to share the plan (or sections of it)—on a confidential basis, of course—with some or all of the following folks:

- ◆ The CEO
- ◆ Product managers
- ◆ Sales managers
- ◆ Bankers
- ◆ Venture capitalists
- ◆ Private investors
- ◆ Business partners
- ◆ Affiliates
- ◆ Ad agencies
- ◆ Marketing consultants

- SEO specialists
- Other vendors
- Employees
- Freelancers
- Media reps
- Mastermind circle
- Trusted friends and advisors

You will need the approval of the CEO and other members of the senior management team, assuming you are the marketing director and not the CEO or owner. In traditional organizations, marketing is often at the bottom of the food chain and sometimes treated as a second-class citizen. Copywriter Clayton Makepeace suggests that the typical corporate structure be inverted, so that customers are at the top and marketing right behind them. It's his assertion that marketing is key to the business's success, not an ancillary activity (see Figure 10–1).

FIGURE 10–1. **Clayton Makepeace's Inverted Corporate Hierarchy Puts Marketing above Other Functions**

Write It Down to Get It Done

A written plan is far more likely to be implemented than a plan you have in your head. That alone increases your chances for succeeding in your business. Once you write down everything, you'll have a handy guide to refer to on a daily basis. Your written plan will provide a timetable for getting things done. This will help you stay on track to meet your goals for the year. Also, when something doesn't work, it will be easier to make small adjustments to fine-tune your plan if the initial plan is in black and white.

Gather all your responses to the Action items from the previous chapters. You can find blank forms in Appendix A. If you've completed the Actions in each step, you'll see that you've already written most of your plan.

First, remind yourself of what you're trying to do here: plan how you're going to sell your products or services. For most businesses, that's a multistage process. Use the form shown in Table 10–1

How will I generate as many leads as I want?	Direct mail, articles, speaking, referrals, joint ventures, LinkedIn, Pinterest, email, banner ads, content marketing
How will I qualify leads?	Call after mailing or getting leads from marketing efforts; find out the business's chief growth challenge and how committed they are to marketing; explain how I work and find out if they're interested in proceeding.
How will I get appointments to meet or present (if applicable)?	Call and qualify the lead. If there's a strong win-win potential, ask for the appointment.
What offer will I make to close the sale?	Not sure yet.
How will I follow up with qualified leads until they purchase?	Create a "touches" system to ensure ongoing, monthly contact. Make sure the methods build in value for the prospect.
How will I follow up with new clients after the sale to continue serving and selling to them?	Maintenance plan, referral plan, touches system for clients, joint ventures, surveys.

TABLE 10–1. **Stages in CMP's Selling Process**

Avoid These Mistakes When Buying Marketing and Creative Services

As a business owner you will eventually find yourself in the position of having to buy marketing and "creative services" to help create your marketing campaigns.

Creative services encompasses a wide range of activities including: copywriting, graphic design, content marketing, search engine optimization (SEO), website design, email marketing, public relations, trade show booth design and manufacture, ad specialties (promotional giveaways), PowerPoint design, mailing lists, marketing plans, Google ad campaigns, enewsletters, and many others.

Buying marketing and creative services is an activity that many entrepreneurs have limited experience in and don't do well. When you hire a suboptimal marketing or creative vendor, or hire a skilled one and then change everything she has done, you are begging for suboptimal results.

One of the mistakes entrepreneurs make is, when they receive the work from the vendor, to immediately say "I don't like it."

But whether you like it or not is really the wrong question to focus on. The real question is whether it will work and get the desired results. There is often no correlation between advertising that people like (e.g., they find it creative, beautiful, entertaining, or humorous) and advertising performance. Often ugly, copy-heavy, "uncreative" ads bring in the most response, leads, and orders—precisely what you want.

There are so many vendors in almost every category listed above today that a Google search will quickly find dozens if not hundreds of them. The problem is you don't know how good they are. My colleague J.S., a marketing consultant, complains, "With a Google search my prospects will find other vendors 1/20th as qualified as I am."

For copywriters, graphic designers, and others who produce tangible work that may be examined, you can refine your search in several ways online.

First, look at the portfolio of sample word on their sites. In particular, look for samples in your niche or industry. If you don't like the samples, they are probably not a good fit for you.

Second, examine the client list. Is it long, impressive, and are their companies on it that are in your industry?

Third, read the testimonials, paying special attention to those talking about the results the vendor has achieved for his clients in terms of response rates, conversion rates, leads, and sales.

Does the vendor have a reputation for excellence in his particular skill set? When you ask others for a recommendation, does his name come up frequently? These are the vendors you want to hire.

The best way work with any marketing or creative vendor is as follows:

1. Provide the most thorough briefing you can. You can find my "discovery process" online here: www.bly.com/newsite/Pages/documents/HTPFAC.html.

2. Give as much guidance as you can. If you have certain preferences—for instance, you don't like Garamond type or purple in design—let the vendor know so as to avoid disappointment later on.

3. Show the vendor past promotions you have done in the genre (e.g., print ads, landing pages) and give the results. This tells the vendor the style and tone you are comfortable with, and most vendors can accommodate that to a degree.

More and more these days, when I ask clients about deadlines, a client who called me on Tuesday will say they want the copy Thursday.

This is not smart. When you ask a creative vendor for a rush job, you are getting their first thought, not their best though. Allowing sufficient time to do the job right—at least a week or two—will yield a better result.

As in virtually any service field, squeezing the marketing or creative vendor to a rock bottom price is also counterproductive, as you usually get in this life what you pay for.

(there's a blank form in Appendix A) to identify the tactic(s) you'll use at each stage of your own selling process. If a stage doesn't apply to your selling process, skip it.

Create a One-Year Plan

Now that you know what you need to do to be successful at each stage of the selling process, make sure you include the tactics you identified in your action plan. A lot can change in three years, so start with a one-year plan. You already set a goal for what you want to accomplish during the next year, created strategies to succeed in achieving that goal, and identified the top three to five tactics you'll employ to implement the strategies. Now, it's time to detail the actions you'll take.

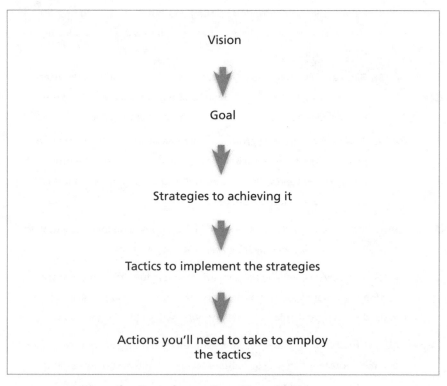

FIGURE 10–2. **Steps in Creating a One-Year Plan**

Identify Your To-Dos

Table 10-2 lays out the action plan for implementing one of CMP's strategies:

- ◆ Column 1: The goal
- ◆ Column 2: The strategies identified to achieve the goal
- ◆ Column 3: The tactics to implement each strategy
- ◆ Column 4: The to-dos to implement each tactic
- ◆ Column 5: The timeline for completing the series of steps
- ◆ Column 6 (not pictured): Who is responsible for carrying out the actions

See Chiropractic Marketing Plans, Inc.'s full one-year plan in Appendix B.

Goal	Strategy	Tactic	To Do	Due
Increase sales from $150K to $200K by December 31	Become well known for writing marketing plans for chiropractors because no one else in CMP's coverage area is doing this.	Direct-mail campaign to CMP's list four times during the year to build and nurture relationship	Identify four hot buttons for these practices. Focus on one in each of the four mailings. Identify a way to add value to each of the mailings so recipients have a reason to both read and keep the mailing. Decide what action we want chiropractors to take after reading the mailing. Decide what kind of offer to include. Decide who will write the letter. Decide who will put the mailing together. Follow up postal mail with an email blast four weeks later.	Jan. 15 April 15 (mail after tax deadline) July 15 Sept. 15

TABLE 10-2. **Stages in CMP's Selling Process**

Goal	Strategy	Tactic	To Do	Due
		Article marketing campaign	Write articles for both online and offline magazines. Get four articles published in offline magazines targeting chiropractors. Use the articles in mailings to CMP's list and on their website. Write five articles initially by Jan. 31 to send to online article directories, then add one new article each month. Add all articles to the CMP website. Decide whether to hire a ghostwriter. Begin researching and interviewing ghostwriters.	April 1 May 1 June 1 Oct. 1 Jan. 31 End of each month
		Speak to chiropractic groups	Identify networking groups that local chiropractors belong to or attend. Create four or five presentations that will appeal to our ideal client. Hire a virtual assistant. Have VA assemble speaker's kit and begin contacting organizations to get speaking gigs. Speak once a month.	Jan. 31 Mar. 1 Mar. 31 April 1

TABLE 10–2. **Stages in CMP's Selling Process,** continued

Goal	Strategy	Tactic	To Do	Due
		Institute a strong referral program	Determine what the referral program should do for CMP. Decide how the program should benefit those who make referrals. Decide benefits for those who schedule appointments through referrals. Create the referral program. Add it to website and all direct mail. Look for other opportunities to promote the program.	Jan. 31

TABLE 10–2. **Stages in CMP's Selling Process,** continued

Budget

The annual marketing budget is often determined as a percentage of the total annual sales revenues. The table below shows these percentages for a variety of businesses. These are rough guidelines only and not precise. They also ignore the stage the business is in: For startups, which have limited current revenues and desperately need to make sales and add customers, marketing budgets can be many multiples of the percentages seen in Table 10–3.

Industry	Advertising Budget as a Percentage of Sales
Advertising agencies	0.1%
Agricultural production, crops	2.9%

TABLE 10–3. **Advertising Budget Percentages by Industry**

Industry	Advertising Budget as a Percentage of Sales
Air courier services	2.1%
Air transportation, certified	1.8%
Aircraft and parts	0.5%
Auto dealers, gas stations	0.5%
Auto rental and leasing	2.9%
Auto repair services and garages	4.0%
Bakery products	1.9%
Book publishers	3.8%
Business services	5.3%
Catalog showrooms	3.7%
Chemicals (wholesale)	3.5%
Coating and engraving services	2.6%
Computer program and software services	3.5%
Communications and signaling devices	4.1%
Commercial printing	1.2%
Computer equipment	1.9%
Computer stores	1.0%
Computers, micro	5.1%
Connectors	1.2%
Construction, special trade	9.8%
Dairy products	4.9%
Data processing services	1.2%
Detective and protective services	0.2%
Drugs	4.4%
Educational services	5.0%
Electric appliances, wholesale	0.8%
Electric lighting	1.1%
Electronic components	2.3%
Engines and turbines	1.8%
Engineering, architect, survey services	0.8%

TABLE 10–3. **Advertising Budget Percentages by Industry,** continued

Industry	Advertising Budget as a Percentage of Sales
Farm machinery and equipment	1.6%
Financial services	0.7%
Food	7.3%
Freight forwarding	3.6%
Hardware, wholesale	6.4%
Health services	3.3%
Hospitals	5.8%
Hotels	0.4%
Industrial controls	1.7%
Industrial machinery and equipment, wholesale	2.0%
Insurance agents and brokers	0.6%
Lumber, wholesale	2.2%
Machine tools	2.0%
Material handling equipment	1.0%
Medical laboratories	0.9%
Metalworking equipment	5.4%
Management consulting	1.8%
Motor vehicle parts and accessories	1.6%
Motors and generators	1.0%
Musical instruments	3.3%
Newspapers	3.9%
Office automation systems	2.3%
Office furniture	1.4%
Optical instruments and lenses	1.5%
Outpatient care facilities	1.1%
Paint, varnish, and lacquer	3.1%
Paper and paper products	3.8%
Personal services	3.7%
PR services	1.8%
Office supplies	5.2%

TABLE 10–3. **Advertising Budget Percentages by Industry,** continued

Industry	Advertising Budget as a Percentage of Sales
Photofinishing laboratories	1.8%
Photographic equipment and supplies	3.2%
Plastics, resins, elastomers	1.6%
Pollution control machinery	0.8%
Prefabricated metal buildings	0.7%
Pumps	1.2%
Real estate agencies	2.8%
Savings and loan associations	0.7%
Securities and commodities brokers	3.8%
Semiconductors	1.2%
Ship and boat building and repair	2.3%
Soaps and detergents	7.6%
Telephone communications (wire, radio)	1.9%
Textile mill products	1.1%
Tires and inner tubes	3.1%
Training equipment and simulators	1.6%
Valves	1.0%

TABLE 10–3. **Advertising Budget Percentages by Industry,** continued

Budget Allocation

Once you have a marketing budget, you have to allocate it by month or season and by marketing medium. The worksheet shown in Figure 10–2 on page 177 can be used to do this.

Plot Major Campaigns First

Major campaigns require more resources and time to get things done than the typical marketing actions you'll take. So plan for those first.

As you saw in the action plan above, CMP has decided to do four major direct-mail campaigns to all the family wellness chiropractic practices on their target list. The mailings will go out in January, April, July, and October.

Advertising Expenditures by Month and by Medium												
Medium	Jan $	Feb $	Mar $	Apr $	May $	Jun $	Jul $	Aug $	Sep $	Oct $	Nov $	Dec $
Print:												
Newspaper												
1)												
2)												
3)												
Consumer Magazine												
1)												
2)												
3)												
Trade Publications												
1)												
2)												
3)												
Radio:												
AM												
1)												
2)												
3)												
FM												
1)												
2)												
3)												
Satellite												
1)												
2)												
3)												

FIGURE 10–2. **Advertising Budget Allocation Worksheet**

Medium	Jan $	Feb $	Mar $	Apr $	May $	Jun $	Jul $	Aug $	Sep $	Oct $	Nov $	Dec $
Television												
1)												
2)												
3)												
Specialty												
1)												
2)												
3)												
Direct Mail												
1)												
2)												
3)												
Point-of-Purchase												
1)												
2)												
3)												
Co-op												
1)												
2)												
3)												
Content Marketing												
1)												
2)												
3)												
Social Media												
1)												
2)												
3)												
Other												
1)												
2)												
3)												

FIGURE 10–2. **Advertising Budget Allocation Worksheet,** continued

Use a major campaigns calendar like Table 10–4 to help you think through the resources you'll need to complete your actions (a blank form is in Appendix A). That way, you won't be delayed because you failed to anticipate something you need until the last minute.

Month	Campaign	Expected Cost	Actual Cost	Resources	Expected Results	Actual Results
January	Direct mail (referral and new client letters)	$500		List, sales letter, offer	1 new client	
February	Touch 1	$200		Article	3 new clients	
March	Touch 2	$200		Postcards	2 new clients	
April	Direct mail	$500		List, sales letter, offer	3 new clients	
May	Workshop; Touch 3 (calls)	$600		Location, handouts	5 new clients	
June	Touch 4	$200		Case study	3 new clients	
July	Direct mail	$500		List, sales letter, offer	3 new clients	
August	Touch 5	$200		Email blast	3 new clients	
September	Touch 6	$200		Infographic on Pinterest	3 new clients	
October	Direct mail	$500		List, sales letter, offer	4 new clients	
November	Touch 7 (calls); seminar	$1100		Location, manuals	6 new clients	

TABLE 10–4. **CMP's Major Campaigns for 2015**

Month	Campaign	Expected Cost	Actual Cost	Resources	Expected Results	Actual Results
December	Touch 8 (Happy Holidays)	$300		Cards	1 new client	
Comments:		Campaigns to repeat:			Campaigns to drop:	

TABLE 10–4. **CMP's Major Campaigns for 2015,** continued

Break It Down

Now that you have a plan, it might at first glance look like a lot to take on. The best way to tackle your plan is to break it down into manageable segments. This is why we began by plotting the big stuff, the major campaigns, first. It gives us time to think about what each campaign will require: the actions to complete it, the resources needed, when it has to begin to be ready on time, and a tracking system to evaluate whether it did what it was supposed to do.

Here's an easy way to approach this challenge:

◆ Remember, you set a one-year goal and created strategies to achieve that goal. It makes sense to ask yourself what you need to accomplish by the halfway mark to stay on track to complete the annual goal. So begin with your six-month goals.

◆ The halfway mark between six months and one year is nine months. Ask yourself what you'll need to complete by nine months to meet the one-year goal.

◆ Now, the halfway mark between your starting date and six months is three months. Ask yourself what you'll need to complete during the first three months of your plan to stay on track to meet your six-month goal.

◆ Three months will come and go quickly without progress unless you're taking regular action toward meeting your goals. It's easy to wrap your mind around needing to have specific actions completed within the next month. So ask yourself what you must accomplish during the next month to stay on track to meet your three-month goals. Near the end of that month, do the same for the following month—knowing that you now have only two months left to hit your three-month markers.

Marketing activity and expenditures are usually not constant throughout the year. Your business may have busy seasons and slow seasons. Accounting and tax preparation firms, for example, are enormously busy from January 1 through April 15. Your marketing and media activities and budget can be used in any of the patterns shown in Figure 10–3. A business that has constant work all year,

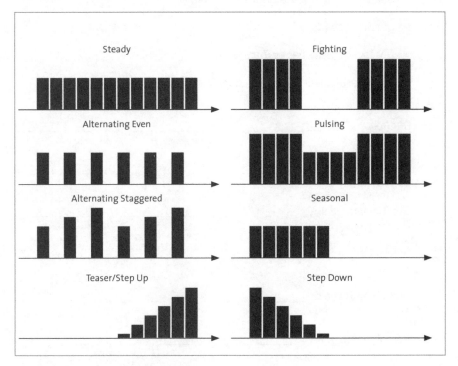

FIGURE 10–3. **Media Scheduling**

such as an electrical contractor, might use the steady pattern and spread their marketing efforts equally over the months. A business that is hit with periodic slowdowns could use the fighting or pulsing pattern to combat these turndowns.

Action...

Write Your Plan

- ◆ Our Vision (Use Chapter 1 answers)
- ◆ Our Niche (Use Chapter 2 answers)
- ◆ Our Ideal Client (Use Chapter 3 answers)
- ◆ Our Competition (Use Chapter 4 answers)
- ◆ Our Strategy (Use Chapter 5 answers)
- ◆ Our Tactics (Use Chapter 7 answers)
- ◆ Our Measurement Stick (Use Chapter 9 answers)

Our Action Plan: _____

Our 30-day goals: _____

Our 3-month goals: _____

Our 6-month goals: _____

Our 9-month goals: _____

Our 12-month goals: _____

Ten Ways to Stretch Your Marketing Budget

Most small businesses have modest marketing budgets, which means you have to make every dollar count. Here are ten ways to get big results from a small budget:

1. *First, use your ads for more than just space advertising*. Ads are expensive to produce and expensive to run. But there are ways of getting your advertising message in your prospect's hands at a fraction of the cost of space advertising.

   The least expensive is to order an ample supply of reprints and distribute them to customers and prospects every chance you get. When you send literature in response to an inquiry, include a copy of the ad in the package, either hard copy in the mail or PDF attached to an email. This reminds a prospect of the reason he responded in the first place and reinforces the original message.

   Distribute ads internally to other departments—engineering, production, sales, customer service, and R&D—to keep them up-to-date on your latest marketing and promotional efforts. Make sure your salespeople receive an extra supply of reprints and are encouraged to include a reprint when they write to or visit their customers.

   Turn the ad into a product data sheet by adding technical specifications and additional product information to the back of the ad reprint. This can be a PDF with product description on the front and the ad on the back. This eliminates the expense of creating a new layout from scratch. And it makes good advertising sense, because the reader gets double exposure to your advertising message.

   Ad reprints can be used as inexpensive direct-mail pieces. You can mail the reprints along with a reply card and a sales letter. Unlike the ad, which is "cast in concrete," the letter is easily and inexpensively tailored to specific markets and customer groups.

Use the ad graphic as a banner on your homepage. Turn the ads into an HTML email campaign.

If you've created a series of ads on the same product or product line, publish bound reprints of the ads as a product brochure. This tactic increases prospect exposure to the series and is less expensive than producing a brand-new brochure.

If your ads provide valuable information of a general nature, you can offer reprints as free educational material to companies in your industry. Or, if the ad presents a striking visual, you can offer reprints that are suitable for framing.

Reuse your ads again and again. You will save money—and increase frequency—in the process.

2. *If something works, stick with it.* Too many marketers scrap their old promotions and create new ones because they're bored with their current campaign. That's a waste. You shouldn't create new ads or promotions if your existing ones are still accurate and effective. You should run your ads for as long as your customers read and react to them.

   How long can ads continue to get results? The Ludlow Corporation ran an ad for its erosion-preventing Soil Saver mesh 41 times in the same journal. After 11 years it pulled more inquiries per issue than when it was first published.

   If a concept still has selling power but the promotion contains dated information, update the existing copy—don't throw it out and start from scratch. This approach isn't fun for the ad manager or the agency, but it does save money.

3. *Don't overpresent yourself.* A strange thing happens to some entrepreneurs when they get a little extra money in the ad budget: They see fancy four-color brochures, gold embossed mailers, and fat annual reports produced by Fortune 500 firms. Then they say, "This stuff sure looks great—why don't we do stuff like this?"

   That's a mistake. The look, tone, and image of your promotions should be dictated by your product and your market—not by what other companies in other businesses put out.

   Producing marketing materials that are too fancy for its purpose and its audience is a waste of money. And it can even *hurt* sales—your prospects will look at your overdone literature and wonder whether you really understand your market and its needs.

4. *Use "modular" product literature.* One common advertising problem is how to promote a single product to many small, diverse markets. Each market has different needs and will buy the product for different reasons. But on your budget, you can't afford to create a separate brochure or white paper for each of these tiny market segments.

   The solution is "modular literature." This means creating a basic brochure layout that has sections capable of being tailored to meet specific market needs. After all, most sections of the brochure—technical specifications, service, company background, product operation, product features—will be the same regardless of the audience. Only a few sections, such as benefits of the product to the user and typical applications, need to be tailored to specific readers.

   In a modular layout, standard sections remain the same, but new copy can be used for each market-specific section of the brochure. This way, you can create many different market-specific pieces of literature on the same product using the same basic layout. Significant savings in time and money will result.

5. *Use article reprints as supplementary sales literature.* Marketing managers are constantly bombarded by requests for "incidental" pieces of product literature. Engineers want data sheets explaining some minor technical feature in great detail.

   Reps selling to small, specialized markets want special literature geared to their particular audience. And each company salesperson wants support literature that fits his or her individual sales pitch. But the ad budget can only handle the major pieces of product literature. Not enough time or money exists to satisfy everybody's requests for custom literature.

   The solution is to use article reprints as supplementary sales literature. Rather than spend a bundle producing highly technical or application-specific pieces, have your sales and technical staff write articles on these special topics. Then, place the articles with the appropriate journals.

   Article reprints can be used as inexpensive literature and carry more credibility than self-produced promotional pieces. You don't pay for layout or printing of the article. Best of all, the article is free advertising for your firm.

   Have a page on your website where you post all the articles written by or about your firm and your product. A large online article library will improve your ranking with the Google search engine.

6. *Explore inexpensive alternatives for lead generation, such as banner advertising, organic search, LinkedIn, and PR.* Many smaller firms judge marketing effectiveness solely by the number of leads generated. They are not concerned with building image or recognition; they simply count bingo-card inquiries.

New-product press releases lead the list as the most economical method of generating leads. Once, for less than $100, I wrote, printed, and distributed a new-product release to a hundred trade journals. Within six months, the release had been picked up by 35 magazines and generated 2,500 inquiries.

In another campaign, we bought a text ad in an on-line newsletter for $1,000. It ran daily for a full week and generated 140 downloads of our free white paper. That's a cost of just $7 per inquiry.

Post all of your press releases in a Media or Press section of your website. Optimize your press releases with key word phrases to draw more organic search traffic.

7. *Do not overpay for outside creative talent.* Hire freelancers and consultants whose credentials—and fees—fit the job and the budget.

Top advertising photographers, for example, get $1,000 to $2,000 a day or more. This may be worth the fee for a corporate ad running in *Forbes* or *Business Week.* But it's overkill for the employee newsletter or a publicity shot. Many competent photographers can shoot a good photo for your website for $200 to $250.

When you hire consultants, writers, artists, or photographers, you should look for someone whose level of expertise and cost fits the task at hand.

8. *Do it yourself.* Tasks such as distributing press releases or creating simple squeeze pages can usually be done cheaper in-house than outside. Save the expensive agency or consultant for tasks that really require their expertise.

If you do not have a marketing manager or assistant, consider hiring a full-time or part-time administrative assistant to handle the detail work involved in managing your company's marketing. This is a more economical solution than farming administrative work out to the agency or doing it yourself.

9. *Get maximum mileage out of existing content (text and images)*. Photos, illustrations, layouts, and even copy created for one promotion can often be lifted and reused in other pieces to significantly reduce creative costs. For example, copy created for a corporate image ad can be modified for use on your homepage. Also, you can save rough layouts, thumbnail sketches, headlines, and concepts rejected for one project and use them in future ads, mailings, and promotions.

10. *Pay your vendors on time*. Reason: You'll save money by taking advantage of discounts and avoiding late charges when you pay vendor invoices on time. And, you'll gain goodwill that can result in better service and fairer prices on future projects.

Chapter 11
WORK IT!—
IMPLEMENTATION

You now have a plan for how you're going to create the business you envisioned. But a plan that just sits on the shelf—as so many marketing plans written by high-priced consultants do—is worthless. Remember, the marketing plan is not the end. It's a means to an end.

Those ends are more leads, customers, orders, and sales—and a profitable small business that generates the income required to live the lifestyle you seek. So, the time for reading, thinking, planning, and writing your plans is over, at least for now. The next step is the most important of all: action.

It's time to hit the ground running. How? Lay out the actions you'll take for the next 30 days. Decide the first thing you need to do. Then, do it. Decide the next action you need to take. Then, take it, and so on. Keep taking the next step and completing the next action, and before you know it, your dream will no longer be just a dream.

Budgeting Your Plan

To market a product, you must unfortunately have money to do the marketing. Some marketing options, like prime-time TV commercials on major networks, are costly. Others, such as writing articles for the web, are cheap. How much money should you spend on marketing this year? There are six traditional methods for determining your annual marketing budget.

Method 1: Percentage of Sales

The most widely used budgeting technique is to set your promotion budget as a fixed percentage of your sales. Let's say you sell $50,000 in handwoven baskets every year. If you set the promotion budget at 2 percent of sales, you will allocate $1,000 for promotion.

What sales do you base the percentage on? It's up to you. You can base it on past sales (either last year's sales or an average of the past several years), on future sales (as predicted by your sales forecast), or some combination of past and predicted sales.

What percentage of sales should you choose as the promotion budget? It varies from industry to industry. Defense contractors spend very little on promotion—about 0.15 percent of sales. Some large consumer companies spend 15 percent or more.

The percentage-of-sales method is simple to use. Its major benefit to small business is that these percentage guidelines can tell you whether your budget is reasonable or way out of line. On the negative side, basing promotional expenditures on sales is somewhat illogical: It implies that promotion is the result of sales when, in fact, sales are the result of promotion. Also, the percentage-of-sales method does not take into account the economy, the market, the competition, and your own planned sales objectives. Therefore, at best, it is a rough guideline and not the final word.

Method 2: Unit of Sales

This variation of the percentage-of-sales method bases promotional expenditures on units of product sold rather than on the gross dollar

What Kind Of Results Can You Expect from Your Marketing?

One of the toughest aspects of writing a marketing plan is forecasting results from your marketing tactics.

If you work for a company, your boss will ask you: "What percentage response will we get from the direct-mail piece? How many clicks will our Google ad campaign produce? What will be the conversion rate on our landing page? How many prospects will download our white paper?"

The problem with making a marketing plan based on these forecasts is that they are not really forecasts. At best, they are rough guesses.

The fact that so many seem not to understand is that no one can predict or say for sure what results a given marketing tactic will produce. A postcard mailed to your customer list can produce between 0 percent and 100 percent response. And I am not really being facetious when I say that.

Neither results is likely, but in truth 0 is more realistic than 100. Some marketing campaigns get the results you expect or desire. Others exceed those results and everybody is happy. But others underperform expectations.

When that happens management often becomes upset and angry with both the marketing people in the organization and the agency or freelance who created the campaign. The one thing you need to understand before you write and execute your marketing plan is that marketing is done with risk capital.

By that, I mean you have to assume that in a worst-case scenario, your campaign bombs, generates no response or sales, and the money you spent on it is lost. "Risk capital" means you only spend money on marketing that you can afford to lose.

Often entrepreneurs come to me wanting me to create say a direct-mail package, and when I tell them the cost, they gasp. I ask, "If we do this campaign and spend this money and it bombs, have we just lost your rent or mortgage money?"

If they admit the answer is yes, I refuse the job, even if they want to take the chance and still hire me to do the mailer. Why? I do not want people to lose money they in fact cannot afford to lose.

Are you a small company with an extremely limited budget and shallow pockets? Then in the marketing plan you write, substitute inexpensive marketing tactics for the more traditional and expensive marketing methods.

Jay Conrad Levinson coined the term "guerilla marketing" for marketing done on a shoestring. Instead of an ad in the newspaper, for instance, sponsor the town's Little League team. Instead of paying thousands of dollars for a booth at your industry's biggest trade show, offer to give one of the breakout presentations which, aside from the cost of getting to and from the exposition, costs you practically nothing.

I am an advocate of combining online and offline marketing into integrated multichannel campaigns. But if money is tight, lean more heavily toward online options, which generally cost a lot less than offline tactics.

The internet has made many marketing ploys more affordable. When I started out in marketing in the 1970s, making and airing a TV commercial cost many thousands of dollars. Now you can have your own "TV commercial" on the internet at virtually no cost by posting a video on YouTube. And you can shoot it yourself, for free, without hiring an expensive professional cameraman.

But whatever tactics you use, understand that you can't really forecast the results with any degree of certainty. What you can and should do is try the tactic on a small scale. If it works, do more. If it doesn't, try something else.

amount of sales. Say past experience has taught you that it takes 20 cents, worth of promotion to sell one can of baked beans. If your goal is to sell 100,000 cans of beans, you will need to spend $205,000 on promotion.

This method can be helpful when you are selling high-value durable goods, such as TV sets and washing machines, or small-value goods, such as canned food, toilet paper, and motor oil. It is not a valid approach for setting a budget for a service business.

Method 3: Match the Competition

Some companies play follow-the-leader by basing their promotion budget on what their competitors are spending. It is good business sense to recognize the impor- tance of competition. But by matching your competitors' promotions dollar- for-dollar, you assume they are trying to achieve the same sales and marketing ob- jectives as you are—and that is probably false. Besides, your competitors may not

> By all means, pay attention to the competition. But don't follow them automatically.

know how to budget and execute promotions effectively, in which case you would be mimicking their errors. Of course, if a compet- ing firm is much larger than you are, you can't possibly match its budget dollar-for-dollar. But you could spend what it's spending on a percentage-of-sales basis.

By all means, pay attention to the competition. But don't follow them automatically. Instead, develop a plan that suits your goals, your company, your products, and your marketing philosophy.

Method 4: All You Can Afford

With the all-you-can-afford method, you first appropriate money for es- sential operating expenses: rent, raw material, taxes, insurance, labor, postage, and inventory. Whatever is left over is allocated to the pro- motion budget.

This technique can help fledgling business ventures survive. But if you are past the stage where you're struggling just to pay the landlord, avoid the all-you-can-afford method, because it implies that promotion is a luxury and not an essential part of running a growing business. And chances are, if you are reading this book that is not the case.

Method 5: Historical

The easiest way to set a promotion budget is to say, "Let's spend what we spent last year, plus 10 percent for inflation." This method has essentially the same advantages and disadvantages as the percentage-of-sales method. Use it as a rough guideline only.

Method 6: Objective and Task

This is the most effective method: to define the sales and marketing objectives that promotion should accomplish, then appropriate the budget needed to achieve these objectives. Let's say a freelance graphic artist wants to promote his services, and his *sales objective* is to earn $80,000 by getting assignments from a dozen or so different advertising agencies. The *task* that can best accomplish this *objective* is a direct-mail campaign aimed at ad agency creative directors. Thus, his simple promotion budget would look like this:

Sales Objective	Task	Cost
To get $80,000 in work from 10–15 different ad agencies	Direct mail to 1,000 creative directors	$1,000
	Phone follow-up	$100
	Second mailing to 1,000 creative directors	$2,000
	TOTAL BUDGET:	$2,100

Methods 1 through 5 set a budget, then allocate funds for specific tasks. The objective-and-task method takes the more logical approach of building a budget based on the tasks you want to complete. It ensures that promotional dollars are spent on those projects that will most benefit your business.

A disadvantage of the objective-and-task method is that the budget will probably be much more than you can afford. If that happens, you must rank objectives in order of importance and concentrate on those at the top of your list.

Tactical Execution

While marketing plans can keep your ship on course, there are many marketing plans that never leave the port. By that I mean many small-business people are more comfortable writing marketing plans than actually going out and doing marketing or sales.

> Marketing plans are ideas, and without action, plans and ideas have no value and generate no revenue.

Marketing plans are ideas, and without action, plans and ideas have no value and generate no revenue. A well-thought-out, beautifully written, handsomely published marketing plan that sits on the shelf and is never referred to or acted on is completely without value.

When you follow the marketing planning process outlined in this book, the result will be a plan packed with tactics—promotions you should be doing to generate more leads, prospects, and customers. Executing these tactics—not planning them, thinking of them, or writing them down in a marketing plan—is what makes things happen.

The late professional speaking guru Dottie Walters, a gracious lady, once called me "a magnificent idea man." But I didn't like that. Ideas are a dime a dozen; an idea and a five-dollar bill will get you a cup of coffee at Starbucks.

Action is what makes marketing plans come to life. As a copywriter, I have spent much more time writing marketing campaigns than planning them, to good effect.

Preventing Marketing Bottlenecks

One of the advantages of having a written marketing plan vs. creating your promotions off-the-cuff is that with a plan, you know way in advance what you are doing, when, and the resources required to complete marketing tasks.

Without planning, marketing campaigns are invariably launched late, which, at best, delays the ROI they produce and, at worst, makes you miss important milestones, such as emailing webinar invitations with sufficient advance notice to potential attendees.

There are many fancy tools you can use to plan marketing campaigns, including wall boards, Gantt charts, and software. I use my Outlook calendar to record dates for the intermediate steps as well as the launch date.

Here is a simple example of a bottleneck: A company asked me to write an online promotion for a consumer product and wanted to launch in six to eight weeks. I made it clear in our planning that I needed a sample of the product in my hands to complete my research and copywriting. There was no reason they could not have overnighted the product. But because of their corporate bureaucracy, I did not receive it for two weeks! Then we all had to scramble to make up for the delay and hit our launch date, which we did, because of a delay that was totally preventable. A little planning can easily eliminate such absurd bottlenecks.

> There are many fancy tools you can use to plan marketing campaigns, including wall boards, Gantt charts, and software.

Improving Quality and Results

You have a marketing plan full of promotions and a schedule for implementing them (see the appendices). But it is not enough to meet the schedule; you have to meet it with quality work. That is, the better the execution of your tactics, the more money following your marketing plan can help you make!

Here are some of the key factors with the biggest effect on the quality of your marketing and the results they produce:

- *Copywriting.* I have seen good copy increase response rates from 25 to 100 percent or more over weak copy, yet many marketing managers and business owners do not understand the value and importance of A-level copy.
- *Graphic design.* Although marketing pundits say design is far less important than copy, good design enhances copy, making it more readable and, therefore, able to do its job of lifting response better.
- *Lists.* I have seen one list pull up to a 200 percent greater response than other lists purported to reach the same audience.
- *Offer.* I have seen one offer generate a 10 to 900 percent greater response than another offer for the same product. Elements of the offer include price, terms, conditions, guarantees, and premiums.
- *Media.* You must test different media to see what works best for your offer. The performance of varying media and formats can vary from product to product and market to market. I have seen some products where a direct-mail letter in an envelope far out-pulled a postcard. But I have also personally beaten traditional sales letters for other products by using postcards! You have to test to know what works.

Cost Control

Earlier in this chapter we looked at six methods of setting the annual marketing budget. But when it comes time to execute the plan, the implementation always seems to cost more than we bargained for while the budget suddenly seems inadequate.

My solution is to be a marketing tightwad. I am a cheapskate and practice that philosophy with my internet business and my copywriting clients. All else being equal, I would rather spend a modest sum than be extravagant.

One of the problems with Madison Avenue ad agencies and branding consultancies is that their emphasis on creativity means that aesthetics, not return on marketing dollars (ROMD), is what drives them—and aesthetics make campaigns more expensive while in many cases reducing ROMD. These ad agency and branding types look to produce campaigns that are both beautiful and entertaining, which usually costs more money. Direct marketers, like me, look to maximize ROMD, which means reducing marketing costs while boosting response rates, and I recommend that latter approach to you too.

One advantage of creating marketing campaigns "on the cheap" is that it is easier to get a higher ROMD when you haven't spent that much in the first place. If a $100,000 campaign produces $100,000 in sales, you break even. But if a $1,000 campaign produces $100,000 in sales, you have multiplied your money a hundredfold.

> Making your layouts simple and plain may actually increase response rates, as counterintuitive as you may find that.

Also, and this is a secret most Madison Avenue types either don't know or deliberately avoid, "dirty" layouts—ads with plain, down-and-dirty design—often outpull ads that are fancy, beautiful, and elegant. So making your layouts simple and plain may actually increase response rates, as counterintuitive as you may find that.

Copy: The Foundation of Implementation

A radio program for a vocabulary source notes, "People judge you by the words you use." Nowhere is this truer than in marketing. To implement your marketing campaign, you have to know the fundamentals of good copy, whether you write your own copy or hire an ad agency to do it for you. Copy is dependent on using the right words, and testing proves that something as simple as word choice can have a huge impact on the result.

Write the Way Prospects Talk

Almost universally, the great writing teachers tell us to avoid jargon and to use small words instead of big ones. But in copywriting, there are exceptions to this rule—times when a bigger or fancier word, or a piece of jargon, can command readers' attention and persuade them more effectively than everyday prose.

The first exception is the use of big words to create a perception of enhanced value. For example, Mont Blanc doesn't call their products "pens" in their catalog. They sell "writing instruments." Reason: People will pay $150 for a writing instrument, while they can buy a perfectly functional pen at CVS for a dollar.

In a similar vein, almost no one sells used cars any more. Today, a used car is called a "certified pre-owned vehicle." "Vehicle" sounds more impressive than "car." "Pre-owned" removes the stigma of "used." And who certified your pre-owned BMW or Lexus? BMW and Lexus, of course.

Another reason to use jargon is to create a sense of affinity between the writer and the reader. You want prospects to feel that you are part of their group, or at least that you know and understand them. But don't use insider jargon when writing to nonspecialists. Sociologist Susan Brownmiller defines jargon as "language more complex than the word it serves to communicate."

> Another reason to use jargon is to create a sense of affinity between the writer and the reader.

The third application of jargon is in writing about technical topics, and a huge number of business-to-business marketers sell technical products to technical audiences. Is it safe—even advisable—to use jargon in these situations? When writing about technical products or marketing to a technical audience, it's important to note the difference between technical terms and jargon. Technical terms are words that precisely describe the technology, process, or idea we want to convey. "Operating system" is a technical term, as is "broadband network." We should use them. They are familiar to our readers, and to avoid them would require substituting lengthy and unnecessary descriptions. Technical terms were invented to concisely and clearly communicate technical information to audiences with varying degrees of education and experience.

Jargon, on the other hand, is language that is unnecessarily complex—more so than the idea it is meant to convey. The advantage of using jargon is that with some audiences (e.g., IT professionals), it creates an affinity with the reader. The disadvantage is that, aside from sounding pompous, it is not as clear or direct as simpler substitutes, and therefore, your reader may wonder what you really mean.

> Technical terms are words that precisely describe the technology, process, or idea we want to convey.

What about acronyms, an insidious subcategory of jargon particularly rampant in certain industries, such as telecommunications? The rule is to spell out the term on the first use, with its acronym following in parentheses; e.g., short messaging service (SMS), electronic data interchange (EDI).

However, this rule is typically not applied when using acronyms so commonplace that the initials communicate your idea more quickly and clearly than the term spelled out. Examples include DNA (deoxyribonucleic acid), EST (Eastern Standard Time), and scuba (self-contained underwater breathing apparatus). You can minimize confusion when using acronyms by being consistent in your usage. Don't randomly jump from USA to US to U.S.A. to US of A; pick one and stick with it throughout your document.

Even when using legitimate technical terms and acronyms, don't overdo it. A sentence packed with too many acronyms and technical terms seems cold, inhuman, and almost unreadable. The optimal ratio is no more than one technical term for every ten words in the sentence.

Writing Great Headlines

The headline is the most important part of your copy. David Ogilvy, founder of the ad agency Ogilvy & Mather, estimated that 80 percent of the selling power of an ad is in the headline. Therefore, it pays to spend extra time developing strong headlines.

The best way to get ideas for headlines when you are stuck is to keep a swipe file of successful headlines and consult it for inspiration when you sit down to write a new ad or mailing. As a shortcut, here's a partial collection of such headlines from my vast swipe file, organized by category so as to make clear the approach being used:

- ◆ *Ask a question in the headline.* "What Do Japanese Managers Have That American Managers Sometimes Lack?"
- ◆ *Tie in to current events.* "Stay One Step Ahead of the Stock Market Just Like Martha Stewart—But Without Her Legal Liability!"
- ◆ *Create a new terminology.* "New 'Polarized Oil' Magnetically Adheres to Wear Parts in Machine Tools, Making Them Last Up to 6 Times Longer."
- ◆ *Give news using the words "new," "introduction," or "announcing."* "Announcing a Painless Cut in Defense Spending."
- ◆ *Give readers a command—tell them to do something.* "Try Burning This Coupon."
- ◆ *Use numbers and statistics.* "Who Ever Heard of 17,000 Blooms from a Single Plant?"
- ◆ *Promise readers useful information.* "How to Avoid the Biggest Mistake You Can Make in Building or Buying a Home."
- ◆ *Highlight your offer.* "You Can Now Subscribe to the Best New Books—Just as You Do to a Magazine."
- ◆ *Tell a story.* "They Laughed When I Sat Down at the Piano . . . But When I Started to Play."
- ◆ *Make a recommendation.* "The 5 Tech Stocks You Must Own NOW."
- ◆ *State a benefit.* "Managing UNIX Data Centers—Once Difficult, Now Easy."

- *Make a comparison.* "How to Solve Your Emissions Problems—at Half the Energy Cost of Conventional Venturi Scrubbers."
- *Use words that help readers visualize.* "Why Some Foods 'Explode' In Your Stomach."
- *Use a testimonial.* "After Over Half a Million Miles in the Air Using AVBLEND, We've Had No Premature Camshaft Failures."
- *Offer a free special report, catalog, or booklet.* "New FREE Special Report Reveals Little-Known Strategy Millionaires Use to Keep Wealth in Their Hands—and Out of Uncle Sam's."
- *State the selling proposition directly and plainly.* "Surgical Tables Rebuilt—Free Loaners Available."
- *Arouse reader curiosity.* "The One Internet Stock You MUST Own Now. Hint: It's NOT What You Think!"
- *Promise to reveal a secret.* "Unlock Wall Street's Secret Logic."
- *Be specific.* "At 60 Miles an Hour, the Loudest Noise in This New Rolls-Royce Comes from the Electric Clock."
- *Target a particular type of reader.* "We're Looking for People to Write Children's Books."
- *Add a time element.* "Instant Incorporation While U-Wait."
- *Stress cost savings, discounts, or value.* "Now You Can Get $2,177 Worth of Expensive Stock Market Newsletters for the Incredibly Low Price of Just $69!"
- *Give the reader good news.* "You're Never Too Old to Hear Better."
- *Offer an alternative to other products and services.* "No Time for Yale—Took College At Home."
- *Issue a challenge.* "Will Your Scalp Stand the Fingernail Test?"
- *Stress your guarantee.* "Develop Software Applications Up to 6 Times Faster—or Your Money Back."
- *State the price.* "Link 8 PCs to Your Mainframe—Only $2,395."
- *Set up a seeming contradiction.* "Profit from 'Insider Trading'—100 Percent Legal!"

◆ *Offer an exclusive readers can't get elsewhere.* "Earn 500+ Percent Gains with Little-Known 'Trader's Secret Weapon.'"

◆ *Address readers' concerns.* "Why Most Small Businesses Fail—and What You Can Do About It."

◆ *"As crazy as it sounds . . ."* "Crazy as it Sounds, Shares of This Tiny R&D Company, Selling for $2 Today, Could Be Worth as Much as $100 in the Not-Too-Distant Future."

◆ *Make a big promise.* "Slice 20 Years Off Your Age!"

◆ *Show ROI for purchase of your product.* "Hiring the Wrong Person Costs You Three Times Their Annual Salary."

◆ *Use a "reasons-why" headline.* "7 Reasons Why Production Houses Nationwide Prefer Unilux Strobe Lighting When Shooting Important TV Commercials."

◆ *Answer important questions about your product or service.* "7 Questions to Ask Before You Hire a Collection Agency ... and One Good Answer to Each."

◆ *Stress the value of your premiums.* "Yours Free—Order Now and Receive $280 in Free Gifts with Your Paid Subscription."

◆ *Help readers achieve a goal.* "Now You Can Create a Breakthrough Marketing Plan Within the Next 30 Days . . . for FREE!"

◆ *Make a seemingly contradictory statement or promise.* "Cool Any Room in Your House Fast—Without Air Conditioning!"

More Copy Tips

"Amateurs may talk about creativity, but professionals insist on structure," copywriter Martin Chorich recently said to me. In direct marketing, structure is key: If your copy does not follow the formula for persuasion, it won't work, no matter how creative you get.

There have been numerous formulas for writing persuasive copy throughout the years. The most famous of these is probably AIDA, which stands for *attention, interest, desire,* and *action.* In copywriting seminars, I've taught a variation on AIDA known as the "motivating sequence."

The five steps of the motivating sequence are as follows:

◆ *Step 1: Get attention.* Before your promotion can do anything else, it has to get your prospect's attention. It must get the prospect to stop, open the envelope, and start reading the materials inside instead of tossing your mailing in the trash. You already know many methods of getting attention, and see dozens of examples of them in action every day. In TV and magazine advertising, sex is often used to gain attention for products ranging from soft drinks and cars to diets and exercise programs. Or you can make a bold statement, cite a startling statistic, ask a curiosity-arousing question, put a bulky object in the envelope, or use a pop-up graphic. You get the idea.

◆ *Step 2: Identify the problem or need.* Most products fill a need or solve a problem a group of prospects are facing. But what are the chances that the prospect is thinking about this problem when he or she gets your promotion? Probably not great. So the first thing you have to do is to focus prospects' attention on the need or problem your product addresses. Only then can you talk to them about a solution. For instance, if you are selling an economical office telephone system, instead of starting off by talking about your system, you might say, "Are you sick and tired of skyrocketing long-distance phone bills?"

◆ *Step 3: Position your product as the solution to the problem.* Once you get the prospect to focus on the problem, the next step is to position your product or service as the solution to that problem. This can be a quick transition. Here's an example from a fundraising letter from the Red Cross: "Dear Mr. Bly: Someday, you may need the Red Cross. But right now, the Red Cross needs you."

◆ *Step 4: Proof.* As Mark Joyner points out in his book *The Irresistible Offer*, one of the questions on the tip of your prospect's tongue upon receiving your promotion is, "Why should I believe you?" You answer that question by offering proof. That proof is of two sorts: The first type of proof goes to credibility. It convinces the prospect that you, the seller, are a reputable firm or individual, and, therefore, someone to be trusted. The second type of proof has to do with the product and convinces the buyer that your product can do what you say it can do. Testimonials, case histories, reviews, performance graphs, and test results are examples of proof in this category.

◆ *Step 5: Action.* The final step is to ask for action. Your goal is usually to generate either an inquiry or an order. To ask for action in direct marketing, we make an "offer." I define the offer as "what readers get when they respond to your promotion, combined with what they have to do to get it." In a lead-generating direct-mail package, the offer might be as simple as "Mail back the enclosed reply card for our free catalog." In a mail-order online promotion, the offer might be "Click here, enter your credit card information, and purchase our product on a 30-day money-back trial basis for $49.95, plus $4.95 shipping and handling."

I am willing to wager that every successful piece of copy you have ever mailed or emailed follows the five steps in the motivating sequence to some extent, even if you've never heard of it before. That's because you have an instinct for how to sell, and that instinct leads you to organize your selling arguments according to the motivating sequence.

So, if you can sell instinctively, then what use is knowing AIDA, the motivating sequence, or other persuasion formulas? The answer is this: When you have the steps written out in front of you, you can more consciously make sure you've handled all five steps fully and in correct sequence, and make sure no step is shortchanged or left out, increasing your odds of writing a winner.

Schedule Your Action Steps for the Next 30 Days

Knowing what you must accomplish within the next month will add a sense of urgency to your work. It will propel you to follow through on the things you said you would get done today. Create a 30-day marketing calendar (see Table 11–2) detailing your actions for the next 30 days. Be sure your 30-day schedule takes into account the results you hope to produce in the next three months or so after implementing your action plan.

> If you are planning to put up a new website, one of your action steps would be to find and reserve a domain name.

Table 11–2 lets you see your goal for each week and what you need to do each day to achieve it. What do we mean by action steps? Well, if you are planning to put up a new website, one of your action steps would be to find and reserve a domain name. Another would be to implement whatever software you need to run the site, such as a content management system and shopping cart.

Action Plan January 2015						
	Goals	**Daily Actions**				
		Mon.	Tues.	Wed.	Thurs.	Fri.
Week 1						
Week 2						
Week 3						
Week 4						
Comments/Results						

TABLE 11–2. **30-Day Marketing Calendar**

Follow These Keys to Success

Once you fill out your calendar, use it, and follow a few keys to success:

- *Begin each day by reading your goals and the list of actions for that day that will take you closer to your goals.* Knowing you have only 30 days to complete the actions will keep you focused.

- *Review your full plan regularly.* Visualize the completed goal and your rewards. See your new home; smell the leather seats in your new car; hear the sounds of excited children creating their own dreams in your new youth center; enjoy the new employees you've been able to hire as your business has grown; savor the moment of your hole-in-one. Then, each night, right before you go to bed, repeat the process. This process will start both your subconscious and conscious mind working toward the goal. This will also begin to replace any of the negative self-talk you may have and replace it with positive self-talk.

- *Visualize your goal as a done deal.* Zig Ziglar said we must "see the reaching, before we reach the reaching."

- *Every time you need to make a decision during the day, ask yourself, "Will this take me closer to or farther from my goal?"* If the answer is "closer to," then do it. If the answer is "farther from," well, you know what to do.

- *The program will give you a constant reality check.* You can see if it's working.

- *Review every day for the first 30 days.* This will keep you focused and energized. You'll also quickly get a sense of what's working.

- *Near the end of the 30 days, assess your results.* Look at what remains to be done to meet your three-month goals. See what's working and what's not. With this additional knowledge, schedule your next 30 days.

Chapter 12
REVIEW AND TROUBLESHOOT YOUR PLAN

Despite the wisdom and many benefits of creating a rock-solid marketing plan, virtually all marketing plans contains the same flaw: They are written to cover a yearlong period, but inevitably, circumstances change, sometimes dramatically, during those 12 months. And many of those changes are significant enough to render some or all of your beautifully crafted plan incorrect or obsolete. Therefore, it is exceedingly common to alter the plan, or at least a number of its tactics, to adjust midstream based on current market conditions and the results of implemented tactics to date. Says CPA and financial planner James Lange, "All good plans need to be modified and adjusted due to changing circumstances."

No plan is perfect. No matter how solid your assumptions are and how thorough you are in putting together your plan, expect to make adjustments as you learn more. Reviewing your plan on a regular basis is so critical to your success that you should schedule review dates.

Decide what you'll review, how you'll approach troubleshooting, and what you'll do when things don't quite go according to plan (see

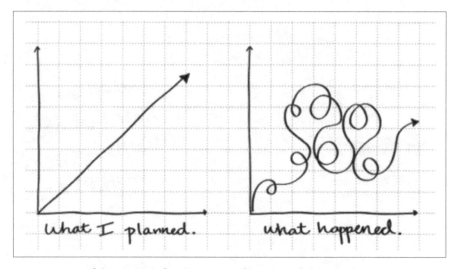

FIGURE 12–1. **Things Rarely Go According to Plan!**

Figure 12–1). Once you make any needed adjustments, it's time to do it all again.

There are two major signals that it's time to rethink and revisit your marketing plan. The first is when you launch one or more campaigns based on your stated core value proposition—promoting your new or flagship product—and those promotions start bombing.

You test some emails or postcards, and the results are terrible. Time to change the market plan? Not quite yet. Instead, rework the copy and design. Test different formats, offers, pricing, lists, and media. If these tests begin yielding positive results, crisis averted. On the other hand, if test after test produces little or no sales, you know your plan—or one or more of its major assumptions—is flawed at the core. Time to gather in the conference room and rethink strategy, approach, and messaging.

So it is a growing stream of failed promotions that's the first sign your marketing plan may need retooling. The second signal that the marketing plan may require adjustment is sudden and negative unexpected changes in conditions—changes in the market, the competitive landscape, technology, and any other factors affecting your business. For a stock market newsletter publisher, for instance, a market shift from bearish to bullish may render the marketing plan written only a few months ago ineffective or even obsolete.

How often should you stop and review your plan's progress? The frequency with which I evaluate my progress and make corrections in my sales and marketing depends on the business. In my copywriting business, my jobs are typically two to four weeks in duration. So my cash flow may be uneven. Therefore, I look at my month-to-date and year-to-date gross sales at the end of every month to see whether I am on track. I also check on a weekly basis the number of active jobs and pending jobs, for which I keep two separate lists.

In my internet marketing business, where I sell products instead of services, each sale is made in a minute online. So I look at a one-week sales report that tells me, among other things, my revenues for the week. I look at this twice a week: once at the end of the week to see how well I did, and once in the middle to see whether I am on track to make my weekly sales goal. I also check my sales revenues daily, again to see if each day I have earned the average dollar amount needed to achieve my weekly and annual revenue goal.

What You Should Review

You review to stay on top of how much progress you're making. So, of course, you'll review your actual results vs. those you expected. Is there a variance? If so, why? Ask yourself, "Why were we wrong in our expectations? Did we do something wrong? Did we stick to our plan?" Think this through, looking at your actions and numbers. Then adjust your tactics, actions, or expectations as needed.

> You review to stay on top of how much progress you're making.

Major changes in your business or the marketplace may mean you need to update your plan. These changes can include:

♦ You add a new niche or service.

- A major company enters the niche and changes the costs of doing business—consider hardware stores when Home Depot moves in.
- New technology has rendered the way you do things antiquated and inefficient.
- You take on a partner.
- You have competition from overseas (e.g., your customers are outsourcing to cheap labor in India).
- Your sales or profits dive.
- There is a recession or economic downturn causing your customers to cut back on their spending.
- You have many more competitors than you did a few years ago.
- Demand for the product or service you offer is declining.

A Sales Tactic for Overcoming Price Resistance

One of the negative effects of the recession on small-business owners is that it creates a buyer's market rather than a seller's market. In a buyer's market, consumers feel more empowered and are more likely to exhibit price resistance. An article in *Time* magazine reports that 72 percent of consumers surveyed said they had recently tried to negotiate with retail outlets other than auto dealerships, and of those, 80 percent were successful in getting the merchant to lower the price. So as a business owner, you must be prepared for prospects who want to haggle over price and know in advance how you will handle price objections.

> One of the negative effects of the recession on small-business owners is that it creates a buyer's market rather than a seller's market.

Many of us won't ask the prospect how much he or she wants to pay because we feel that it is somehow sleazy and that doing so will create an uncomfortable situation. But if you did know how much your buyers wanted to spend, your sales closing ratio would shoot through the roof—because you'd be quoting prices you knew they could afford and were willing and prepared to spend. How do you ascertain what the buyer wants to spend without the awkwardness of asking outright?

When it's time to discuss price, ask the buyer, "Do you have a budget?" Note that you are not asking, "What is your budget?" You are instead asking the much less threatening question, "Do you have a budget?" The buyer can only give one of two answers: yes or no, with about half of prospects saying yes and the other half saying no.

If the buyer says yes, then you ask, "Would you mind sharing with me what your budget is?" Those prospects who tell you their budget have just given you the range under which your price quotation must fall to be accepted.

> When it's time to discuss price, ask the buyer, "Do you have a budget?"

But what if the buyer says, "No, we don't have a budget"? Then you ask, "Do you have a dollar figure in mind of what you would like it to cost?" Even if they do not have a budget worked out, many people, when asked the question in this way, will come back at you with an answer like "I was figuring to spend around $1,000 and not more than $3,000." In effect, they really do have a budget—$1,000 to $3,000—but just never wrote it down or said it out loud before.

A few people, however, will not share their budget, no matter how you ask. "I don't want to give you my budget," they will say. "I want *you* to tell *me* what it will cost." In such cases, use the "good, better, best" method of price quotation. Let's say you are quoting on selling the prospect a half-acre lot with a custom-built home. Instead of just quoting your top-end home, which is $500,000, you give the prospect three options to choose from.

The first option, which you call "good," is a basic three-bedroom home with a fireplace and unfinished basement. It is $300,000—the cheapest you can offer while still giving the buyer a decent home and yourself a decent profit. The second option, which you call "better," is the same home, but with a finished basement and an added sitting room in the master bedroom suite. It is $400,000—your middle-of-the-road model. The third option, which you call "best," is the same home as in the "better" option, but with top-of-the-line landscaping, a second fireplace, and a fourth bedroom. It is $500,000—your top-of-the-line model.

You outline all options for the prospect, including the prices. Then, instead of asking whether they want a home, you ask, "Which do you want—good, better, or best?" This strategy increases the chances that your price quotation will fall within the dollar amount the prospect wants to pay.

Also, very few people want the lowest-quality of three choices. So, some buyers who were looking to pay $300,000 will find a way to pay $400,000 (even if it means a bigger mortgage or borrowing from Uncle Joe), and more will select "better" over "good."

We find a similar pattern in marketing nutritional supplements by mail. If we offer three options—one bottle, three bottles, six bottles—the average unit of sale will be about 3 ½ bottles.

Testing Your Marketing Campaigns

I once heard on the radio that the Florida Marlins, with 23 wins and 14 losses, had at that time the best record in Major League Baseball at the time. That means the best-performing team in professional baseball loses nearly 4 out of every 10 games it plays. And remember—that's the best record in baseball.

What's ironic is that businesspeople who accept this statistical truth about baseball without a second thought absolutely go bonkers when even one of their marketing programs fails. Experienced marketers expect a percentage of their test campaigns to underperform the control or even lose money. They accept this fact without despair, because they know

> Experienced direct marketers expect a percentage of their test campaigns to underperform the control or even lose money.

that if one test mailing in every two, or every three, or even every five is a winner, they can make a lot of money.

Inexperienced direct marketers don't get this, however. As a result, countless small businesses test direct marketing once every few years, and if they don't hit a home run the first time at bat, they loudly proclaim that "direct mail doesn't work" and abandon it wholesale.

If you're a business owner or marketing professional, is there a better way to get direct marketing to work for you? Yes. You simply do more testing than you do right now. For example, let's say you are planning to mail 5,000 postcards to drive people to a web page, but you can't decide which of two headlines you like: "Tastes Great" or "Less Filling." If you subjectively pick just one, your risk of selecting the wrong sales appeal—and therefore having your postcard mailing bomb—is 50 percent. A much better approach is to split the postcard mailing into two batches, half with the headline "Tastes Great" and the other half with "Less Filling." Each drives traffic to a different URL, so you can measure the click-through and conversion rates and then see which generates the most leads.

> Especially on the web, testing different variations in headlines, copy, graphics, and format is relatively quick, easy, and inexpensive.

Especially on the web, testing different variations in headlines, copy, graphics, and format is relatively quick, easy, and inexpensive (called *multivariate*, or *Taguchi testing*, for this method, you test multiple versions of multiple variables simultaneously). Therefore, if you create a long-copy landing page to sell a product on the internet and your conversion rate is poor, don't give up on the product. Instead, test different headlines, visuals, pricing, offers, premiums, subheads, and copy leads. You'll notice that one headline pulls slightly better than another, or one price generates 40 percent more orders. Start incorporating the winners of these tests into your landing page, and in no time flat, you can take the promotion from marginally profitable to a real winner—all courtesy of testing.

How to Troubleshoot Your Plan

How should you approach troubleshooting your plan? Begin with the data you set up as benchmarks. If you see significant variances, dig deeper and ask yourself a few basic questions:

- Is the recession affecting your business?
- Are you getting fewer leads and new business opportunities than normal?
- Are your sales up, down, or flat?
- Has the dollar value of your average order declined?
- Do sales take longer to close?
- Are customers seeking concessions on pricing and terms?
- Which marketing activities seem to be working well?
- Which marketing activities have seen results fall off lately?
- Can I trace new clients or increases in sales to specific sources or actions?
- Are my actions generating the expected revenues? Are they costing more than they're bringing in?
- Which actions have been most fruitful?
- Which have been least productive in terms of generating sales and clients?
- Has anything been a disaster?
- Are there any tactics or actions that have completely fallen flat?
- Are there significant changes in my industry or marketplace affecting my business?
- Which of my services is generating the most revenue?
- Which is generating the least? Why?
- Should I replace it with another tactic or action now? Next year? Why?
- What do I need to do more of?
- Are my refund rates steady or increasing?

Pinpoint which elements of your strategy are not working by looking at the numbers. (Are you getting the new clients you wanted? Are you increasing your retention rate as you desired? Are you getting the referrals you anticipated? Are those converting to new sales?) Look at each piece of your strategy to try and pinpoint what's falling short of your goals. Is your competition more successful than you expected? Why? What are they doing that you can learn from?

What to Do When Your Marketing Is Not Working

If things are not working, don't despair. You have options. If the deviation from your expected results is minor, you probably only need to fine-tune your actions. But if you're clearly not hitting the mark, here are a few suggestions for getting back on track:

◆ Adjust your service to address your niche's needs more closely.

◆ Repackage your product and service options to create offers with lower price points.

◆ Make your credit policies more liberal and offer payment plans with flexible terms and low rates.

◆ Massage your message. Perhaps your language is not quite connecting with your ideal client, or maybe you're mistaken about what he or she values most. Find that hot button and drive home your message right into its most sticky and most painful parts.

◆ How's your credibility? Do you need to enhance it with some testimonials, case studies, or online video demonstrations? Maybe strengthening your guarantee can help overcome any reluctance to give your service a try.

> You might need to fine-tune your niche selection to something that more closely fits what you offer.

◆ What new capabilities can you develop that will give you an advantage to offer clients?

◆ Are your sales coming from your niche clients or another demographic group? You might need to fine-tune your niche selection to something that more closely fits what you offer.

◆ Don't get into a price war, but do make sure you're not pricing yourself out of the market. If your prices are higher than the competition's, be sure your clients perceive your services as more valuable. This is a function of positioning properly and then building your branding or image to fit that positioning.

Consistency is important when you're trying to implement a long-term plan, so resist the temptation to abandon a strategy. Give it time to work. Remember, change and growth come in stages, often in spurts. What you're looking for is significant movement toward meeting your goals. What's significant? Those are numbers you'll need to decide as you set your benchmark measurements.

When does it make sense to change marketing strategies? Consider shifting gears if there is a fundamental shift in the basic assumptions you made about your niche, the competition, or the environment you operated in when you formed your strategy.

How to Keep Working Your Plan

1. *Every day, be renewed by your vision.* Your mind can be your greatest asset or your most tiring obstacle. So begin your day by renewing your mind with the clarifying power of your vision. When W. Clement Stone and Earl Nightingale both said, "Whatever the mind of man can conceive and believe, it can achieve," they knew these were far more than simple words on a page. There simply is no substitute for the power of belief. When you believe, obstacles that would throw your entire day into chaos suddenly become bleeps that you just intuitively know how to solve without expending valuable time or energy. Don't laugh this off as touchy-feely. This is one of the most inexpensive and profitable investments you'll ever make in yourself. Just do it.

2. *Focus on your niche.* Become the expert in all things involving your niche. Don't limit your knowledge to the services you offer. The more you know about your niche's priorities and challenges, the more valuable a resource you can become to

them. Become familiar with other professionals who can assist your niche with challenges outside your expertise. When you're tempted to work with clients outside your niche, make sure the time and payoff will be worth it and won't draw you away from your commitment.

3. *Stay close to your ideal client.* Networking, surveys, online community forums, trade magazines, and associations are all great ways to keep sharp about the things that matter to your ideal client. Also, stay on top of the news, and ask yourself how your client's needs will be affected by changes in the business and world environment.

4. *Keep your eyes on your competition.* If your clients stop thinking that you offer a competitive advantage in addressing their needs, you lose and the competition wins. Enough said. Don't be the last to know what your competition is doing.

5. *Make sure you're positioned to win.* If you're doing the first four steps, you'll know when it's time to change your tune, tweak your message, and speak a new language that's more in tune with what your ideal client needs. Ask yourself, "Is my unique selling proposition still unique? Does anyone do it better? What one thing can I do to serve my clients better?" That's how you stay unique.

> Stick close to your plan. Follow your schedule. Complete the actions you say you will complete in your daily schedule.

6. *Take action every day.* Stick close to your plan. Follow your schedule. Complete the actions you say you will complete in your daily schedule. At the end of the week, give yourself a grade for effort. Then, give yourself another one for accomplishment. If you're getting A's for effort and C's for accomplishment, troubleshoot.

7. *Focus on one marketing project at a time.* One of the greatest mistakes people make in setting goals is trying to work on too

many things at one time. There is tremendous power in giving focused attention to just one idea, one project, or one objective at a time.

8. *Ask yourself good questions.* As you think about your goals, instead of wishing for them to come true, ask yourself *how* and *what you can do* to make them come true. The subconscious mind will respond to your questions far more effectively than just making statements or wishes.

9. *Congratulate yourself.* You're halfway home. You've done something that less than 3 percent of the population has done—set goals and created a plan for achieving them. Every study on the subject tells us you're far more likely than most to succeed with your plans if you will only do one thing: *take action!*

Be that external force. Plan your work, then work your plan, and you'll have an unstoppable moneymaking system that can grow your business beyond even your most amazing vision.

Chapter 13

CONTENT MARKETING

Over the past five to six years, a number of marketing trends have either emerged or grown more prevalent. Content marketing is certainly near the top of the list of growth areas in marketing activity. Others include data analytics (see Chapter 9), mobile marketing (see Chapter 14), search engine optimization (especially with Google now penalizing nonmobile-friendly websites with lower rankings on their search engine results pages), and social media (see Chapter 15).

As part of your marketing plan, you will want to think about content marketing, which is using content to bring in customers who would be interested in your products and services. If you sent out an email to get potential customers to sign up for your newsletter subscription, you might offer them a free report or a white paper on one of your products or a new service you are offering. For an example, see the sign-up box for *The Direct Response Letter*, my enewsletter: www.bly.com/reports.

Content is information that can be found in magazines, books, reports, websites, radio shows, online videos, and other media—both print and electronic—on subjects of interest to your readers.

Content marketing is useful, practical information that explains how to perform a task or solve a problem, most typically related to the tasks your products help customers with, or the problems you help customers solve. In the sales cycle, content is considered a "soft sell" that is focused on providing information and educating the customer. A "hard sell" is an advertisement that promotes a call to action to make a product purchase.

> A "hard sell" is an advertisement that promotes a call to action to make a product purchase.

Among the many formats and media for content publishing are special reports, white papers, case studies, blog posts, ebooks in PDF format, Kindle ebooks, paperbound books, pamphlets, YouTube videos, webinars, podcasts, and presentations using PowerPoint or some other visual software program, often published online on SlideShare—in short, anything that helps build a connection and trust with customers who want to know what you know. The content sells; your copy sells.

Therefore, content marketing is not a direct selling process, but it encourages customers to make a future purchase because now they know more about what you have to offer them and can see how the product or service will benefit them. Content marketing helps answer questions that customers may have about what you are offering—its methodology, technology, and application—rather than just seeing an advertisement about the new product. In retrospect, content marketing is about telling a story that most people can relate to in one context or another.

Keep in mind that content does not have to be printed or electronic text. There are four basic modes of learning—reading, watching, listening, and doing—and there are multiple content formats to accommodate each mode (see Table 13–1 on page 223).

White Papers

A white paper tends to be more technical than most other content marketing pieces and is commonly used in the business-to-business

Mode of Learning	Content Format
Reading	Books
	PDF ebooks
	Kindle ebooks
	Minibooks
	Special reports
	White papers
	Blogs
	Articles
	Enewsletters
	E-lessons
Watching	DVDs
	Streaming mp4 video
	SlideShare
	TV
	Flash/rich media
	Infographics/tipographics
	Comic books
	YouTube
	Pinterest and Instagram
Listening	Audio CDs
	Downloadable mp3s
	Podcasts
	Internet radio
	Speeches
	Teleconferences
	Webinars
Doing (experiential learning)	Seminars/workshops
	Classes
	Boot camps
	Executive retreats
	Conferences
	Demos
	Software

TABLE 13–1. **Matching Content to Prospects' Preferred Learning Mode**

(B2B) side of commerce, especially for selling software and other technical products to IT professionals. It presents a point of view, such as in government policy-making circles, or describes a product or service, using proven facts, statistics, and technical product or service information in great detail.

White papers can be as short as four pages, but should be large enough to give all the information needed to help customers make purchasing decisions. A full-length white paper is typically 8 to 10 pages. The target audience also determines how the white paper will be written, and, as part of a marketing strategy, several may need to be developed for different audiences, such as the company presidents, marketing research strategists, supply chain managers, or IT managers.

For the IT professional, the white paper would use more terminology concerning programming languages than it would for a CFO. Some audiences may need to see how the product or service will cut down production costs, so a comparative table of before-and-after costs may need to be shown.

Although formats, styles, and approaches to white papers vary widely, many follow a similar outline:

- Front cover, title, and subtitle
- Table of contents
- Executive summary
- A look at the problem the white paper addresses
- Body, including alternative solutions explored and final solution recommended
- Conclusions
- Contact information and call to action
- About the author, including details on the company publishing the paper

The best white papers are not just "information dumps" but are written to solve a specific marketing problem. For instance, one company sold a high-end, expensive content management system (CMS) software package. The marketing challenge was not explaining features and benefits; prospects understood what a CMS is and what it does: allow subject matter experts and content owners to update the corporate website without help from IT. The problem was that this CMS was very expensive, and the potential customers' senior management team—mainly the CEOs and CFOs—did not see how they would recover the cost of their investment in the CMS, as beneficial and convenient as having it would be.

The solution was to publish a white paper showing how to calculate the ROI for a new CMS. By doing so, the CMS vendor could help prospects see that buying the CMS was a profit center, not a cost center—one that would pay back its cost in about six months and generate substantial savings in time and money from that point on.

Case Studies

Case studies use a story format to narrate how a problem faced by a company or an individual was solved by using a particular product or service. More than just a story with a happy ending, case studies are high-powered sales collateral. By profiling a wide cross-section of customers, case studies deliver information that's relevant to each target audience and in a way they will relate to.

> What makes case studies so attractive to marketers and consumers alike is that they're based on real-life experiences.

Written properly, case studies are excellent tools for generating leads. Because of their versatility, case studies can be used in nearly every facet of marketing, and can be targeted for dozens of different market segments based on industry, demographic, or geography, to name just a few.

What makes case studies so attractive to marketers and consumers alike is that they're based on real-life experiences. Case studies are viewed as credible, third-party endorsements that carry a high degree of believability. That gives case studies a big advantage over traditional advertising, which consumers often view with skepticism.

A survey by Forrester Research shows that 71 percent of buyers base their decisions on trust and believability. Relating your customers' positive experiences with your product is one of the best ways to establish credibility in the marketplace. Giving your customers confidence in what you're offering dramatically increases the likelihood they'll do business with you.

> A case study will present the problem first, along with any limitations or conflicts that might have been in place at the beginning.

A case study has some of the same elements of a white paper, but tells a story as to how the product or service effectively solved a problem for a particular customer or business. Most case studies are developed over two to three pages, with about 750 to 1,500 words, and have more of a human interest storyline, rather than presenting technical specifications. A case study will present the problem first, along with any limitations or conflicts that might have been in place at the beginning.

Customers with similar issues will see how the problem and solution matches theirs, providing a stronger incentive to purchase the product or service. Building trust and believability with customers is essential; a case study provides this when they see a real-life situation in action, rather than reading sales literature.

Most case studies follow this basic outline:

- Who is the customer?
- What was the problem? How was it hurting the customer's business?
- What solutions did they look at and ultimately reject, and why?
- Why did they choose our product as the solution?
- Describe the implementation of the product, including any problems and how they were solved.
- How and where does the customer use the product?
- What are the results and benefits they are getting?
- Would they recommend it to others and why?

Special Reports

Investors, technical support people, teachers, consumers, small-business owners, scientists—anyone with a problem would find a properly targeted downloadable special report helpful and valuable.

The internet is perfect for research. That's why so many folks turn to Google when faced with a problem. The internet makes it easy for them to find helpful advice on just about any subject. This advice often comes in the form of a downloadable special report.

Special reports are widely used by internet marketers to drive website traffic and increase sales. They are popular, because they work. As Michael Stelzner, founder of Social Media Examiner, points out, "If you give readers something of value, prospects and customers will give you their loyalty, and ultimately, their business."

Readers love special reports because they are focused. The report is about a single, specific problem and gives practical, proven ideas for solving it; for example, how to set up an email strategy using an outside provider, as well as which strategy is the most productive. Another report might detail how to conduct effective cold calls and what to say, using certain types of scripts for every customer response. Building a library of different reports is very effective in presenting you as a knowledgeable content marketing specialist, and such reports can be used over and over. For instance, you can use one as a free bonus gift when customers make an online purchase of an ebook you are promoting.

> Special reports are widely used by internet marketers to drive website traffic and increase sales.

Over time, when you have developed enough reports, you can compile a number of them and repurpose them into an ebook or PDF book that you can use as a lead magnet—an added incentive for prospects to respond to your emails and other marketing promotions. Other types of reports, ebooks, and PDF books can also be created as resource guides, which are valuable for customers who do not know where to obtain needed products and services (e.g., go to www.bly. com and click on "Vendors" to see my online resource guide). You can also develop content that contains commonly used checklists, such as how to set up an online business or how to make the right decision when purchasing a corporate jet.

Minibooks

Looking for a great "lead magnet"—a free content giveaway to generate leads? Try a new kind of lead magnet, the MiniBük (not a misspelling)—an ultrashort book format more likely to be read by more people. A MiniBük is a tiny 3.5-by-5-inch printed book. It stands out from all the PDF lead magnets, because it is a physical premium sent via mail. Designed with a high-impact cover, titling, and copy, plus a layout pleasing to the eye, it earns the opportunity to be read.

With its small size, readers expect the value gained will exceed their reading time, and with a well-written one, readers will "get" your message. The MiniBük offers several additional advantages over traditionally formatted content:

- ◆ The unique format gains attention and makes your content stand out from the mound of white papers and other content your prospects receive.
- ◆ The small size makes it easy for your prospects to carry your miniature book in their pockets or bags so they can read it when they have a few minutes, such as waiting for a bus or train.
- ◆ The limited number of pages mean there is less writing for you to do vs. producing a full-length book. Where a trade paperback book like this one is typically 80,000 to 100,000 words, a MiniBük is about one-tenth that length, so you can not only write it faster, but it will cost less to produce.

MiniBük authors have had many successes, finding the highest value when the book is used to sell products or services many times its cost. For details or samples, call (800) 900-2499; for an overview, visit minibuk.com.

Audio-Visual Presentations

Audio-visual presentations include online videos, such as YouTube or other platforms, and webinars, which show pictures with detailed information, important for an audience to see as they gather their information on your product or service. PowerPoint presentations can be available on your website as streaming video, on YouTube, and on SlideShare.

Podcasts are also very popular and selected podcasts can be subscribed to through Apple iTunes. Audio CDs are another way to provide information, such as recorded online interviews with popular authors or industry experts who are happy to tell you how they achieved success.

Speeches or video scripts can be written, as well as any text applied within a visual product or service demonstration that shows graphs and charts, such as in a PowerPoint presentation. The principles of the white paper and case study also apply here, although it may not be quite as detailed. Other examples are YouTube videos that show people how to do something, such as some type of craft. Viewers are taken step-by-step through the creative process and shown what tools to use and how to use them. Content like this provides links back to the website where interested customers can find other videos, sign up for newsletters, and purchase products used in the videos.

If you are creating a program on how to design and manufacture outdoor sheds, then consider putting the program on a DVD and sell it or give it away to generate leads, along with a PDF book that shows in detail how to find and check the lumber you want to buy, cut the required lumber into specific sizes, and join the wood together using

> Podcasts are also very popular and selected podcasts can be subscribed to through Apple iTunes.

a sturdy corner-notching process. The more detail you can show, both in the PDF book and on the DVD, the happier your customers will be for making their construction project easier.

Infographics

An infographic is, as the name implies, a graphic designed to convey information. Today's infographics communicate complex data in a mix of design, writing, and analysis—in a visual shorthand of text and images—effectively making deep data *comprehensible* to the viewer in an entertaining way. Although wildly popular, some old-school-types like author Stephen Few, an expert in the effective visual communication of data, claim infographics are overused and misleading. Says Few: "Infographics could be used for good if we could only figure out when to use them and how to properly design them. Research is needed, but in the meantime, organizations are spending bundles of money on silly posters that are rarely more effective than a simple written document." Yet most marketers will tell you infographic marketing has the potential for growing your audience, generating engagement, earning links, enhancing brand recognition, and improving Google rankings.

> An infographic is, as the name implies, a graphic designed to convey information.

Figure 13–1 on page 231 shows a typical infographic: a vertical format with dimensions proportional to a letter-size piece of paper or a poster. Rather than presenting information in linear written fashion, as a white paper does, the infographic conveys it through multiple factoids, call-outs, graphs, charts, and pictures. The best infographics are tightly focused on a single, narrow topic, like the white paper infographic shown.

Providing detailed information, such as tables and graphs showing counts and percentages, is important for your audience to know, but may be boring. Design an infographic with a picture of the product or

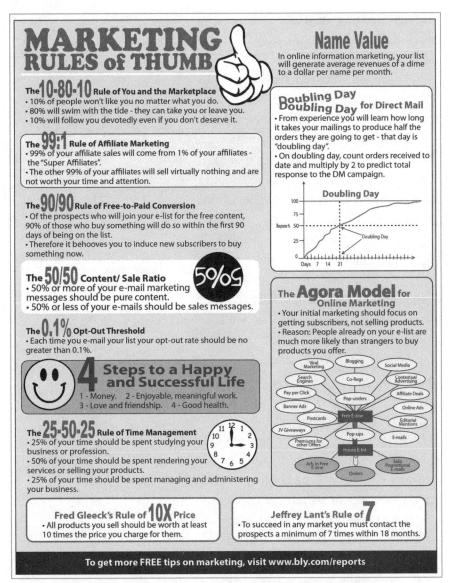

FIGURE 13–1. **Infographic in 8.5-x-11-Inch Vertical Format**

central theme in the center, and then include one informative graph in the upper right-hand corner, text content in the upper left corner, then other related smaller pictures or other information, filling in the remaining white spaces. The objective is to provide the central point, surrounded by visually supporting documentation that is easy to view and remember.

There are websites where you can design visually engaging infographics for free: *Venngage* (https://venngage.com), *Infogr.am* (https://infogr.am), *Piktochart* (http://piktochart.com), Canva (www.canva.com), and Easel.ly (http://www.easel.ly). Author John Kremer has invented an alternative to the infographic, the tipographic. It too is a content-containing graphic, only shorter and much plainer in design (see Figure 13–2). Early results show tipographics work as well as infographics, or better. But they take far less time, effort, and money to produce. I was quoted $1,000 by one graphic designer for an infographic but only $100 for a tipographic.

Infographics should have a call to action, typically but not always toward the bottom of the page. This call to action is usually a hyperlink to the marketer's landing page or website. You generate traffic by posting the infographic on Pinterest and Instagram where it can gain a viewing audience.

Blogs

In your site's ranking on the Search Engine Results Page (SERP), Google penalizes static sites that never

15 Tips
for Profitable PDF E-Book Publishing

1. Use an 8 ½ X 11-inch page size.
2. Aim for 50 pages – around 15,000 words.
3. Create a landing page to sell the e-book. Example: www.myveryfirstebook.com
4. Write as an expert, not a journalist.
5. Don't just collect and rewrite articles from Google.
6. Interview subject matter experts.
7. Participate in the skill or activity you write about.
8. Pack your book with practical tips.
9. Give step-by-step how-to instruction.
10. Use real-life examples.
11. Don't give a lot of theory or background.
12. Write in simple and straightforward prose.
13. Give away a free bonus report with purchase.
14. Offer a 90-day money-back guarantee.
15. Price the e-book between $19 and $49.

For more tips on e-book profits:
www.myveryfirstebook.com

FIGURE 13–2. **Tipographic**

change and rewards sites that add new content on a regular basis. One of the easiest ways to add new content is with a blog. Write two to three 300- to 500-word posts each week, and you'll more than satisfy Google for updating site content.

In the upper right corner of your blog, have icons that allow your visitors to subscribe to your blog via an RSS feed. The more subscribers to your blog, the more exposure your blog content garners.

Blogs can be a bit more personal than white papers and other more formal content marketing vehicles, but the most effective blogs present valuable information rich in both ideas and how-to instruction. A blog gives you freedom to express your opinion of an idea or methodology more vociferously than, say, a special report, but you cannot merely rant and rave; within your essay, you must give solid advice.

> When visitors or subscribers comment on your posts, you should reply when appropriate.

"People who visit your blog want to be informed," writes Ogi Djuraskovic in his ebook *How to Start a Blog*. "They want to learn more or stay up-to-date on specific topics. There is never enough information for the voracious appetites of collectors and enthusiasts. They desire more, and you can give them that."

Read your own blog regularly. When visitors or subscribers comment on your posts, you should reply when appropriate. Blog readers like two-way communication with the blog owner, and some enjoy a good debate or argument. If appropriate, give it to them, but with a tone of being helpful and inquisitive, not arrogant or argumentative.

Enewsletters

Another powerful vehicle for content marketing is online newsletters, also known as enewsletters or ezines. I have 65,000 subscribers to my enewsletter *The Direct Response Letter*, which covers marketing and related business topics.

There are two styles of enewsletters. One is a compendium of short articles or items, just a few paragraphs each, and maybe five to seven short entries per issue; in the newsletter trade this type of newsletter is called a digest. The other ezine approach is to make each issue a longer essay on a single topic. I use both formats; my online essays typically run 400 to 700 words each.

The frequency of your enewsletter can be monthly, twice a month, weekly, or even multiple times per week. How do you know when you are emailing your newsletters too frequently? People will begin to send you emails complaining that you are sending too frequently, and others will opt out of your list, known as unsubscribing.

> The frequency of your enewsletter can be monthly, twice a month, weekly, or even multiple times per week.

Enewsletters can be plain text or colorful HTML; I prefer the former. Text emails are faster, easier, and cheaper to produce. "It's ugly but easier to read, because of all the short lines," says email marketing expert Ben Settle. "Plus, to make matters worse, a lot of people use HTML tables that are way too wide. On even a bigger screen like my phone, I have to swipe over to read an entire sentence, then swipe back for each single sentence. And what may read fine on one person's phone could be way too wide for someone else's."

Keep an archive of past issues of your enewsletters on your website. This is another way to ensure that you meet Google's preference for a constant stream of fresh content on your site.

As with blog posts, make your enewsletter articles interesting and useful; a little controversy goes a long way in generating greater excitement and interest among your readers. For a major telecom company, we produced an article saying their wireless protocol was better than the competitor's protocol.

You may decide to generate additional revenue by selling products and services in your enewsletter. If you do, at least 50 percent of your ezine must be useful content, with less than half being sales copy for your products. If more than half of what you publish is pure sales, your subscribers will rapidly become disgusted with you and stop reading what you send.

How to Double Your Responses with Content Marketing

Content marketing requires a strategic plan of deciding how often you want to publish a blog or send an email. Create an editorial calendar of when you want to publish content and who you want to see the message. Fit this into your 30-day action plan from Chapter 11. You can develop new content, but if you do not have a lot of time available, then repurposing older content works well too.

The key is to collect information and store it in relevant files associated with different topics, or you can use an application like Evernote, which collects and saves interesting internet pages of information. If you have written an ebook, select a small portion from the book and rewrite it as an interesting topic that is relevant to many of your readers. Then decide what platform the message will work well on, such as Facebook, Twitter, Pinterest, or an email blast. In some cases, the message may need to be redesigned for several platforms.

> It may be necessary to change your posting strategy for different time periods and with different content.

If you have been watching your social media interactions for a time, you will notice which people check in and what time of day they do so. If you were sending out a message to the morning crowd, then you can send it again to the evening crowd. Review your site statistics that tell you how many people are seeing your posts, taking action on a link in the message, and whether you have less responses this week than last week.

It may be necessary to change your posting strategy for different time periods and with different content. If it is working well, then do not change it. Evaluate your content and make sure it is interesting and fresh. Using keywords within the content is also important, and developing this strategy requires a bit of research to see what words pull up best.

Another way to engage potential customers is to joint venture with other businesses online and ask if they will share your blog, while you share something of theirs back on your site. Guest blogging on other sites is also effective and helps promote you and your product or service.

Finding Content Sources

Aside from doing your own research to create your content, you can also interview experts in your field. Getting quotes from recognized experts in the content subject will add much more to your credibility. For lesser-known experts, make sure that they are credible sources by checking out their websites and what content they may have produced in their industry. This is particularly true of websites that offer connections with experts, such as HARO (Help a Reporter Out). Other websites where you can find experts are ProfNet.com, AllExperts.com, Business Wire's ExpertSource.com, and Experts.com. There are plenty of similar websites, so chances of finding the right expert is fairly high.

> Getting quotes from recognized experts in the content subject will add much more to your credibility.

Look for industry groups where you can sign up to access member businesses in specific industries, such as Thomasnet.com, which caters to customers looking for industrial and commercial suppliers, and industry-specific products and materials. There are over 700,000 suppliers listed nationwide, which can be selected by company type, location, ownership, and certifications. A brief description is given of the company, and the website can be accessed through the provided link. Additionally, if you specialize in writing for this industry, you can sign up as a service provider, offering marketing content services to the industry members. Check to see if the industry group would like content written for their newsletter or look into advertising on their website. You can also find the latest industry news by signing up for the ThomasNet newsletter.

Government websites also offer a wealth of information, which can be useful for building your content, such as USA.gov and the Government Printing Office (GPO.gov), where you can access the catalog of U.S. government publications. From there, you can also link to the Federal Depository Library, or use the MetaLib federated search engine, which can access numerous U.S federal government databases. Most government publications are in the public domain and can be used in your content, so long as you note the source.

In designing a content theme, you can check for royalty-free content, such as books and other publications, which are now in the public domain because the copyright ran out and was not renewed. Any publication written prior to 1923 is considered to be in the public domain. However, you must always check the U.S. Copyright Office database at copyright.gov/records/. When the copyright is verified as being expired, you can use that content to repurpose into new content of your own and sell it.

There are numerous websites where you can research for copyright-free content, so only a few are provided here as a starting point: Gutenberg.org, archive.org, Alibris.com, and classic-literature. co.uk/. Once you find a copyright-free publication, you can repurpose it, using additional content relevant to your theme or program, and add in quality illustrations and photographs. The only fees you pay may be to the photographers and illustrators, for which you also note their contributions in the publication. Retitle the work, copyright it, and you are ready to sell it.

Signing up for targeted news feeds from major news publications provides a way of getting news of interest delivered to you as it is published. Google Alerts also provides the ability to select information

> Signing up for targeted news feeds from major news publications provides a way of getting news of interest delivered to you as it is published.

you are searching for and having it sent to you at your email address. Use Twitter to get targeted breaking news in your industry delivered to your account by setting up an automated keyword search in Hootsuite.com.

The Four R's of Content Management

Managing your content so it remains relevant to your needs and those of your customers is essential for maintaining successful engagement and, ultimately, future sales. As part of your content distribution calendar, always review your content before posting it, even if it worked well before. Develop a strategy for the Four R's of management that follow.

Refresh

When you pull out content that you posted last year for another posting, read it through carefully and make sure that each component is still relevant and up-to-date. For example, you might have posted last year that ABC Media was the best place for finding royalty-free photographs. If you do not use ABC Media yourself, then go to the website first and make sure they are still in business and offering royalty-free photographs.

> There is nothing worse than sending your customers to a website that has changed its practices or no longer exists.

There is nothing worse than sending your customers to a website that has changed its practices or no longer exists. If they are out of business, then do some quick research for other websites that offer royalty-free photographs. In fact, you might want to add in a couple of similar sites, not just one.

Recycle

Recycling your content refers to using sections from other content pieces, such as blogs or ebooks, and then expanding that message a little more to develop your new message. You can also use content sent out in your blog a year ago, particularly if you use a link to one of your reports, products, or services, and just change some of the text around, while still keeping the link.

If you showed your customers how to do a process in one of your ebooks, take that information and turn it around into a visual presentation as a video or series of photographs. It is the same information that was written in the book. Alternatively, if you had a webinar on how to start a crafts business, turn all that information into an ebook and sell it. Better yet, provide both as a complete package.

> If you had a webinar on how to start a crafts business, turn all that information into an ebook and sell it.

Retire

Some content will become outdated over time as technology and processes change, which happens almost on a daily basis. What was once a unique process of gathering customer information several years ago through email strategies may no longer be relevant if you are using an outside vendor who can do it far better than your long, drawn-out process, mainly because it is what the vendor does, professionally and efficiently. Many customers will be more interested in who you use to take care of that side of your distribution and information collection. Therefore, that content piece should be retired.

Replace

As noted in the previous section, you will need to retire content from time to time. It is important, however, to also replace it with a new content piece, such as a list of the best companies to use for taking care of your email list. Show the importance of best practices in gathering customer information, handling subscriptions and deletions, and also maintaining your content distribution schedule. Provide pertinent criteria on how to choose the best vendor.

Every content piece has value, and while you may need to replace an old blog post, for example, you can update it with fresh, new information, even while keeping in a link that is still good and, most likely, has search engine optimization (SEO) attached to it. When you get ready to repost the updated version, use an editor's note at the top under the title, or at the bottom, indicating when the post was first published, noting that it has been updated for new information.

Content Curation

Content curation is the process of collecting information from a number of sources, which are then presented as part of a themed package on a given topic. As an example, someone may gather photographs from numerous photographers around the web as part of a theme on U.S. national parks. It is important to note that photographers are listed with their photographs as part of copyright regulations, so it is always important to note where the photograph, or information, came from. There may be fees involved, which are paid to the photographer, in order to show such photographs on a curated site.

> Content curation is the process of collecting information from a number of sources, which are then presented as part of a themed package on a given topic.

A successful content curation strategy is to mix or alternate curated content with fresh content created by you, which will reflect what you are promoting, whether it is a theme, your products, or a service. The importance of such a strategy is to develop a relationship with your customers, particularly when operating on a timed schedule. Customers will begin looking for your content when you can deliver interesting and thought-provoking material. Kristina Cisnero, inbound marketing specialist for Hootsuite (http://blog.hootsuite.com/beginners-guide-to-content-curation), notes that the team produces a weekly post called "This Week in Social" where the latest news in social media and new technology is presented, aside from regular content postings, a content curation process which nearly every business could use.

When curating content from other sources, make sure that you read each piece completely before sharing it under your brand. In some cases, the headline and initial theme may match the entire story and reflect something you may not agree with; yet you have posted it, meaning that you do agree with it. Avoid such a calamity at all costs.

> When curating content from other sources, make sure that you read each piece completely before sharing it under your brand.

There are numerous content curation tools that can help you compile information for resharing to your audiences. Check them out to see which one will work best for you. TweetedTimes.com produces a newspaper-styled compilation of news shared by followers on your Twitter list. Pinterest is another curation tool, as is Feedly.com, Storify.com, List.ly, and Bundlr.com. Learning how to use one or more of these tools may be useful as part of developing your content curation strategy as well as giving you new ideas for future content marketing development.

Chapter 14
MOBILE MARKETING

There are two really good reasons to jump into mobile marketing. The first comes directly from Google. As mentioned earlier in this book, to provide users worldwide with relevant, high-quality search results optimized for their devices, on April 21, 2015, Google expanded their use of "mobile-friendliness" as a ranking criterion. In short, websites that are not mobile-friendly will be penalized with lower search rankings. The fact is no entrepreneur really serious about making money would be willing to undermine their online marketing success by ignoring this Google pronouncement.

The second reason is equally as persuasive: *A mobile device is the closest you can get to your consumer.* Whether cell phone or tablet, there really is no more personal or pervasive device as a mobile one. In 2011, Americans spent 2.7 hours per day socializing on their mobile phones—more than twice the time they spent eating! People have their phones with them at all times of the day, even in the bathroom. That's a level of "closeness" you can't ignore.

Here's how pervasive this medium is: As of October 2014, 64 percent of Americans owned a smartphone. Jump ahead five *months,* to April 2015, when it was reported smartphones reached nearly 77 percent penetration in the United States (a number that is expected to grow to 80 percent or beyond by December 2015). The percentages may change, but the trend is obvious: Mobile is growing. In fact, in August 2014, we reached the *tipping* point: when mobile had officially overtaken fixed internet access. Here are a few more facts about mobile marketing:

◆ *Mobile devices outnumber humans on earth.* That means there are over 7.2 billion mobile devices. Not surprisingly, the figure continues to increase—more than five times faster than the human population. No other technology in human history has impacted us like the mobile phone. Think of it: from zero to 7.2 billion in less than three decades. Amazing.

◆ *Mobile will surpass desktop in search ad dollars spent in 2015.* Mobile ad spending in the U.S. will jump 50 percent in 2015, but is predicted to jump to 60 percent in 2016. Here's something else: The largest portion of ad spending, by a 3–1 margin, is taking place inside apps, not the mobile web.

◆ *Nineteen percent of people have dropped their cell phones in the toilet.* And 59 percent of smartphone owners say they would reach into the toilet to retrieve it. Maybe that's not surprising: "Help, I dropped my cell phone in the toilet" and "My phone fell in the toilet, what should I do" are two popular Google search phrases.

◆ *Seventy-five percent of Americans bring their phones to the bathroom.* Men seem to be more attached to their phones; 30 percent couldn't go to the restroom without their mobile device. But women are not far behind: 20 percent bring their phone to the bathroom every time.

◆ *Fifty-six percent of American adults are now smartphone owners.* That figure is up from 35 percent in 2011. At the same time, the number of adults with no cell phone fell to an all-time low of 9 percent.

◆ *Thirty percent of U.S. shoppers research products and services on a smartphone before making an in-store purchase.* And 40 percent of U.S. shoppers engage in *showrooming*, which is when consumers research in-store and purchase via digital commerce channels. Ninety-three percent of consumers use or are interested in using their smartphone to shop on-the-go, and 90 percent use, or are interested in using, their smartphone to shop from home. Approximately 8 in 10 consumers are digital shoppers, which are defined as those who regularly research and purchase products via the internet.

◆ *Within five years, half of today's smartphone users will be using mobile wallets as their preferred payment method.* Despite a slower rate of adoption in the U.S., when compared to global figures, it is projected that by 2018, mobile in-person payments will increase 600 percent, reaching $23 billion, up from $3.73 billion in 2014.

◆ *Cyber Monday sales are up 30 percent, and mobile sales are up 96 percent since 2011.* While total Cyber Monday sales were up close to 9 percent in 2014, mobile sales increased by a whopping 29.3 percent and accounted for 1 in 5 transactions. Cyber Monday reached $2 billion in desktop online spending in 2014, up 17 percent from 2013. It was the heaviest online spending day in history.

◆ *Sixty-four percent of survey respondents who have smartphones have made a mobile purchase after seeing a mobile ad, but nearly three-quarters (74 percent) haven't received mobile ads from their favorite brands.* Consumers exposed to mobile ads for consumer packaged goods (CPG) products showed a 75 percent increase in store visits and a 96 percent lift over the general population. And it seems smartphone owners were slightly more likely to click on a mobile ad, with 43 percent saying they had, compared with only 37 percent of those using tablet computers.

Here's something else you may not know: Nielsen (www.nielsen.com) has found that 84 percent of smartphone and tablet owners say they use their devices as second screens while watching TV at the same time. It's obvious: Savvy digital marketers will add "mobile" to their "fixed" internet presence right *now*. Without doubt, no other medium enables you to connect with the right people, at the right place, and the right time.

> Smart entrepreneurs and small-business owners use a combination of traditional and digital marketing channels.

Mobile marketing is really nothing more than a set of practices enabling businesses to communicate with these connected consumers in an interactive, relevant way, via a cellular (or mobile) device. Smart entrepreneurs and small-business owners use a combination of traditional and digital marketing channels.

But there are distinct advantages in choosing to put the emphasis on mobile channels, not the least of which have already been mentioned: Mobile is personal and pervasive. All you need do to understand is look around you: People carry their cell phones everywhere (and if you watch closely, you'll see most people won't even share their cell phone with anyone). This means your marketing messages can be read and acted on immediately. As if that's not enough, the mobile phone:

♦ *Is available at the point of creative inspiration.* Phones today feature a number of tools that let users act on creative impulse, from taking photos and videos to becoming a scribbling pad on which to jot down ideas. These features can be used to encourage interactivity within campaigns especially created for mobile. It presents the mobile as a useful tool in viral campaigns based on consumer–generated content.

♦ *Can provide accurate audience measurement.* Every transaction made on a mobile phone can be uniquely tracked to that mobile phone number, whether the transaction is a voice call, an SMS message, or accessing the internet. The aggregated data can provide extensive profiling and segmenting opportunities for targeting the right audience. Be aware that the networks determine the data they are willing to share with the marketing company. This limits the information available.

◆ *Captures the social context of media consumption.* Because mobile phones can accurately track transactions to any phone number (user), they can also track transactions between mobile numbers (users). This means that sophisticated data mining can identify patterns that indicate information and preferences of mobile phone users. This rich data can then be used to both create and market your products, content, and services online.

Plan Your Mobile Strategy

When you set about integrating mobile into your marketing plan, you should begin with the basics: the "who, what, and how" of your mobile strategy. And you do that by getting the answers to these questions:

> When you set about integrating mobile into your marketing plan, you should begin with the basics: the "who, what, and how" of your mobile strategy.

◆ Who are your customers and who are you trying to reach?
◆ Who will want to engage with your mobile content?
◆ What tasks and needs does your audience have?
◆ What mobile channels will you use?
◆ What tone or angle will you use to inspire your audience to get involved?
◆ Why do your customers need information from you in a timely manner?
◆ How will your target audience access your mobile content (which type of handheld device will they use)?

- How will they use your content in their daily lives?
- How will you make your mobile content sticky and engaging?
- How will you cross-pollinate between the selected channels?
- How will you create sharing opportunities?
- How will you fuel the momentum of your mobile campaign?

Of course, you'll also want to clearly define your mobile marketing goals. Do you want to increase the number of newsletter sign-ups, generate leads, or make sales? When you set a goal, remember to make sure it's SMART: *specific, measurable, action-oriented, realistic* and *timely* (refer back to Chapter 5 if you need a refresher). Let's get started by taking a closer look at available mobile channels.

Mobile Websites

Some business owners create a subdomain set up specifically for mobile phones. Then if a mobile user types www.theirdomain.com into a smartphone, the site automatically determines the inquiry source and automatically redirects them to a mobile-friendly subdomain. The trick is to create a mobile site that loads quickly and provides a simple, streamlined experience. Many other business owners use web hosting companies, which offer low cost, semi-automatic cookie-cutter mobile sites.

> Some business owners create a subdomain set up specifically for mobile phones.

Short Message Service (SMS) Messaging

If you doubt the value of SMS text message marketing, you should ponder this statistic: 95 percent of your customers who have opted into your text messaging program open (and read) your mobile messages within three minutes of receiving it. Now, that's effective. SMS message marketing are purportedly both complicated and hampered by regulation, but the truth is these regulations serve the marketer as well as the consumer (protecting the latter from spammy marketing, and protecting marketers from spam-related accusations). First and foremost is the fact they are both permission-based, which means you should always be completely transparent about your text marketing program, practice full disclosure, and always get everything in writing.

Mobile Apps

There are countless mobile apps designed to serve up informative tips and educational snippets, help you to track your caloric intake, mark exercise milestones, guide you in meditation practice, or simply to entertain you with engaging games—yet consumers are always looking for more, and better, apps.

What this means to marketers is simple: You can boost brand awareness and consumer affinity with apps, but you must have a thorough understanding of your audience so you can provide them with an app that is functional (such as a calculator) or entertaining (like a video, game, or music); or provide some sort of social connectedness, such as an app for a user community. You may want to consider offering a free version of your app and let users decide if they are willing to invest in a premium version with more features and content. (This was the model used by Rovio Entertainment when they began marketing the *Angry Birds* game. They offered a free version, while paid subscribers were given access to more challenging levels and other free add-ons.)

> You may want to consider offering a free version of your app and let users decide if they are willing to invest in a premium version with more features and content.

Mobile Coupons

A growing number of businesses, like Target, Sephora, Bath and Body Works, and Olive Garden deliver coupons via mobile devices in an effort to appeal to consumers, many of whom would never think of clipping or carrying coupons. To redeem a mobile coupon, all users need to do is show the coupon bar codes to the cashier, who will scan them like a regular coupon. Location-based shopping coupons using mobile devices are also gaining popularity.

Mobile Campaigns and Ads

Mobile marketing presents a distinctly unique way to create interactive dialogues with customers. But it requires matching creativity to a smaller screen size; designing messages that are short, instantly understood, and effective; and creating a call-to-action with a minimal number of steps.

Here's a fact worth remembering: Research indicates that mobile ads perform about *five times better* than internet ads. (The most common mobile ads are simple text links and display ads that are sold based on cost per click, cost per acquisition, and cost per thousand.)

Mobile marketing is not about your convenience. The benefits of receiving the information or discount via a mobile device must be valuable enough to the recipient. It has to make sense to the recipient as a benefit and not seen as an intrusion. Make offers that are in tune with the recipient's buying habits. You have to sync your messaging with your customers' purchase history or favorites. If you are sophisticated enough to delve into mobile advertising, you should have access to a consumer's buying records to know what the individual needs and wants. Hey, you can go so far as to ask your customers what they want using Twitter, then show them you listened by making those same offers. This goes back to the idea of creating a dialogue, rather than a monologue. You really need to be strategic about what content you send out using mobile media.

> Make offers that are in tune with the recipient's buying habits.

A major consideration when establishing a mobile marketing strategy involves identifying the benefits to the consumer, then integrating the message in your overall marketing campaign so you can communicate those benefits through all other marketing and social media channels.

No Website? Choose Your Mobile Website Configuration

Google recognizes three different configurations for building mobile websites:

1. *Responsive Web Design (RWD).* Serves the same HTML code on the same URL regardless of the users' device (desktop, tablet, mobile, nonvisual browser), but can render the display differently (i.e., respond) based on the screen size. Responsive design is Google's recommended design pattern. Google's algorithms should be able to automatically detect this setup if all Googlebot user agents are allowed to crawl the page and its assets (CSS, JavaScript, and images).

> Responsive design is Google's recommended design pattern.

2. *Dynamic Serving.* Uses the same URL regardless of device, but generates a different version of HTML for different device types based on what the server knows about the user's browser. Dynamic serving is a setup where the server responds with different HTML (and CSS) on the same URL depending on the user agent requesting the page.

3. *Separate URLs.* Serves different code to each device, and on separate URLs. This configuration tries to detect the user's device, then redirects to the appropriate page. In this configuration, each desktop URL has an equivalent different URL serving mobile-optimized content.

Already Have a Website? It's High Time to Make It Mobile-Friendly

Because mobile internet usage is increasing at such a high rate, it's *extremely* important that your website is mobile-friendly. Right now, if you've got a website designed solely for desktop users, Google will penalize you for your lack of a mobile presence. That means it's high time you make your site equally favorable for both desktop and mobile users, and responsive web design will get it done for you.

> Because mobile internet usage is increasing at such a high rate, it's *extremely* important that your website is mobile-friendly.

A responsive design simply means a website that has been constructed so that all the content, images, and structure of each site page remain the same on any device. You want to be able to deliver a full site experience but on a smaller screen, and with responsive website design, you don't have to have worry about having different websites for various devices or making sure your site runs properly on a mobile device.

But letting go of worry is just one reason why you should make the switch to responsive design. Here's the big one: Responsive design can increase coveted conversion rates, effectively turning shoppers into buyers.

Here's another great reason to "go responsive": It allows you to do some important high-end heatmapping and A/B testing. In marketing, A/B testing refers to an experiment with two variants, "A" and "B." A/B testing is a simple way to test changes to your web page against the current design and determine which ones produce positive results. It's a way to validate higher conversion rates before making any proposed design changes.

Web *heatmapping* is based on technology that monitors eye movements as a means of studying how people interact with text or online documents. The results of heatmap testing are used for identifying areas of a web page most frequently scanned by visitors.

This analytical data can lead to insights you can't find using other methods, which can greatly increase your conversion rate. You'll be able to segment mobile users and gain a better picture of how those users are interacting on your site. When you do this, you can discover what sales tactics and marketing strategies are effective, as well as those that are not.

> This analytical data can lead to insights you can't find using other methods, which can greatly increase your conversion rate.

So how do you make your current website mobile-friendly? Google makes it easy with a set of valuable resources, including their Mobile-Friendly Test (www.google.com/webmasters/tools/mobile-friendly/) to see if pages on your site are already friendly to mobile users. You'll also want to check the Mobile Usability Report in Google's Webmaster Tools to fix any potential mobile issues found on your site.

If you're using a CMS (content management system) such as WordPress or a platform offered by your hosting provider to build your site with themes, designs, and templates, you'll want to see if the software or platform is listed in Google's Customize Your Software tutorials. (Fortunately, each tutorial has step-by-step instructions on making your website themes and templates mobile-friendly).

Does Google give a stronger mobile-friendly ranking to pages using responsive web design (which uses the same URL and the same HTML for the desktop and mobile versions) vs. hosting a separate mobile site? No, mobile-friendliness is assessed the same, whether you use responsive web design (RWD), separate mobile URLs, or dynamic serving for your configuration. If your site uses separate mobile URLs or dynamic serving, Google recommends reviewing the Mobile SEO guide to make sure the search engine is properly crawling and indexing your mobile pages.

Avoid These Common Mobile Website Mistakes

Google is the ultimate arbiter of mobile-friendliness, and fortunately, they are very clear about what is required for your current site to be considered mobile-friendly. Again, you'll want to access Google's Webmaster's Mobile Guide, a comprehensive resource for creating and improving a mobile-friendly site; but here's a short look at the common mistakes marketers make when attempting to "go mobile" using their existing website.

- ◆ *Blocked JavaScript, CSS, and image files.* For optimal rendering and indexing, you've got to allow Googlebot access to the JavaScript, CSS, and image files used by your website so the system can see your site like an average user. If your site's robots.txt file disallows crawling of these assets, it directly harms how well Google's algorithms render and index your content. In short, this can result in suboptimal rankings.

- ◆ *Unplayable content.* Some types of videos or content are not playable on mobile devices, such as license-constrained media or experiences that require Flash or other players that are not broadly supported on mobile devices. Unplayable content, when featured on a page of any website, is always frustrating for end users.

- ◆ *Faulty redirects.* If you have separate mobile URLs, you must redirect mobile users on each desktop URL to the appropriate mobile URL. Redirecting to other pages (such as always to the homepage) would not only be incorrect, but it would be ineffective.

- ◆ *Mobile-only 404s.* When completing internet searches, who likes to arrive at a "404" page? No one; and unfortunately, many sites serve content to desktop users but show a 404 error page to mobile users. To ensure the best user experience, if you recognize a user is visiting a desktop page from a mobile device and you have an equivalent mobile page at a different

URL, redirect them to that URL. You'll also want to make sure that the mobile-friendly page itself is not an *error* page!

♦ *App download interstitials.* Many webmasters promote their business's native apps to their mobile website visitors. If not done with care, the interstitial pages can cause indexing issues and disrupt the visitor's usage of the site.

♦ *Irrelevant cross-links.* A common practice when a website serves users on separate mobile URLs is to have links to the desktop-optimized version, and likewise, a link from the desktop page to the mobile page. A common error is to have links point to an irrelevant page, such as having the mobile pages link to the desktop site's homepage.

> A common error is to have links point to an irrelevant page, such as having the mobile pages link to the desktop site's homepage.

♦ *Slow mobile pages.* Did you know the majority of smartphone users expect websites to load in four seconds or less? And most of the time they are disappointed, because the average website takes nine seconds—more than twice that amount of time to load. Having a fast mobile website is all about making the hard decisions and getting rid of what doesn't add a lot of value to the user's experience and remove it. (There are ways to speed up your mobile site, including reducing the number of file download dependencies and required client-side JavaScript processing, and making image sizes smaller.)

Getting the Most from Mobile Email

About 72 percent of mobile users read their emails in bed, first thing in the morning. That's because most people use their phones as an alarm clock, so they commonly turn off the alarm and hit the email icon. Here's another number worth remembering: 77 percent of participants reported that they check their email "everywhere" or "obsessively." (These readers have notifications set to alert them when an email arrives; they tend to check their mobile device immediately upon feeling that telltale buzz or hearing the alert tone.) If over three-fourths of mobile users check their email obsessively, you've got a captive market for your email messages. But what kind of emails should you send? You've got a choice: HTML or plain text, so which should you use?

HTML or Text: The Pros and Cons

It may be hard to believe, but the mobile email open rate, which is the standard measure of how many people on an email list view a particular email campaign, has seen explosive growth over the past three years. In 2011, 11 percent of emails sent to mobile devices could be labeled as an "open"; today the percentage is holding rather steady at 45 percent, which is an increase of over 300 percent. But there's more: During this same time period, desktop opens have decreased 53 percent, while web-based email accounts (webmail) opens decreased 10 percent.

Let's break it down to make it easy to remember: Plain text email is better if you are worried about deliverability into the inbox, concerned about your email visuals not breaking or appearing incorrectly in email service providers, expecting replies to be sent to your email, or don't have the development and design resources to create a well-tested, tightly coded html email template.

HTML email is better if your main objective is to convert a sale, the information needs to be visually organized, or you have the in-house resources to create a workable and successful email template. Certainly, conversion is an issue to all digital marketers, so let's get out of the "either/or" mindset and say "send both"!

It is important to understand that the open rate is *not* a 100 percent accurate measure. Recording an "open" can only happen if the reader's email client is capable of displaying HTML with images, and that option is turned *on*. So if you are sending text-only emails, there is no way to record open rates. Similarly, people reading your HTML email without images showing will not be recorded as "opens."

Current Trends in Email Open Rates

There are certainly some broad trends in open rates that are worth noting here:

- As list size goes up, the open rate tends to fall. Could it possibly be because smaller companies are more likely to have personal relationships with their list subscribers?
- Companies and organizations that are focusing on enthusiasts and supporters, like churches, sport teams, and nonprofits, see higher open rates.
- More specific niche topics, like some manufacturing areas, also typically have higher open rates than emails on broader topics.
- Typically 50 percent of opens occur in the first six hours after the email is sent and about 80 percent within 48 hours.

Adhere to Mobile Email Best Practices

With over 80 percent of subscribers reporting that they will delete an email if it doesn't look good on their mobile device, it's *essential* for you to optimize your emails for mobile subscribers, especially if they're a big chunk of your audience. Using mobile email best practices ensures that designs are legible and easy to interact with not only on mobile devices, but also on tablets and desktop environments. Here are some tips for making your emails look great on mobile.

- *Enlarge fonts.* It might not seem obvious to you, but readers in their mid-40s and older mention having trouble reading tiny text on mobile devices. Fortunately, the Apple-recommended font size of 17 to 22 points in mobile emails satisfies most mobile readers. Tiny text is hard to read on a desktop comput-

> Tiny text is hard to read on a desktop computer, never mind on the small mobile screen.

er, never mind on the small mobile screen. To avoid illegible fonts, a size of 14 pixels as a minimum for body copy and 22 pixels for headlines is useful. (Also, you'll want to note that Apple's IOS will automatically resize fonts under 13 pixels, making them larger on your behalf.)

♦ *Use thumb-friendly buttons.* As the descriptive model of human/computer interaction known as Fitt's Law suggests, increasing the size of an interaction target decreases the time and effort required to reach it. That means you'll want to use thumb-friendly buttons for your "Read More," "Buy Now," and social media links. Big buttons are not only more visible on a mobile screen, but they're also easier to interact with. If you really want to use text, keep the sizing guidelines in mind. But please note that some readers mention that it helps to have links underlined in mobile emails to make them stand out. When it comes to reading emails on mobile, your call-to-action (CTA) *must* be touch-friendly. It's recommended you follow the *fat-finger rule*: Put the CTA front and center and, if you're using a button, make it a minimum size of 44 x 44 pixels.

♦ *Streamline content.* Evaluate the content in your email and get rid of the less useful or relevant links, copy, and images. Also be concise, but still approachable. The shorter the copy, the easier it is for people to scroll on mobile.

♦ *Use single-column layout.* While many online newsletters are multicolumn, mobile-friendly emails should consider switching to a single-column layout. This approach accommodates smaller screens and can help increase legibility.

♦ *Ditch detailed navigation bars.* When viewed on a mobile device, navigation bars can break, are too small to tap, or simply aren't relevant to the email content.

♦ *Image-blocking techniques.* Like webmail and desktop clients, there are numerous mobile email apps that block images by default. As a result, it's important to optimize your emails to be viewed without images. Luckily, there are a number of strategies to help combat image blocking. ALT text, which is short for *alternative text*, is one of the best ways to get around clients that block images by default. When your email reader doesn't display the image, you see in its place the alt text. Luckily, adding ALT attributes is extremely easy—all it takes is adding an attribute to the image tag. Here's a hint from the experts: You can take your ALT

> Like webmail and desktop clients, there are numerous mobile email apps that block images by default.

text to the next level by adding a bit of inline CSS to change the font, color, size, style, and weight. This technique, known as *styled ALT text*, is a great option for maintaining branding and adding some fun to your images.

- *Use a balance of live text and imagery.* This ensures your emails are accessible, eliminates the HTML-to-text ratio spam issue, and allows for the email to be legible and easy to interact with regardless of whether images are present or not.
- *Optimize content in upper-left corner.* Many mobile email apps, including some Android and BlackBerry apps, will only display the upper left-hand corner of your email. (This happens when the lack of *autoscaling* cuts off the right side of emails and forces users to scroll left-and-right in addition to up-and-down to view your entire message.) As a result, it's important to place important information and CTAs in the upper-left corner of your email.
- *Be aware of the perils of Android presentation.* Emails typically look the same on most Android devices. Any differences in appearance usually relate to how the Android user chose to set up their device for email and in what app they choose to read their email. If you know you're sending to an Android-heavy readership (remember the need for market audience research), take these tips into consideration:
  - If you're using a two-column template (which is not recommended), consider using a smaller left column and wider

right column. Research has found if the right column takes up the entire screen on initial download, the reader doesn't always remember that there may be an additional "hidden" column. (Android users seem to have an easier time reading single-column and left-sidebar designs.)

— Watch the margins and padding on the edges of your email. For instance, when a client uses the Gmail app, if your text is right against the edge of the screen and your reader scrolls too far horizontally to read the text, they'll scroll to the next email instead of to the end of the text or image they're viewing.

— Give them a second chance by letting them "save" your email for later by adding an Instapaper (www.instapaper. com) link to your articles.

— Modify content delivery using media queries. These are a way to change content delivery according to media types and features. Media queries help you change the width of your email from a set pixel width on desktop to 100 percent of the screen when viewed on a mobile device. Additionally, if you're using media queries, a single-column layout is your best bet.

Test, Learn, and Improve

There needs to be a well-developed, clearly stated plan of action for testing, which details what will be tested, how it will be measured, and subsequent action steps. In mobile marketing, as in any other facet of marketing your business, consistently applying a *test, learn, improve* model will ensure the program gets smarter.

Chapter 15
SOCIAL NETWORKING

You know what a *social network* is; it's a group of people who have something in common. They share a certain social *reality*. And that knowledge leads directly to the definition of a social networking website (SNS), which is one that "enables users to create public profiles within that website and form relationships with other users of the same website who access their profile." Social networking sites can be used to describe community-based websites, online discussions forums, chat rooms, and other social spaces online. Social networking sites allow users to share ideas, pictures, posts, activities, events, and interests with people in their network.

In spite of the concerns of social scientists who argue popular social networking sites like Facebook and Twitter are doing more harm than good, there are many valid reasons to add social media to your marketing plan.

The first is the fact that social media is ubiquitous. For example, with close to one and a half *billion* accounts, 1 out of every 7 people on earth is on Facebook. YouTube boasts over 800 million members,

LinkedIn has over 332 million users, and Twitter has 302 million active tweeters; Google+ has over 300 million active accounts. Pinterest has 70 million users (and 85 percent of them are female).

When it comes to social media, the word "user" packs a wallop. In July 2012, Americans spent 74 billion minutes on social media via a home computer, 40.8 billion minutes via apps, and 5.7 billion minutes via mobile web browsers, a total of 121.1 billion minutes on social networking sites. According to recent data, the average user logs 1.72 hours per day on social platforms, which represents about 28 percent of all online activity.

> According to recent data, the average user logs 1.72 hours per day on social platforms, which represents about 28 percent of all online activity.

Who uses social media? As of January 2014, close to 72 percent of all men and over three-quarters of all women regularly using the internet are also using social networking sites. Today, 56 percent of Americans have a profile on a social networking site, and 22 percent use one or more of these sites *several* times per day. (A whopping 23 percent of Facebook users admit to checking their account *five or more* times *every* day.)

And the most recent findings about Twitter? In 2010, research found that only 47 percent of Twitter users actually sent tweets, but that's all changed. The overwhelming majority of new Twitter users are active tweeters, driving the average way, way up to 76 percent. When it comes to use percentages for specific social networking channels, as of September of 2014:

- ◆ 71 percent of online adults use Facebook.
- ◆ 23 percent of online adults use Twitter.
- ◆ 26 percent use Instagram.
- ◆ 28 percent use LinkedIn.

Statista, self-described as an online "statistics portal" featuring statistics and studies from more than 18,000 sources, reports during the third quarter of 2014 that LinkedIn had 332 million members, which is up from 296 million members in the first quarter of that year (an increase of over 12 percent). Other key findings about social networking site users, gleaned from the 2014 *Social Media Report* from the Pew Research Center:

◆ Multiplatform use is on the rise: 52 percent of online adults now use two or more social media sites, a significant increase from 2013, when it stood at 42 percent of internet users.

◆ For the first time, more than half of all online adults age 65 and older (56 percent) use Facebook. This represents 31 percent of all seniors.

◆ For the first time, roughly half of internet-using young adults ages 18 to 29 (53 percent) use Instagram; half of all Instagram users (49 percent) use the site daily.

◆ For the first time, the share of internet users with college educations using LinkedIn reached 50 percent.

How Social Networks Can Help Build Your Business

As fascinating as these facts are, we're here to focus on how social media can help you to connect with (and engage) your current and prospective consumers. Social networking really does work: 65 percent of small-business owners said social media helped them stay engaged with customers, while 51 percent of Facebook users (and 64 percent of Twitter users) have been found to be more likely to buy the brands they follow online. This increased brand recognition is just one benefit of effectively using social channels. Others include:

◆ *Improved brand loyalty.* In 2013, the academics over at Texas Tech University found brands who engage on social media channels enjoy higher loyalty from their customers, and

"A strategic and open social media plan could prove influential in morphing consumers into being brand loyal."

recommended companies take advantage of the tools social media gives them when it comes to connecting with their audience. Their conclusion? "A strategic and open social media plan could prove influential in morphing consumers into being brand loyal."

◆ *More conversion opportunities.* Every post, comment, and tweet is a chance for someone to react, and every reaction could lead to a site visit, and eventually a conversion. While not every brand interaction will result in a conversion, every positive interaction increases the likelihood of an eventual conversion.

◆ *Higher conversion rates.* Social media marketing results in higher conversion rates in a few distinct ways. Perhaps the most significant is that brands are *humanized* by interacting in social media channels. Here's something else: Studies have shown that social media has a 100 percent higher *lead-to-close* rate than outbound marketing, and a higher number of social media followers tends to improve trust and credibility in your brand, representing social proof. As such, simply building your audience in social media can improve conversion rates on your existing traffic.

◆ *Increased inbound traffic.* Think of each social media profile you create as a path leading back to your website. Remind yourself every piece of content syndicated on those profiles is another opportunity for a new visitor. The more quality content you syndicate on social media, the more inbound traffic you'll generate, and more traffic means more leads and more conversions.

Still not convinced you should put effort into developing a social side to your marketing plan? Maybe you'll be impressed by these reasons: Your website will rank higher in the search engines, provide your customers and prospects with a richer brand experience, and decrease marketing costs.

Let's not forget you can greatly improve your understanding of current and prospective customers by actively monitoring the activity in your social channels. This monitoring, often called *social listening,* can also provide clear insights into who your competitors are and what they are doing. The understanding gleaned from this social listening will then drive the development of new products and services as well as define your social marketing and content syndication efforts.

There are quite a few free ways to easily "listen in," including Google Alerts (www.google.com/alerts), which is a basic way to discover when a website is posting about you. But it doesn't capture everything, and it certainly doesn't cover social media or most blog sites. Still, it's a good, automated, entry-level way to get some feedback about any kind of search query emailed to you. Here's a tip: If you want instant results from Google Alerts, you'll want to mark "as-it-happens" under "how often." IceRocket (www.icerocket.com) specializes in blog searches, while Social Mention (www.socialmention.com) collects aggregated data across multiple platforms, and they offer some basic analytics that help you determine if the sentiment is positive or negative. Topsy (http://topsy.com) is very similar to IceRocket and Social Mention; the main focus is around social media, especially multimedia and blogs. None of these tools are all-inclusive. They catch only bits and pieces of what is out there, but if you run a search every day, it will only take a few minutes to scan through anything new. Your reputation matters, so make social listening a habit.

> Here's a tip: If you want instant results from Google Alerts, you'll want to mark "as-it-happens" under "how often."

As to when to post content to social sites, while all audiences are different, you can use the times given under each of the following sections as a general guide. Trends being what they are, they are sure to change over time. So how do you know what's trending? What's being called "the social search engine," HashAtIt (www.hashatit. com) gives you a way to find out what's hot across multiple social networks in real time. The site collects status updates, tweets, and other posts, allowing users to search for the most popular hashtags on Facebook, Twitter, Instagram, and Pinterest—all in one place, and all for free.

Five Steps to Crafting Your Social Marketing Plan

The first step to any social media marketing strategy is to establish objectives and goals that you hope to achieve. Having these objectives also allows you to quickly react when social media campaigns are not meeting your expectations. Without these goals, you have no means of gauging your success and no means of proving your ROI.

You don't want to get carried away; too many goals are worse than none. That's why you should limit yourself to two primary goals and two secondary goals. For example, a primary goal could be to raise brand awareness or increase customer loyalty. A secondary goal could be to generate more traffic to your website or build your list of newsletter subscribers. Based on these goals, you'll choose the social networking sites you'll use.

> It's important to assess your current social media use and how it is working for you.

Step two involves conducting a social media audit. It's important to assess your current social media use and how it is working for you. This requires figuring out who is connecting to you via social media, which social media sites your target market uses, and how your social media presence compares to your competitors'. It will become evident which accounts need to be updated and which need to be deleted altogether.

Once you've audited your accounts, it's time for step three, when you hone your online presence. Fill out all profiles completely. If you don't already have social media profiles on each network you focus on, build them from the ground up with your broader goals and audience in mind. If you do have existing accounts, it's time to refine and update them for your best possible results.

If authenticity is as important as experts say, you'll want your social presence to be honest and unique. So in step four, you'll find your social voice and tone. It can be valuable to turn to your competitors for inspiration when it comes to what content types and information get the most social media engagement.

Your consumers can be equally as inspiring, not only through the content they share but in the way they phrase their messages. Don't forget to turn to industry leaders for inspiration too. Many companies have managed to distinguish themselves through advanced social media strategies. Follow them faithfully and learn everything you can.

> Your consumers can be equally as inspiring, not only through the content they share but in the way they phrase their messages.

Here's the essential truth of any social marketing plan: You need great content. So in step five, you'll get specific about the content itself, adding these specifics to a comprehensive editorial calendar. Your plan should answer the following questions:

- What type(s) of content do you intend to post and promote via social media?
- How often will you post the content?
- How can you target the specific audience for each type of content?
- Who will create the content?
- How you will promote the content?

When it comes to posting frequency, recent research has found you want to post consistently, but not too often. Top brands on Pinterest post five times per day, tweet three times each day (although engagement does decrease slightly after the third tweet), and post three times per day consistently on Google+. You can post twice per day on Facebook before likes and comments begin to drop off, and once a day (20 posts per month) on LinkedIn is sufficient to reach 60 percent of your audience.

Your editorial calendar should list the dates and times you intend to post blogs, Facebook posts, Twitter updates, and other content you plan to use during your social media campaigns. It's suggested you create the calendar and then schedule messaging in advance, rather than updating constantly throughout the day.

Here's one more thing: Despite the need to be specific in step five, your social media plan should be constantly changing. As new networks emerge, you might want to add them to your plan. As you attain goals, you want to adjust them or find new goals for each network. This is a plan that is meant to change, so be flexible and open to changes.

Measure, Monitor, and Grow Your Online Influence

Klout (https://klout.com) is a company that quantifies people's online influence. A San Francisco startup, Klout was founded in 2008 (when Twitter was still in its infancy). The rationale behind Klout is to measure users' influence across Twitter (and to a lesser degree Facebook, Google+, and LinkedIn) and rank users accordingly. It assigns users a Klout score, which purports to measure (on a scale of 1 to 100) a person's social media influence on various topics. At this time, Klout is free to all users.

There's no doubt that social marketing can be time-consuming, and its effectiveness is often in question. Its success or failure is often dependent on how frequently members of your target audience check their Facebook News Feed or Twitter stream. But if you can get something in front of the right people, they'll forward it to others in their network. Social networking analysts have found most Facebook page posts fade off into the ether three to five hours after getting published. That's okay when it comes

> Social networking analysts have found most Facebook page posts fade off into the ether three to five hours after getting published.

to Aunt Martha's birthday photos, but it can be disheartening for marketers.

Recently Klout unveiled an analytics dashboard, Klout for Business, to help brands pinpoint their influencers. It can tell businesses the identity of the influencers among their Twitter followers and Facebook fans, including age groups, gender, and location; and, of course, what topics they're influential on.

Klout also recently announced a new content tool that will help users improve their scores. You can do this by sharing a link to your own content, sharing content created by others (Klout generates suggested content for you), or you can combine both methods. This is designed to increase your social engagement levels by increasing the chance of your content being retweeted or responded to on Twitter.

Other things to know about Klout: It provides every user with a personalized content stream based on their specific topical interests and what's likely to resonate with their network. You can filter your stream by individual topics, making it easier to find and share content likely to engage your audience. The "create" tab helps you to find shareable articles likely to resonate with your audience. You can also create original posts easily, simply by clicking an icon in the corner of the "create" tab.

Klout offers marketers a personalized scheduling tool, which recommends the best times to publish, based on when your audience is online and most likely to engage with you. By publishing at these times, you're more likely to share the right message at the right time with the right people.

There are some dos and don'ts when it comes to using Klout—the first of which is obvious: Don't post stories with no value to your audience. You can use Klout to help you create a content strategy mix of original (created by you)

> These days, more and more social networkers are looking to boost their Klout rating and show others the power of their social influence.

and aggregated content. Once created or aggregated, you can use the

Klout scheduling tool to "prime the social media pump" with a steady flow of content to your audience.

These days, more and more social networkers are looking to boost their Klout rating and show others the power of their social influence. But never artificially manipulate your Klout score. Always remember, if you keep focused on your network and content strategy, you'll succeed.

How can you generate a higher Klout score? There are some simple ways to climb up the ladder of social influence.

- ◆ *Build a network.* The key to increasing a Klout score is similar to finding success on the social web in general: Build a targeted, engaged network of people who would be legitimately interested in you and your content.
- ◆ *Create meaningful content.* Adopt a strategy to create or aggregate meaningful content that your network loves to share with others. Provide links!
- ◆ *Engage.* Actively engage with others in a helpful and authentic way. Ask questions, answer questions, and create a dialogue with your followers.
- ◆ *Interact with everyone.* Don't be afraid to interact with Klout users with lower scores—it won't hurt your own score. In fact, it helps build their score and, in turn, makes you more of an influencer.
- ◆ *Publish continually.* Access to free publishing tools such as blogs, video, and Twitter have provided users with an opportunity to have a real voice, so take advantage of these many platforms.

There are other no-cost reputation-monitoring websites around, one of which is Kred (http://kred.com), which is intended to measure both social influence and outreach, and provide you with a score for each on your profile. Your influence is measured by assessing retweets, replies, mentions, and follows on Twitter. Outreach is a cumulative score based on how often you retweet, reply, share, and mention other people. Each social action by you or your followers results in a certain number of points, and there is an activity page where you can see exactly what has contributed to your Kred score, a fact which makes it the most transparent of the two monitoring sites.

The Top Social Networks

We'll devote the rest of the chapter to covering the basics of the top social networks to use in your social media marketing strategy. You don't have to use all of them; which ones you use depends on your target audience (see Chapter 3).

Facebook

www.facebook.com

Recent research confirmed Facebook continues to be the most popular social media site. In October 2014, the site announced that the number of active monthly users reached 1.35 billion, roughly equal to the population of China, and 9 percent larger than that of India. It's estimated 71 percent of internet users are on Facebook.

> Recent research confirmed Facebook continues to be the most popular social media site.

More important than the number of users is the fact that Facebook's users continue to be very active. Seventy percent of users engage with the site daily (and 45 percent do so several times a day). In short, Facebook acts as "home base" for many internet users. Here are recommendations for connecting with your audience in this most popular social channel.

First things first: Fully optimize your Facebook page. Your page's cover photo is the first impression people get of your Facebook page. It also shows up in several other ways on Facebook—if someone hovers over your page name in a post, in suggested pages, and in other places. If possible, have a tagline on the photo that states the main reason why someone should like your page.

The next thing you'll need to optimize is the "About" section. You'll want to add critical keywords here because this section is indexed in Google, and you get the chance to tell people more about what you do. Link to special places on your website you want to highlight and maybe even add some testimonials from satisfied clients or customers.

We've already talked about the need for you to have a well-thought-out content strategy; after all, the most notable way people are going to interact with your Facebook page is through your posts. That means it's critical to know what you're posting and how often. It's best to have a mixture of business news, tips, photos, links, and also humor.

Facebook posts have an extremely short visibility shelf life (three to five hours). This means if you're only posting a couple times a week, you're in real danger of dropping off your audience's radar. It's recommend you post on Facebook at least twice a day during the week to increase your visibility.

> One of the best ways to grow your presence on Facebook organically is to connect and comment on other complementary business pages.

One of the best ways to grow your presence on Facebook organically is to connect and comment on other complementary business pages. It's easy to see how this new audience has the potential to see your name in the comments of that post, giving your page more visibility (and creating goodwill with the owners of these complementary pages).

And, if you are the face of your business, use your personal profile when posting. What's the thinking behind this recommendation? Your personal profile is more visible to your network than your business page, and by occasionally sharing your business news on your personal page, it's argued you'll have an increased chance of your most important announcements being seen.

Google+

https://plus.google.com

Think of it: There's a wealth of Google products (Gmail, Google Reader, Google Maps, just to name a few), and Google+ is intended to be the amalgamation of all those products into one that ties people together across all of Google.

Your Google+ account is based on your Google profile. You can build a personal bio, share information like your address, phone number, and email, and add in links to your personal or professional websites.

The main activity on Google+ takes place in a stream, which is a lot like the wall on Facebook. It's where you'll see status updates from the people you've chosen to follow in your circles. (A circle is a collection of people you're connected to. A Google+ account comes with three predefined circles: friends, family, and acquaintances, but you can also create your own customized circles. Status updates can be shared with specific circles, or narrowed even further to share with individual users.

> The main activity on Google+ takes place in a stream, which is a lot like the wall on Facebook.

It's interesting: Google+ perplexes more marketers than any other channel. In truth, most business owners keep their Google+ page up-to-date simply because it's Google, and updates can help with search rankings.

Despite the confusion (and lack of analytical metrics), there are content recommendations based on the most shared post type on Google+: Photos rank highest, followed by links, video, and at the bottom of the list are text-based posts. (When compared to the average post, photos got 149 percent more "+1s," 136 percent more comments, and 133 percent more reshares.) Other recommendations:

◆ Overall, posts with more than 100 characters had a better engagement rate than those with less than 100 characters.

- ◆ Link dropping (sharing links with less than 100 characters) is a pitfall, offering low engagement across all metrics.
- ◆ Photo posts with more than 100 characters are the winning formula for interaction and engagement.
- ◆ Text-only posts, whether above or below that magic number of 100 characters, are worthwhile for both +1s and comments but not reshares.

What is a "+1"? When someone likes your content, they have the option of using the +1 button, a feature Google describes as a way for you to tell those in your network "this is something you should check out." In that sense, the Google +1 button is similar to Facebook's "like" button. The +1's you receive are collected in your Google profile and displayed when people within your Google social circle search for something you've recommended. Here's a truism: Because it's Google, you can expect changes to the platform, so stay informed.

Instagram

https://instagram.com

Instagram is a mobile photo-sharing app and a social network created in 2010. (Amazingly, just two years later, Facebook purchased the service for $1 billion.) Unlike other social networks, Instagram is completely photo/video-centric, so users can post only images and short videos (up to 15 seconds), but not text updates like they can when using other social channels. About half of Instagram users engage on the platform daily.

> Instagram is free in both the Apple App Store and Google Play, but if you don't have a mobile device, you're out of luck.

Because it's a mobile app, you must download it to your mobile device before you can sign up for an account. Instagram is free in both the Apple App Store and Google Play, but if you don't have a mobile device, you're out of luck.

Even if you do have the app, the fact the channel allows users to post only two types of content (photos and videos) may limit its usefulness to you. But if you're creative, you may find it worthy of your time. As always, start with clear goals. Instagram also advises marketers to "choose authentic storylines best conveyed through captivating imagery"—sound advice, but hard for many marketers to manage. They suggest working with a creative team to produce well-crafted images and videos. But if you don't have such a team, do your research and learn from already-popular Instagrammers. Other things Instagram advises you to be aware of:

Even if you do have the app, the fact the channel allows users to post only two types of content (photos and videos) may limit its usefulness to you.

- If you're not going to use your business name, you need to choose an account name that's easily tied to your brand.
- Your profile image should be your brand's logo or a graphic symbol, but you need to realize the image will be cropped into a circle and appear as a 150 x 150 pixel image on most phones.
- Photo captions should be short. Instagram suggests incorporating a few hashtags (no more than three).
- When it helps tell the story of the image, you should include the location of your photo or video.
- Use the Add People feature to tag accounts in your image, which will help you reach a broader audience.
- Edit your images with filters and other tools available in the Instagram app. These effects give images that unmistakable "Instagram look" that people respond to.
- Post photos and videos of beautiful and unexpected moments that also feel authentic and immediate. Whether your subject is a person or an object, capture it in a context that gives a sense of your brand's identity or point of view.

And, here's a "no-brainer": When it comes to Instagram or any other social channel, ask questions to engage people in your audience. The corollary to that, of course, is to respond in a timely way.

Pinterest

www.pinterest.com

Pinterest was started in 2008, right as the recession was really getting underway. It's a free website requiring registration, where users can upload, save, sort, and manage images and video content—known as pins—through collections known as "pinboards."

Achieving wide acceptance has been a rocky road for the platform (only 17 percent of Pinterest users engage on the platform daily), but today, at least for some companies, Pinterest can be a remarkable online marketing opportunity. How do you take advantage of it? Take a look at some of the big names using the platform. For example, Martha Stewart's organization uses the strategy of dedicated boards covering a single topic. They have over 126 boards, close to 13,000 pins, and almost half a million followers. You've got to admit, when you plan for a large number of boards and pins, being organized is a major key to success.

> To really make the most of the platform, you need to think visually.

You also want to pin regularly. The *Today Show*'s Pinterest team has been doing an amazing job of pinning consistently. This keeps your profile's pins in the feed of each pin's category, thus growing followers and repins. In 2013, the show had over 23,000 pins and more than 106,000 followers—and those numbers have grown considerably.

To really make the most of the platform, you need to think visually. In late 2013, Etsy (www.etsy.com) had more than 317,000 followers on Pinterest, each of whom can see what types of products are available from Etsy's sellers. By visually promoting their own products, Etsy is able to increase sellers' revenues while also driving traffic to its website.

L.L. Bean focuses on customer habits. In 2013, they boasted 5.6 million followers on Pinterest, which can only mean they must like its activity-based approach: Their boards cover everything from the catch-all board labeled "Outdoor Fun" to the more specific. Here are other ways marketers use this engaging platform:

> By visually promoting their own products, Etsy is able to increase sellers' revenues while also driving traffic to its website.

- ◆ *Make sharing easy.* It's all about the sharing, isn't it? In 2013, Sephora had grown its Pinterest following to almost 200,000 followers, partly because it made Pinterest sharing extremely easy on their ecommerce product pages, a fact which has made Pinterest one of the top ten referrers for its website.
- ◆ *Be creative with naming your boards.* Whole Foods has a growing Pinterest presence; in 2013, they had more than 140,000 followers. Board names like "Cheese is the Bee's Knees" and "How Does Your Garden Grow?" give viewers an idea of what they will find on the board, and in a lighthearted way.
- ◆ *Stay relevant. Self* magazine had over 200,000 followers in 2013, partly because it changes its bio to reflect something unique about each season of the year.
- ◆ *Feature what's most creative.* After all, Pinterest is all about creativity: creative ideas, products, and services—presented creatively.
- ◆ *Customize your board covers.* Make your presence uniquely yours.
- ◆ *Be sure to link back to your website.* After all, social is all about connectedness.
- ◆ *Populate your board with pins.* Pin at least 20 to 30 pins on each board, so it doesn't look bare.

- *Make the Pinterest experience fun for your followers.* The platform is rather like Facebook in that regard: People want to be entertained and inspired, but most of all, they want to have fun.
- *Post prices.* It's more than interesting to note Pinterest pins with prices get 36 percent more "likes" than those without. Why not inspire a purchase when you can?
- *Publish a blog post, then pin an image from the article to a board.* Copy the URL of the pin; then use the same image for a post on your Google+ page.
- *Show your pins to newsletter subscribers* by including a few of your best Pinterest pins in your weekly newsletter or your regular email.
- *Use Pinterest group boards to reach more people* to get repins, followers, and traffic.
- *Send an email mentioning Pinterest and feature a Pinterest profile widget* at least once a month.
- *Add a (free) Pinterest app to your Facebook account.* Always think about cross-platform promotion.

Be sure to use other platforms to promote your Pinterest presence: Tweet about Pinterest two to three times a week and update your audience on Facebook once a week (at the very least, every two weeks). You don't have to remain clueless about your Pinterest success (or lack of it). It's easy to discover how your customers and prospects interact with your pins using the Pinterest Analytics tool.

LinkedIn
www.linkedin.com

Being what it is, a professional network for professional people, LinkedIn is the perfect platform to position yourself as a thought leader. That means providing users with serious, meaningful, intelligent, well-researched, and inspiring (or provocative) articles is the name of the game for promoting your LinkedIn company profile and sparking conversation and even some debate in your LinkedIn group.

You can also use LinkedIn to spy on your competition. In truth, there is all kinds of information to be gleaned from a company's profile page. With this information, you can really get to know what you're up against.

LinkedIn also gives you an unparalled opportunity to find highly targeted customers and connections, stay on your customers' radar, and easily grow your email list. It's recommended you draft a "thank you" letter to be sent to your connections, inviting them to be a part of your email list. You'll want to let them know exactly what they will receive by signing up for your list and add some goodwill reciprocity: Offer to look at something of theirs in return.

LinkedIn-sponsored updates give you a way to push your LinkedIn updates and posts into an individual's LinkedIn feed. This "pay-per-click" or "pay-per-impressions" feature offers demographics similar to other social platforms (location, gender, and age), but one key differentiation is the ability to customize based on company name, job title, job function, skills, schools, and groups. Sponsored updates offer an effective way to promote thought-leadership content (white papers, ebooks, or eguides) to a highly targeted niche audience. Experts agree: LinkedIn is a powerful platform for growing the reach of your business and attracting new clients or customers. It also presents a terrific opportunity to stay top of mind. But how do you start? As is true with any of these social channels, to achieve long-term, sustainable success, you'll need to develop a comprehensive and consistent LinkedIn marketing plan.

> Experts agree: LinkedIn is a powerful platform for growing the reach of your business and attracting new clients or customers.

Tumblr

www.tumblr.com

Tumblr is both a blogging platform and a social network. As with other blogging platforms, users create their own blogs in order to post original content in the form of text, photos, and videos. Or they can reblog the posts of others. Users can also follow blogs, which is similar to following someone on Twitter or Facebook. Today, Tumblr, launched in 2007, is one of the hottest social blogging platforms not only on the traditional web, but on mobile devices too. Although accurate numbers are hard to find, as of 2014, the blogging site was believed to have 420 million users, 217 million blogs, and almost 114 million posts each day. (Tumblr recently made headlines when it was acquired by Yahoo! for over a billion dollars.)

If you're looking to start a new Tumblr blog, you'll need a spot of good luck with getting a simple Tumblr URL to go with it. (You'll likely have to incorporate at least two or three words into the URL since most obvious words and names have already been taken.) But don't worry: There are a few simple ways you can come up with great Tumblr blog URLs if you're having a hard time. Use an online thesaurus to see what synonyms there are to use, or visit Word Generator (www.wordgenerator.net). You could even make a list of those words you like from WordGenerator and plug them into Thesaurus.com to see what else you might be able to come up with.

> Tumblr is both a blogging platform and a social network.

You may find you'll need to use more than one word—even two or three—and some experts even advise using misspelled words or numbers in place of letters (though this isn't a very good option for a business Tumblr blog). Keep in mind your Tumblr URL isn't set in stone. You can change it any time you want by accessing your settings, selecting your blog, and changing the URL.

With its highly social and visual interface, and a user base that has collectively created over 217 million blogs, Tumblr is well positioned in regard to other social networks like Twitter and Facebook. But before adding Tumblr to your social network marketing plan, you should determine whether your audience is using Tumblr. If the answer is yes, it might be worth setting one up.

Twitter

www.twitter.com

There are remarkable engagement opportunities available to you on Twitter. According to recent findings, there are 974 million existing Twitter accounts, but most of these users are inactive. Don't worry: In the last quarter of 2013, Twitter claimed to have 241 million active users—defined as people who logged in at least once a month—and that's more than enough activity to make Twitter worthy of inclusion in the social networking component of your marketing plan. Fully completing your Twitter profile is the first step to creating a personal brand presence here. Avoid posting an incomplete or vague description of you and your business (this is true for all social networking sites). Remember, too, that Twitter lets you include links in your profile, so use this space strategically. Always include your name in your profile so people can recognize you easily.

Finding the right people to connect with on Twitter can be confusing. For example, lots of people think that if they type several keywords in the search box, Twitter will search for any tweets that contain any of those terms. Unfortunately, that's not how it works. Twitter only searches for tweets that contain all those search terms, as if there is an invisible "and" inserted between your keywords. Instead, you can use the "or" search operator, which tells Twitter you want to search for one term or another. Here's another tip: When you want to search for a phrase instead of a single keyword, you should put the phrase in quotations (single keywords don't need quotation marks).

> Avoid posting an incomplete or vague description of you and your business (this is true for all social networking sites).

You can also find people in your industry to connect with using Twitter Analytics, but you'll need to request advertiser status (this requires you to jump through a few hoops to meet Twitter's expectations). Once your account is changed to advertiser status, you'll log in to see the Twitter Analytics Dashboard, where you'll click the "Followers" tab. Review who your followers follow to find the names of others who are in your niche market. In addition to listing your followers, the Analytics Dashboard gives you the means to review the performance of your tweets and any Twitter Cards you may have created. (Twitter Cards allow you to attach photos and videos to tweets that drive traffic to your website.)

Twitter lists are a useful way to filter information. The basic function of a Twitter list is to group people together based on a similar function, characteristic, or interest. There's something else you should know about creating a list: You can set them to be private or public. What does this mean for you, the online marketer? You can monitor your competitors with a private list, while at the same time, you can show off your impressive roster of clients or brand advocates in a public list. You can also share your lists with other users, which is a good way to find new followers and attract people to your profile. Here's a tip: A quick way to grow your Twitter community is to notify people that you've added them to a list. Those users may then reply or retweet as a thank you for sharing their profile with your followers and list subscribers. In short, creating and sharing lists positions you as an authority in your field and grows your Twitter community as people learn to trust you.

> Twitter lists are a useful way to filter information.

Twitter conducted a study of over 2 million tweets and found that including a photo can boost retweets by up to 35 percent and adding a video can result in a 28 percent boost. While photos and videos can be important for engagement, how you add them to your tweets matters, so check Twitter's Help section (https://support. twitter.com) if you run into difficulties. Twitter is also integrated with video-sharing sites such as Vine (https://vine.co), which is owned by Twitter, and YouTube, both of which help you make the most of your visual content.

YouTube

www.youtube.com

Ten years after its launch, YouTube boasts over 1 billion users. Around 300 hours of videos are uploaded every minute, and those who monitor the site's use tell us people are watching 50 percent more videos every month. The time is right for you to market your business using videos posted on YouTube.

Again, as in all your social networking efforts, you must strive to create *shareable* content that will help you break down any barriers between you and prospective customers or clients. You want to develop content that gives your business a "face" and a "personality," videos that excite viewers enough to recommend them to their friends or colleagues.

You also might consider making a weekly (or biweekly) video of updates in your business. Of course this video blog (vlog) should be fun, entertaining, and sharable. (Be sure to promote it in email marketing messages or through other social channels).

Here's something essential to remember: Your videos must be findable within and outside of YouTube. Google owns YouTube, so make sure to practice good SEO by using targeted keywords in your video titles, tags, and descriptions.

There are a number of useful features available on YouTube, such as their free Audio Library, which offers over 150 royalty-free instrumental backing tracks for use in videos uploaded to the site. You can access it through the Creator Studio menu in the Video Manager section of your YouTube account. You can easily filter the list by genre, mood, instrument, or duration, and then preview the track. Once you've found the perfect background music for your video, you hit the download icon and the music is yours to use in video production.

Then there's YouTube's Fan Finder feature (www.youtube.com/yt/fanfinder), which is nothing more than free channel ad space directed at people who are likely to enjoy your content. The program allows you to submit short videos that show off your brand and content, which will target people YouTube believes are most likely to enjoy your content and become a regular viewer.

You're also able to add a clickable link to a website of your choice using a site annotation within the video player itself. It's a multistep process that requires you to verify ownership of the YouTube account (via a quick two-step telephone process) as well as ownership of the website domain. Once both are verified, you can link it to your YouTube account. In addition to adding a clickable link to your videos, you can also add a three-second animated branding clip and/ or a branding watermark to each of your videos.

You can add YouTube Cards to videos, which include an image, title, link, and call to action. When your audience watches your videos, they no longer have to be prepared to write down the web address you mention: the clickable card gives them all the information they need. There are six types of cards to choose from: merchandise, fundraising, video, playlist, associated website, and fan funding. It doesn't take long to set up YouTube Cards, but make sure whichever card you use is aligned with the goal(s) of your video.

> You can add YouTube Cards to videos, which include an image, title, link, and call to action.

YouTube videos are great not only for promoting your products and services, but they are invaluable for building your status as an authority. Certainly, the video platform allows for a high level of communication creativity; just remember with every social media tool it's important to keep your branding consistent and to engage with your viewers. Changes come and go in the blink of an eye. Stay up-to-date with the latest YouTube video creator tools and program changes by checking in with the Getting Started section of the site (www.youtube.com/yt/creators/get-started.html).

Don't Think Twice

Without a doubt, social media offers you a number of ways to learn about your audience. It can also help you find new customers, expand your audience, and receive instant feedback from your customers and prospects. Social media is also the route to improving market intelligence and getting ahead of your competitors, as well as increasing website traffic and search ranking. And, of course, it makes sharing content easier and faster.

But with all those advantages, social media can be frustrating for anyone expecting immediate results. "If there's one thing I would tell entrepreneurs about social media," says seasoned entrepreneur Gary Vaynerchuk, "it would be: *patience*. Social, unlike SEM and SEO, unlike email marketing, unlike direct mail, unlike most things, is a marathon in a sprint world. Social media is a difficult matrix for people to figure out because it can be at times a sprint, but far more often, it's about lifetime value."

> Without a doubt, social media offers you a number of ways to learn about your audience.

Here are the major steps we've covered in creating a marketing plan with the key worksheets or forms for each. Just fill in the blanks to create your marketing plan!

Step 1: Write Your Vision Statement

It's time to create your own vision statement. Don't worry about trying to make it perfect. What's important at this point is to begin the conversation with yourself about the business you're trying to create.

Begin with a clean sheet of paper. Imagine your business three to five years in the future, and answer the following questions.

- What service(s) do you perform?
- For whom? (What types of clients? If you have specific clients in mind, list them.)
- Where is your business located? Do you work at home or in an office? Describe everything.
- You've just met yourself on the job. What do you do in the business? Are you an owner or a hands-on employee? What is your life like? What about your life makes you happy?
- How much do you and the business earn? (The amounts won't be the same.)
- Do you have employees? If so, how many? What do they do? What value do they add to the business? What skills and training do they have? Be as specific as possible.

- ◆ What does this business look like when you sell it or turn it over to relatives?
- ◆ What does this business do better than any other? What are you known for?
- ◆ How do you feel about this business? What inspires you about this business?
- ◆ What are the four or five keywords you use when describing your business to others? What are the words your clients use when describing what you do for them to others?

Write your vision statement.

_____

_____

_____

_____

_____

_____

_____

_____

Step 2: Describe Your Niche

Write a description of your niche. The following formula can help:

I (We) _____ for _____

(describe the service you perform)   (describe the group you perform your services for)

so they _____.

(describe the results they can expect)

Describe your niche here:

_____

_____

_____

_____

_____

_____

_____

_____

Step 3: Identify Your Ideal Client
Monthly Client Report

Tracking who buys what every month is a great way to learn more about your clients and to identify the potential lifetime value of your average client. You can create a form similar to the one below in Excel, Access, or even Word.

Client Report (Month/Year)								
	Services Purchased	Problem Solved	Date	Amount	YTD $	Last Purchase Date	Client Since (m/d/y)	Lifetime Value to Date
Client 1								
Client 2								
Client 3								
Totals				$	$			$
Comments:								

Client Profiles

Create a client profile for each of your clients, and add to it any time you have any kind of contact with that client. A sample profile you

might build in Access or another database follows. Remember, knowing and understanding your clients' wants and needs better than your competitors do is one of the keys to successful niche marketing.

CLIENT PROFILE	
Contact Information	
Client Name	
Title	
Company	
Phone Number	
Fax Number	
Address, City, State, Zip	
Purchasing History	
Client Since	
Services Purchased (Dates and Amounts)	
Biggest Challenges	
Perceived Value of Solving Their Challenges	
Client's Competitors	
Their Main Clients	
Year-to-Date Purchases	
Referrals Given	
Lifetime Value	
Client Preferences	
Preferred Method of Contact	
Frequency	
Birthday	
Anniversaries	
Favorite Restaurant(s)	

CLIENT PROFILE	
Contact Information	
Spouse	
Children	
Hobbies	
Likes/Dislikes	
World News	
Issues Affecting Them	
Marketing Efforts	
Type/Dates/Results	
Next Action (Schedule It)	

Profile Your Ideal Client

Write a description of your ideal client. Add as much detail as you need to be clear about who this client is. What is your client's most pressing problem? What aspirations does he or she have that might drive buying habits? What influences your ideal client's purchasing decisions?

_____

_____

_____

_____

_____

_____

_____

_____

_____

_____

_____

_____

_____

Describe your current clients.

_____

_____

_____

_____

_____

_____

Comment on how closely your actual and ideal clients match. Describe what they have in common. Describe how they differ. If there is a wide disparity between the two, describe the changes you intend to make to bring them closer together.

_____

_____

_____

_____

_____

_____

_____

_____

_____

_____

_____

_____

_____

_____

What does your ideal client want to experience when doing business with you? Is it the same as what your current clients want?

_____

_____

_____

_____

_____

_____

_____

_____

_____

_____

_____

_____

What do you need to do to find more of your ideal clients?

_____

_____

_____

_____

_____

_____

_____

_____

_____

_____

_____

_____

Step 4: Describe the Competition

Use the table to identify both you and your competitors' strengths and weaknesses. Think back to the things you identified as important to your ideal client. How well are competitors addressing those issues? Do you see any gaps? Opportunities? Competitive threats?

Feature	Your Business	Competitor 1	Competitor 2	Competitor 3	Competitor 4	Competitor 5
What service(s) do they offer?						
Primary focus						

Feature	Your Business	Competitor 1	Competitor 2	Competitor 3	Competitor 4	Competitor 5
Perceived advantage (their strengths vs. your weaknesses)						
Message						
How do they position themselves?						
What do they do well?						
Strengths						
Segments of your niche they ignore						
Things they don't do well						
Reason clients like them						
Reason former clients don't like them						
Things you can learn from them						
Things you do better than they do						
Things you do they can't copy or improve						

Feature	Your Business	Competitor 1	Competitor 2	Competitor 3	Competitor 4	Competitor 5
Things they do that can take business away from you						
How do they price their services?						
How do they package their service? (With special offers, bonuses, guarantees, payment plans, longer service hours, more service providers, etc.?)						
Weaknesses						
Opportunities for you						

Write a summary of what you found in analyzing your competitors. Where are the opportunities for you?

_____

_____

_____

_____

_____

_____

_____

_____

_____

_____

_____

Step 5: Strategize
Positioning Statement and Goal Setting

A general format for writing a positioning statement includes the following:

> "We sell [*your service type*] for [*your ideal client type*] that need/want to [*the problem you solve*] and will buy from us because [*why your solution is different*]."

Remember, your positioning statement should focus on what you do, whom you do it for, and the unique benefit for your clients. Focus on just one promise.

Write your positioning statement.

_____

_____

_____

_____

_____

_____

_____

Write your goals for your business for the next year. Try to focus on no more than three to five major goals. You don't want to be overwhelmed.

_____

_____

_____

_____

_____

_____

_____

_____

_____

_____

_____

Write your strategy for meeting your one-year goals.

_____

_____

_____

_____

_____

_____

_____

_____

_____

_____

_____

_____

_____

_____

_____

_____

Step 6: Identify the Tactics You'll Use

Identify the three to five tactics you'll begin with and why you think they're your best choice given your goals and strategies.

_____

_____

_____

_____

_____

_____

_____

_____

_____

_____

_____

_____

Step 7: Put Your Measurements in Place

- ◆ What data will you measure to track your results?
- ◆ How will you measure each metric?
- ◆ What system will you use?

_____

_____

_____

_____

_____

_____

_____

_____

_____

_____

_____

_____

_____

_____

Step 8: Write Your Plan
Stages in the Selling Process

At every stage of the sales process, there's a dance going on between you and your prospect. Selling requires getting and staying in step with your client. Think through what you need to do at each stage of the selling process to get to the next stage. Then fill in the following table. Keep this in mind as you develop client profiles and tactics for getting your clients' attention.

Stages in the Selling Process	
How will I generate as many leads as I want?	
How will I qualify leads?	
How will I get appointments to meet or present (if applicable)?	
What offer will I make to close the sale?	
How will I follow up with qualified leads until they purchase?	
How will I follow up with new clients after the sale to continue serving and selling to them?	

List your major campaigns.

Major Campaigns for (Year)						
Month	Campaign	Expected Cost	Actual Cost	Resources	Expected Results	Actual Results
January						
February						
March						
April						
May						
June						
July						
August						
September						
October						
November						
December						
Comments:		Campaigns to Repeat:		Campaigns to Drop:		

Advertising Budget Worksheet

| | Advertising Budget | | | | | | | |
Month	Total Marketing Budget	Magazines	Web	TV	Radio	Direct Mail	PR Social
January							
February							
March							
April							
May							
June							
July							
August							
September							
October							
November							
December							
Total							

Marketing Plan Format

- ◆ Our Vision (use Step 1 answers)
- ◆ Our Niche (use Step 2 answers)
- ◆ Our Ideal Client (use Step 3 answers)
- ◆ Our Competition (use Step 4 answers)
- ◆ Our Strategy (use Step 5 answers)
- ◆ Our Tactics (use Step 6 answers)
- ◆ Our Measurement Stick (use Step 7 answers)
- ◆ Our Action Plan (use Step 8 answers)

Our 30-day goals: _____

Our 3-month goals: _____

Our 6-month goals: _____

Our 9-month goals: _____

Our 12-month goals: _____

Step 9: Implement

Plot your to-dos for the next 30 days. Then begin.

Action Plan (Month, Year)						
	Goals	**Daily Actions**				
		Mon.	Tues.	Wed.	Thurs.	Fri.
Week 1						
Week 2						
Week 3						
Week 4						
Comments/Results						

Chiropractic Marketing Plans Inc.'s Marketing Plan

Our Vision

To be the planning resource chiropractors in Southern California think of first when looking for tools to grow their practice, because we know their industry even better than they do.

Our Mission

To give chiropractors the know-how to grow a successful practice, starting with a plan that details how they will proceed.

Our Niche

We develop marketing plans for chiropractors located within a ten-mile radius of our office so they know how to refocus their actions and resources on the clients most likely to help them achieve their vision for their business.

Our Ideal Client

Using the listed resources, we have decided to redefine CMP's ideal client as family wellness chiropractic practices that emphasize care for parents and children. This type of clinic focuses on nutrition, exercises, and massage as part of their care.

We also know the following about the chiropractors located within a ten-mile radius of our office:

♦ 70 percent are in private practice.

♦ 28 percent specialize in family practice.

♦ Another 1 percent specialize in pediatric practice.

♦ They see an average of 127 patients per week.

♦ Their average patient spends $1,200 in the first year.

♦ Their average patient visits 30 times per year and spends $40/visit.

♦ New patients make up 60 percent of their patient load.

♦ They retain 40 percent of old patients.

♦ They average seven new patients each week.

♦ Their average practice billings are $350K to $500K per year.

♦ Their average practice earnings are $110K.

♦ The average chiropractor's age is 42.

♦ They are 80 percent male.

♦ Trigger: They want more acceptance of what they do by the public and MDs.

♦ They get information from the state trade association, association magazines, health magazines and journals, business magazines, and the internet.

♦ They sell pillows, vitamins, and massage services to complement treatments.

♦ Hot buttons: Revenues are stagnant, they need to increase their new patient average, dependence on health insurance payments is growing, they want more referrals from and joint ventures with MDs, and they feel the public still lacks understanding of how much chiropractic treatment can benefit them.

Our Competition

We have found four chiropractic coaching businesses within our niche area. However, none emphasizes marketing plans.

Analyzing Yellow Pages ads, card deck and newspaper ads, and other sources, we learned that these competitors' messages address the same desired outcomes for prospects—growing their practices. So they're indirect competitors, because, even though they don't offer the same service, prospects could view them as a solution.

Three of the coaching services are new, whereas CMP has a successful four-year track record. The coaching is done over the telephone, whereas we work one-on-one, in person, with clients to develop their plans. The in-person conversations create opportunities for more in-depth discussions and often lead to growth approaches the owner had not considered.

So clients see value in the personal meetings. The disadvantage is that they're more time-consuming than telephone consultations. Still, if the meetings result in more satisfied clients and those clients refer others, this is an advantage, and clients perceive it as one.

The main advantage competitors offer is a promise to help chiropractors implement change. This is a more costly alternative. CMP can appeal to those who believe they can carry out their own implementations once they have a plan. Another option is to team with one of the coaches.

So, our main opportunity lies in serving those who want to do their own implementations. For those wanting full-service practice-building assistance, we can team with one or more coaches.

Our Strategy

Positioning statement: Action plans for the family chiropractic practice that wants growth without pain, because the right alignment with the right plan should never hurt.

CMP provides action plans for family chiropractic practices. CMP offers the only growth planning for practices struggling with growth issues.

Goals for this year: Increase revenues from $150,000 to $200,000.

Currently average 29 clients per year throughout Southern California, about two to three each month; current retention rate is 35 percent who renew every year.

Strategy for Achieving Goals This Year

Dominate this field within a ten-mile radius of our office. Forty-two chiropractic practices fit the profile of our target market in our coverage area. We need to close about one-third of those this year.

- ◆ Add 15 net new clients.
- ◆ Increase retention rate to 40 percent.
- ◆ Earn income by matching clients with implementation specialists when plan is complete.
- ◆ Add midyear review service.

Our Tactics

After careful analysis, we believe the tactics most likely to be effective for us are:

- ◆ Form joint ventures with coaches who specialize in building chiropractic practices.
- ◆ Write articles for both online and offline magazines.
- ◆ Institute a strong referral program.
- ◆ Use direct mail.
- ◆ Speak to chiropractic groups.

Our Measurement Stick

Because CMP's goals require increases in revenues, number of clients, and frequency of purchase by clients, we'll use the following data for measurements:

- ◆ Revenue
- ◆ Expenses
- ◆ Break-even sales
- ◆ Cash flow
- ◆ Receivables

- Payables
- Average collection days
- New clients
- Client retention rate
- Cost of acquiring a client or making a sale
- Lifetime value of a client
- Client feedback
- Major campaign costs
- Other marketing costs
- Requests for information from sources we target through major campaigns
- Increase in current clients requesting annual or midyear plan reviews
- Number of purchases
- Close ratio
- New joint ventures with practice-building coaches
- Website visitors
- Page views
- Click-through rates
- Commission
- Taxes
- Earnings (net profits)

We'll use the following type of layout to track our results.

Tracking Results for Month/Year								
				Cost		Outcome		
Goal	Strategy	Tactic	Data	Expected	Actual	Expected	Actual	Source Used
Increase sales by $50K	Increase referrals by 20 percent	Referral program	Referrals received	$100 Direct mail		Subjects for 3 new case studies for articles, website, and direct mail; 3 written testimonials for website; 1 new client		Ask new clients how they heard about us; ask anyone requesting info how they heard about us; responses to direct-mail requests for referrals; testimonials on file
	Become the Expert	Publish one new article each month	Article published; leads; meetings; new client			Ask new clients how they heard about us; ask anyone requesting info how they heard about us; responses to direct-mail requests for referrals; testimonials on file		Magazines in which the articles were published
		Speak once per month to target group	Speaking event; leads; meetings; new client			1 speech; 10 qualified leads; 4 meetings; 2 new clients		Events where the speeches were given

Our One-Year Action Plan

This identifies the major things CMP will need to do over the next year to accomplish our goals.

Goal	Strategy	Tactic	To Do	Due
Increase sales from $150K to $200K by December 31	Become well-known for writing marketing plans for chiropractors because no one else in CMP's coverage area is doing this	Direct-mail campaign to CMP's list four times during the year to build and nurture relationship	Identify four hot buttons for these practices. Focus on one in each of the four mailings. Identify a way to add value to each of the mailings so recipients have a reason to both read and keep the mailing. Decide what action we want chiropractors to take after reading the mailing. Decide what kind of offer to include. Decide who will write the letter. Decide who will put the mailing together.	Jan. 15 April 15 (mail after tax deadline) July 15 Sept. 15

Goal	Strategy	Tactic	To Do	Due
		Article marketing campaign	Write articles for both online and offline magazines. Get four articles published in offline magazines targeting chiropractors. Use the articles in mailings to CMP's list and on their website. Write five articles initially by Jan. 31 to send to online article directories. Then add one new article each month. Add all articles to the CMP website. Decide whether to hire a ghostwriter. Begin researching and interviewing ghostwriters.	April 1 May 1 June 1 Oct. 1 Jan. 31 End of each month
		Speak to chiropractic groups	Identify networking groups that local chiropractors belong to or attend. Create four or five presentations that will appeal to our ideal client. Hire virtual assistant to assemble speaker's kit and begin contacting organizations to get speaking gigs. Speak once a month.	Jan. 31 Mar. 1 Mar. 31 April 1

Goal	Strategy	Tactic	To Do	Due
		Institute a strong referral program	Determine what the referral program should do for CMP. Decide how the program should benefit those who make referrals. Decide benefits for those who schedule appointments through referrals. Create the referral program. Add it to website and all direct mail. Look for other opportunities to promote the program.	Jan. 31
	Dominate our field within a 10-mile radius of our office	Form joint ventures with coaches who specialize in building chiropractic practices	Determine what CMP wants from a JV with a coach. Decide how the JV would work to benefit clients. Identify the qualifications and criteria CMP wants. Contact each of the coaches in our coverage area. Interview to learn their approach, methods, and results. Discuss a joint venture if a win-win. If none of the locals is a good prospect, take the criteria developed and expand the search to a wider area in Los Angeles County. Decide how to promote the JV.	Jan.–Mar.

Goal	Strategy	Tactic	To Do	Due
		Develop "touches" system to ensure list is contacted once a month	List will receive direct mail every three months. Develop contacts for the other eight months. Decide what those eight touches should be. Direct list to CMP website and try to secure opt-in to receive email. Call after every direct mailing. Use the other months to send articles of interest to chiropractors, postcards, marketing tips, and other useful information.	Jan. 31 (develop touch system)
	Add 15 net new clients	Focus on increasing retention, increasing referrals, and adding new clients from lead-generating speeches and articles	Same as under "Develop Referral Program," "Develop Maintenance Program," and DM, article, and speaking tactics. Also, conduct at least one workshop and one seminar during the year.	Jan.–Dec.

Goal	Strategy	Tactic	To Do	Due
	Increase our client retention rate to 40 percent	Develop a maintenance program	Develop list of benefits of reviewing a plan at least annually. Offer incentive for reviewing the marketing plan every year and another for every six months. Develop the offers. Include them to current clients at the time of purchase of services and in direct mail three or four times a year. Include offer for those who make referrals.	Jan. – Dec.

MARKETING PLAN HANDBOOK

Goal	Strategy	Tactic	To Do	Due
	Earn income by matching clients with coaches	Develop a JV program	Survey clients and prospects to see if they would use both services. Find out what they would want/expect. Determine what CMP wants from a JV with a coach. Decide how the JV would work to benefit clients. Identify the qualifications and criteria CMP wants. Contact each of the coaches in our coverage area. Interview to learn their approach, methods, and results. Discuss a joint venture if a win-win. If none of the locals is a good prospect, take the criteria developed and expand the search to a wider area in Los Angeles County. Decide how to promote the JV. Work out the details for introducing the program to clients. Tie in the JV to the workshop(s) and seminar.	Jan. – Mar.

Goal	Strategy	Tactic	To Do	Due
	Add a midyear review service to increase the frequency of usage of our services	Create the service	Outline content of midyear review. Write the program. Price it. Develop list of benefits of a midyear review. Include in direct mail letters and discussions with current clients. Offer to current clients at the time of purchase of services and in direct mail three or four times a year. Create offer in direct mail and touches calls.	Jan. – Dec.

These are the major marketing campaigns we will launch to meet our goals.

CMP's Major Campaigns for 2015						
Month	Campaign	Expected Cost	Actual Cost	Resources	Expected Results	Actual Results
January	Direct mail (referral and new client letters)	$500		List, sales letter, offer	1 new client	
February	Touch 1	$200		Article	3 new clients	
March	Touch 2	$200		Postcards	2 new clients	
April	Direct mail	$500		List, sales letter, offer	3 new clients	
May	Workshop; Touch 3 (calls)	$600		Location, handouts	5 new clients	
June	Touch 4	$200		Case study	3 new clients	

CMP's Major Campaigns for 2015						
Month	**Campaign**	**Expected Cost**	**Actual Cost**	**Resources**	**Expected Results**	**Actual Results**
July	Direct mail	$500		List, sales letter, offer	3 new clients	
August	Touch 5	$200		Special report	3 new clients	
September	Touch 6	$200		Article	3 new clients	
October	Direct mail	$500		List, sales letter, offer	4 new clients	
November	Touch 7 (calls); seminar	$1,100		Location, manuals, meals	6 new clients	
December	Touch 8 (Happy Holidays)	$300		Cards	1 new client	

Breakdown of Our Goals

♦ *30-Day Goals:* Add one new client. Maintain retention rate of existing clients at 35 percent. Stay within $500 marketing budget.

♦ *3-Month Goals:* Achieve 36 percent retention rate. Add six new clients. Start marketing for the seminar in May. Stay within $900 marketing budget. Complete one successful joint venture with a coach; collect $1,000.

♦ *6-Month Goals:* Achieve 37 percent retention. Complete workshop. Add 17 new clients year-to-date. Stay within $2,200 marketing budget. Complete four successful joint ventures.

♦ *9-Month Goals:* Achieve 38 percent retention. Add 26 new clients year-to-date. Complete seven successful joint ventures. Start marketing for the seminar in November. Stay within $3,100 marketing budget.

♦ *12-Month Goals:* Achieve our 40 percent retention of clients. Complete seminar successfully. Add 37 new clients for the year, bringing our total to 49 clients for the year. Complete nine successful joint ventures with coaches with $1,000 fee. Gross $200,000. Stay within $5,000 marketing budget.

CMP's growth has been steady with no obvious seasonal impact. We expect growth to remain steady as we increase our retention rate and add the new review service.

Our Budget

We will review this plan every week for the first 30 days of its implementation and then monthly thereafter.

Service		
Marketing Plans	$185,000	
Reviews	6,000	
Joint Venture Commissions	9,000	
Total Revenues		$200,000
Expenses		
Marketing	5,000	
Operating and Administrative Expenses	82,000	
Total Expenses		**$87,000**
Profit Before Taxes		**$113,000**

Appendix C
MARKETING CONSULTANTS

Working with, or Becoming, a Marketing Consultant

If you do not have the time or desire to write your own marketing plans, or you seek a fresh viewpoint, you can hire a marketing consultant to help you. Or perhaps you are reading this book because you already are a marketing consultant or want to become one. Becoming a marketing consultant offers many career advantages. You can:

- Set your own hours.
- Get a great deal of personal satisfaction from helping businesses grow.
- Take as much vacation time as you want.
- Spend more time with your family and loved ones and more easily adapt your schedule to theirs
- Often get direct and immediate positive feedback on the impact your services are having for your clients (since it is easy to track results).
- Continually expand your knowledge and grow professionally by tapping into a vast array of available resources, including online, print publications, seminars, and special events.
- Enjoy as much work variety as you want, depending on how you structure your consulting practice, which of the many services you wish to offer, and what types of businesses you want to serve.

- Have fun applying your creativity and analytical skills in order to solve marketing problems.
- Earn a six-figure income.
- Avoid long commutes.
- Dress how you want.
- Adopt any work style you like (e.g., you can be a recluse who works by phone and internet and never leaves the house, or work with clients on-site and travel all of the world delivering your services).

Marketing consulting services:

- Are needed by most small to medium-size businesses, because few have all the marketing expertise they need in-house.
- Require almost no startup investment. There are no franchise fees, no expensive equipment to buy, no raw materials or goods to inventory, and no high-priced office that needs to be furnished and rented.
- Offer the ability to sell and deliver multiple services providing almost limitless opportunities to gain additional revenue from existing clients.

Why There Is High Demand for Marketing Consultants

There is high demand for marketing consultants for many reasons, including:

- Increased competition facing most businesses today, resulting in a need for more effective marketing.
- A more rapid rate of change in products, services, and technology in the business world. These new products, services, and technologies necessitate changes in marketing approaches to address what's happening in the world of business.
- The realization by many business owners that being competent in their business niche is not enough. Marketing is increasingly becoming the differentiator in companies that just get by and companies that are highly profitable.

◆ A continually expanding array of marketing communications choices requiring more expertise in picking how to communicate with prospects and customers. Consider the number of channel choices we have on TV today, the number of magazines we can now subscribe to, and the millions of choices of websites to visit. Advertising and marketing channel fragmentation makes deciding where and how to promote your business more of a challenge.

◆ A huge and growing demand for internet marketing assistance. As more and more companies create an internet presence, and as a continuing array of marketing choices and technologies evolve, companies need help deploying effective internet marketing strategies. Although the internet lowers the barriers to worldwide marketing, internet marketing requires a new and constantly changing skill set most businesses don't have or will not invest in internally.

What Is Marketing Consulting?

Marketing consulting is a service provided by solo, freelance consultants, or larger organizations, to help companies improve their sales results in a variety of ways. Following are examples of how marketing consulting can help clients. A marketing consultant can help clients:

◆ Expand market share
◆ Enter a new market
◆ Effectively communicate messages to potential prospects
◆ Improve effectiveness of marketing activities
◆ Identify and solve marketing problems
◆ Identify and deploy new or expanded marketing methods

What Skills Are Required to Be a Successful Marketing Consultant?

The skills required to be a successful marketing consultant vary depending on the nature of the services to be offered. Following is a list of general skills needed for any marketing consultant, followed by additional skills that might be required based on the services that may be offered:

General skills required:

- ◆ Excellent written and verbal communications skills
- ◆ Sales ability
- ◆ Natural curiosity and interest in business, regardless of the type of business
- ◆ High energy level
- ◆ Extensive knowledge of advertising and basic marketing principles
- ◆ Organizational skills
- ◆ Ability to stay focused and work independently
- ◆ Creativity
- ◆ Analytical and problem-solving ability
- ◆ Ability to work well with businesspeople, from the owner of a company to the lowest level employee

Other skills that might be required, depending on services offered:

- ◆ Public speaking
- ◆ Copywriting
- ◆ Graphics design knowledge
- ◆ Online and offline research
- ◆ Internet marketing
- ◆ Internet search engine optimization
- ◆ Publicity and public relations
- ◆ Database marketing
- ◆ Search engine optimization
- ◆ Market research
- ◆ Unique selling proposition development
- ◆ Direct response marketing
- ◆ Broadcast advertising
- ◆ Yellow pages advertising
- ◆ Print advertising
- ◆ Telemarketing script development

- ◆ Knowledge of computer programs, such as Microsoft Word, Excel, and PowerPoint

Fees for Marketing Plan Writers

If you are a small business and pay a professional marketing consultant to write your plan, expect to be charged from $3,000 to $10,000.

- ◆ Low: $3,000
- ◆ Average: $5,000
- ◆ High: $8,000 to $10,000

Higher fees generally reflect the writer's need to do more extensive research on your industry, target market, and clients to complete your plan. They also generally apply to larger companies with multiple products, services, and markets.

When the Marketing Plan Is Part of a Business Plan

A marketing plan is only one part of a total business plan. Unless you're seeking outside funding from a bank or investors, you'll rarely need to produce an entire business plan. (However, if you want to master the workings of your business, producing a business plan for yourself is still a good idea. Look in Appendix D for information on sources for developing a complete business plan.)

Will your marketing plan be different if it's going to be part of a business plan submitted to outside funding sources? That depends.

Funding sources want to know that you have thought through your business and have a realistic view of how you'll generate profits. They're interested in the numbers and anything that affects the numbers, because they need to see how you'll generate the return they expect. They want to see how you've assessed the business environment you operate in, your assumptions about what it will take to succeed, your competition, your strategy for succeeding, and your funding apart from what they might lend you.

So they are interested in your marketing plan, but not necessarily in all the tactical details. Remember, your plan is for you. It tells you what actions you need to take to ensure growth and create your vision. The specific actions are not necessarily of interest to your bankers.

So how would the marketing plan portion differ? It would be more concise and focused on assessing your market, your strategy for serving that market differently from your competitors, and how you plan to apply all your resources to get the highest return.

Appendix D
SOURCES AND RESOURCES

References

Allen, David. 2001. *Getting Things Done*. New York: Penguin.

Antion, Tom. 2005. *The Ultimate Guide to Electronic Marketing for Small Business*. Hoboken, NJ: John Wiley & Sons.

Crispell, Diane. 1993. *The Insider's Guide to Demographic Know-How: Everything You Need to Find, Analyze, and Use Information About Your Customers*. Ithaca, NY: American Demographics Press.

Davis, John. 2007. *Measuring Marketing: 103 Key Metrics Every Marketer Needs*. Singapore: John Wiley & Sons.

Gerber, Michael E. 1995. *The E-Myth Revisited: Why Most Small Businesses Don't Work and What to Do About It*. New York: HarperCollins.

Harding, Ford. 1994. *Rain Making: The Professional's Guide to Attracting New Clients*. Avon, MA: Adams Media.

Hayden, C. J. 1999. *Get Clients Now!* New York: AMACOM.

Hines, Randall and Lauterborn, Robert. 2008. *Print Matters: How to Write Great Advertising*. Chicago: RACOM.

Johnson, Winslow. 2004. *Powerhouse Marketing Plans*. New York: AMACOM.

Joyner, Mark. 2005. *The Irresistible Offer*. Hoboken, NJ: John Wiley & Sons.

Luther, William. 2001. *The Marketing Plan*. 3rd ed. New York: AMACOM.

McDonald, Malcolm and Wilson, Hugh. 2011. *Marketing Plans: How to Prepare Them, How to Use Them.* 7th ed. Burlington, MA: Elsevier.

Ogden, James R. 1998. *Developing a Creative and Innovative Integrated Marketing Communication Plan: A Working Model.* Upper Saddle River, NJ: Prentice-Hall.

Porter, Michael E. 1980. *Competitive Strategy: Techniques for Analyzing Industries and Competitors.* New York: The Free Press.

Rice, Craig S. 1990. *Strategic Planning for the Small Business: Situations, Weapons, Objectives & Tactics.* Holbrook, MA: Bob Adams.

Associations

Direct Marketing Association Inc.
1120 Avenue of the Americas
New York, NY 10036-6700
(212) 768-7277
http://thedma.org/

Direct Marketing Club of New York
224 Seventh St.
Garden City, NY 11530
(516) 746-6700
http://dmcny.org/

International Association of Business Communicators
One Hallidie Plaza, #600
San Francisco, CA 94102
(415) 544-4700
www.iabc.com

National Mail Order Association
2807 Polk St. NE
Minneapolis, MN 55418-2954
(612) 788-1673
www.nmoa.org

Books

Bly, Robert. 2006 *The Copywriter's Handbook: A Step-by-Step Guide to Writing Copy That Sells, Third Edition.* New York: Henry Holt. How to write effective copy.

Cates, Bill. 1996 *Unlimited Referrals.* Wheaton, MD: Thunder Hill Press. How to get lots of referral leads.

Directories

Bacon's Publicity Checklist
332 South Michigan Avenue
Chicago, IL 60604
(800) 621-0561
Media lists for mailing press releases

Directory of Major Mailers
National Mail Order Association
www.nmoa.org/catalog/majormailers.htm
Directory of companies that sell via direct marketing

Encyclopedia of Associations
Gale Research
Book Tower
Detroit, MI 48226
(313) 961-2242
Directory of major U.S. industry and professional associations

O'Dwyer's Directory of Public Relations Firms
J. R. O'Dwyer & Co. Inc.
271 Madison Avenue
New York, NY 10016
(212) 679-2471
www.odwyerpr.com/pr_firms_database/
Lists U.S. public relations firms

Standard Rate and Data Service
1700 Higgins Road

Des Plaines, IL 60018-5605
(800) 851-7737
http://next.srds.com/home
Comprehensive directory of publications that accept advertising

Mailing Lists

Creative Access
3701 N. Ravenswood Avenue, #207
Chicago, IL 60613
(312) 440-1140

Inforgroup Media Solutions
www.infogroupmediasolutions.com

Planning Software

Business Plan Pro
www.bplans.com
Software contains more than 500 sample editable business plans
   for businesses of all types.

Marketing Plan Pro
www.mplans.com
Software contains more than 100 sample editable marketing plans
   for businesses of all types.

Marketing and Business Enewsletters

Bencivenga's Bullets
http://marketingbullets.com
Master copywriter Gary Bencivenga's can't-miss enewsletter based
   on his decades of tested results

Early to Rise
www.earlytorise.com
Daily enewsletter on business success, wealth, and health

Excess Voice
www.nickusborne.com/newsletter
Nick Usborne's enewsletter on online copywriting; informative and
   great fun

Marketing Minute
www.yudkin.com/markmin.htm
Weekly marketing tip from consultant Marcia Yudkin

The Copywriter's Roundtable
http://copywritersroundtable.com
John Forde's superb enewsletter on copywriting

The Direct Response Letter
www.bly.com
Robert Bly's monthly enewsletter on copywriting and direct marketing

The Success Margin
www.tednicholas.com
Ted Nicholas's must-read marketing ezine

Periodicals

Advertising Age
740 N. Rush Street
Chicago, IL 60611
(312) 649-5200
http://adage.com/

Adweek
49 E. 21st Street
New York, NY 10010
(212) 529-5500
www.adweek.com/

Commerce Business Daily
Government Printing Office
Washington, DC 20401

(202) 512-0132
www.cbd-net.com/

DM News
19 West 21st Street
New York, NY 10010
(212) 741-2095
www.dmnews.com/

Public Relations Journal
33 Irving Place
New York, NY 10003
(212) 998-2230
www.prsa.org/Intelligence/PRJournal/index.html

Sales and Marketing Management
633 Third Avenue
New York, NY 10017
(212) 986-4800
www.salesandmarketing.com/

Target Marketing
North American Publishing Co.
401 N. Broad Street
Philadelphia, PA 19108
(215) 238-5300
www.targetmarketingmag.com

Websites

BizStats
www.bizstats.com
Free business statistics, benchmarks, and financial ratios, with a
   special section for sole proprietors

Business Owner's Toolkit: Creating a Written Business Plan
www.bizfilings.com/toolkit/sbg/startup/planning/creating-a-
   written-business-plan.aspx

SCORE Business Planning and Financial Statements Template Gallery

www.score.org/resources/business-planning-financial-statements-template-gallery

The Small Business Advocate

www.smallbusinessadvocate.com

Radio show and website dedicated to small business

Appendix E
GLOSSARY

+1 Button: Similar to Facebook's "like" button, the +1 button is proprietary to Google and is the equivalent to a thumbs-up.

2D Barcodes: Also known as a QRC or Quick Response Code; this is a scannable barcode that can be read by certain mobile applications (by taking a photo of the barcode) and convey information, such as URLs, etc.

Ad Click Rate: Sometimes referred to as click-through, this is the percentage of ad views that resulted in an ad click.

Affiliate Marketing: A system of advertising in which site A agrees to feature buttons from site B, and site A gets a percentage of any sales generated for site B.

Affiliate Program: An arrangement in which a company pays you a percentage of the sale for every online customer they get through a link from your website to theirs.

Affinity Marketing: Marketing efforts, including email promotions, banners, or offline media, aimed at consumers on the basis of established buying patterns.

Agora Model: Online business model in which you build a large opt-in e-list, and then drive sales by sending emails with product offers to your list.

Algorithm: A set of formulas developed for a computer to perform a certain function. This is important in the social sphere as the algorithms for sites like Facebook and Google use are critical for developing content-sharing strategies.

Analytics: Tells you what happened. In general, it involves using technology to gather data which analysts can study. The goal of analysts is to examine this data, looking for patterns in behavior.

Anchor: A word, phrase, or graphic image; in hypertext, it is the object that is highlighted, underlined, or "clickable" that links to another site.

Applet: An application program written in Java that allows viewing of simple animation on web pages.

Application Programming Interface (API): A software-to-software interface, not a user interface. With APIs, applications talk to each other without any user knowledge or intervention. An example of this is the Twitter API.

Archiving: The practice of retaining an organization's social media messages and associated metadata, often for the purpose of regulatory compliance. Archiving has become increasingly important as more and more business communications occur on social media. This data can later be retrieved and analyzed to track the effectiveness of social media activities.

ASP (application service provider): Third-party vendor that develops and hosts internet and intranet applications for consumers.

Avatar: An avatar is an image or username that represents a person online within forums and social networks.

Bounceback: Second mailing sent to a prospective customer who responded to an ad. Bouncebacks are designed to increase response to the initial product information mailing.

Brand Advocate: A customer that is so satisfied with your product that they go out of their way to help you market it.

Broadside: A one-page promotional flier folded for mailing.

Business-to-Business Advertising: Advertising of products and services sold by a business to other businesses.

Cache: A storage area for frequently accessed information.

CGI (common gateway interface): An interface-creation scripting program that allows web pages to be made on the fly based on information from buttons, checkboxes, text input, and so on.

Circles: User-identified clusters of friends on Google+ (users group certain people together, such as colleagues, college connections, family, or neighbors). When you want to share content with only these individuals, the specific Circle is noted as part of the post's sharing options.

Clickbait: Web content with a misleading or sensationalist headline that entices readers to click through to the full story, usually with the goal of generating page views and advertising revenue.

Click-Through Rate (CTR): A common metric for reporting on the number of people who viewed a message or piece of content and then actually performed the action required, such as clicking on the ad or link in an email marketing campaign. The actual metric is calculated by comparing the number of clicks to impressions. The general philosophy is that the higher your CTR, the more effective your marketing is.

Collateral: Printed product information such as brochures, fliers, catalogs, and direct mail.

Common Short Code (CSC): Users send messages to these shortened numbers (4 to 6 digits), usually to get something in return, like a competition entry, for example.

Content Curation: The process of sifting through the web to find the best and most relevant content for an audience and then presenting it to them in a meaningful way. Unlike content marketing, content curation doesn't involve publishing new content. Instead, it's about creating value for your audience by saving them time and effort.

Content Curator: Someone who continually searches out, categorizes, and otherwise organizes the best and most relevant online content on a specific topic or topics.

Content Management System (CMS): An online application that allows you to draft, share, edit, schedule, and index your content. Popular web CMS's make use of simple editors that allow you to create publish content without demanding knowledge of code.

Content Marketing: A marketing strategy based on attracting and retaining customers through the creation and distribution of valuable content, such as videos, white papers, guides, and infographics. Content marketers look to earn customer loyalty and influence decisions by providing useful, entertaining, or educational media.

Content Syndication: The process of pushing your blog, site, or video content out into third-party sites, either as a full article, snippet, link, or thumbnail. The idea is to drive more engagement with your content by wiring it into related digital contexts, either to boost traffic or just get exposure for your brand or your key personalities or products.

Conversion: Getting an online user to take a specific action, typically registering online in exchange for free content or purchasing a product from a website.

Conversion: In online marketing, a conversion is getting a user to take a specific action, typically registering online in exchange for free content or purchasing a product from a website. The action demonstrates that the visitor is "converting" into a customer.

Cookie: A file on your computer that records information, such as where you have been on the web. The browser stores this information, which allows a site to remember the browser in future transactions or requests.

CPC: Cost per click.

CPL: Cost per lead.

CPM: CPM is the cost per thousand for a particular site. A website that charges $15,000 per banner and guarantees 600,000 impressions has a CPM of $25 ($15,000 divided by 600).

CPT: Cost per transaction.

CPTM: Cost per targeted thousand impressions.

Creative Commons: A public copyright license that gives you the ability to use and share otherwise copyrighted material. For social media users, Creative Commons often comes into play when we are looking for images and photos to accompany a social media message or blog post. Sites like Google Image Search and Flickr have filters so you can easily search for photos that fall into this category. Just be careful, as there are different levels of Creative Commons that could restrict whether an image could be used commercially, whether it can be modified, and what kind of attribution is required.

Demographic Overlay: Adding demographic data to a prospect or customer list by running it through the computer and matching it against other lists that already contain the data.

Domain Part of the DNS (domain naming system): Name that specifies details about the host. A domain is the main subdivision of internet addresses, the last three letters after the final dot, and it tells you what kind of organization you are dealing with. There are six top-level domains widely used in the U.S.: .com (commercial), .edu (educational), .net (network operations), .gov (U.S. government), .mil (U.S. military), and .org (organization).

Downscale: Consumers on the low end of the social scale in terms of income, education, and status.

Dynamic Serving: Referring specifically to mobile website development, dynamic serving uses the same URL regardless of device, but generates a different version of HTML for different device types based on what the server knows about the user's browser. Dynamic serving is a setup where the server responds with different HTML (and CSS) on the same URL depending on the user agent requesting the page.

Earned Media: Publicity gained through promotional efforts other than advertising, as opposed to paid media, which refers to publicity gained through advertising.

Embedded Media: Digital media that is displayed within another piece of content, outside its native setting.

Facebook Reach: The number of unique people who have seen content from your Facebook page. Reach is not the same as impressions, which is the total number of times your content is viewed (including multiple views from the same user). Facebook provides two different reach metrics: *total reach* and *post reach*. *Total reach* is the number of unique people who have seen any content associated with your page during the last seven days. Post reach is the number of unique people who have seen a particular Facebook page post in their News Feed. These two primary categories can be further broken down further into *organic* and *paid* reach. Organic reach is free; the term merely refers to the number of unique people who saw your content without you having to pay for them to see it; and *paid* reach refers to the number of unique people who saw your content *because you paid for promoted posts or display ads*.

Firewall: A security barrier placed between an organization's internal computer network—either its IS system or intranet—and the internet.

Flame: An intentionally crude or abusive email message.

Floater: Similar to a pop-up or pop-under message, except it is not blocked by pop-up blockers because it is part of the web page or landing page HTML code. The floater is used to capture the visitor's email address, usually by offering free content.

Follower: A Twitter user who has subscribed to your Twitter account so they can receive your Tweets in their home feed. If you want to send them a direct message, you need to follow them back.

Following: The number of accounts a Twitter user is watching, or *following*.

Follows: The number of accounts that are following a Twitter user.

Four A's: American Association of Advertising Agencies, an industry trade association.

Fractional Ad: An ad that takes less than a full page in a magazine or newspaper.

FTP (file transfer protocol): A protocol that allows the transfer of files from one computer to another. FTP can also be used as a verb.

Geographical Targeting: Also called *geo-targeting* or *geo-locating*, this allows you to see where your visitors come from and also to give them specific information that is relevant to them based on their location.

Geolocation (geotagging): The practice of tagging a photo, video, or message with a specific location. The ubiquity of GPS-enabled smartphones has made geotagging a core aspect of social media.

Geotargeting: A feature on many social media platforms that allows users to share their content with geographically defined audiences. Instead of sending a generic message for the whole world to see, you can refine the messaging and language of your content to better connect with people in specific cities, countries, and regions.

GIF (graphics interchange format): A common compression format used for transferring graphics files between different computers. It supports both static and animated images. Gifs rose to popularity as they allow you to essentially present a short video clip in a far more condensed image format. Only certain social networks support gifs, including Google+ and Twitter.

Global Positioning System (GPS): A satellite-based positioning technology that allows a GPS receiver to calculate its position anywhere on earth with great accuracy.

Global System for Mobile Communications (GSM): A widely used digital wireless telephone technology.

Handle: Another way of saying your account name. It's important that you try to maintain consistent handles on all social network profiles, since people who follow you on Twitter might want to find you on Instagram or Pinterest.

Hashtag: A tag used on Twitter (#) as a way to annotate a message. An example would be: *#yourhashtag*. On most social networks, clicking a hashtag will reveal all the public and recently published messages that also contain that hashtag. Hashtags first emerged on Twitter as a user-created phenomenon and are now used on almost every other social media platform, including Facebook, Google+, Instagram, Vine, and Pinterest.

Host: A server connected to the internet (with a unique IP address).

House Organ: A company-published newsletter or magazine.

HTML: A coding language used to make hypertext documents for use on the web.

HTML-Based Email: An email formatted like a web page with graphics, table columns, and hyperlinks. The HTML code specifies formatting, colors, positioning, and layout.

HTTP (hypertext transfer protocol): A standard method of publishing information as hypertext in HTML format on the internet.

HTTPS-SSL: HTTP with SSL (secure socket layer) encryption for security.

Hyperlink: The clickable link in text graphics on a web page that takes you to another place on the same page, another page, or a whole other site.

Hypertext: Electronic documents that present information that can be read by following many different directions through links, rather than just read linearly like printed text.

Impressions: The number of times an ad, sponsored update, or promoted post is displayed.

Inbound Marketing: A style of marketing that focuses on permission-based marketing techniques that businesses can use to get found by potential customers, convert those prospects into leads and customers, and analyze the process along the way. It leverages tactics, such as SEO, blogging, social media, lead generation, email marketing, lead nurturing, and analytics.

Inquiry Fulfillment Package: Product literature sent in response to an inquiry.

Interstitial: An "intrusive" ad unit that is spontaneously delivered without specifically being requested by a user.

IP Address (internet protocol address): Every system connected to the internet has a unique IP address, which consists of a number in the format, A, B, C, or D, where each of the four sections is a decimal number from 0 to 255.

ISP (internet service provider): A business that provides access to the internet.

Java: An object-oriented programming language created by Sun Microsystems that supports enhanced features such as animation and real-time updating of information.

JPEG (joint photographic experts group): A graphics format that displays photographs and graphic images with millions of colors, compresses well, and is easy to download.

Klout Score: Klout's (www.klout.com) numerical rating of online social influence, ranging from 1 to 100. Klout rates a social media user based on the size of their social networks and how other users interact with their content. The company defines influence as "the ability to drive action" and measures hundreds of signals from Twitter, Facebook, Google+, LinkedIn, Instagram, Wikipedia, and its own network. You can increase your Klout score by connecting multiple platforms to your Klout profile.

Landing Page: Any web page designed to generate conversion or other direct action, as opposed to a page that just provides content or links to more content.

Lift Letter: A second letter included in a direct-mail package; the lift letter is designed to increase response to the mailing. Also known as a publisher's letter because it is primarily used in mailings that solicit magazine subscriptions.

Link Building: Part of SEO (search engine optimization) in which website owners develop strategies to generate links to their site from other websites with the hopes of improving their search engine ranking.

LinkedIn Endorsement: A LinkedIn member's recognition of another person's skill. Endorsements boost your credibility on LinkedIn by indicating that you actually have the skills you say you have. You can only endorse the skills of your first-degree connections.

LinkedIn Influencer: This individual is a top industry leader or other high-profile professional who has been invited to publish on LinkedIn. Although every LinkedIn user can use the social network as a publishing platform, the LinkedIn Influencer program is invitation-only.

LinkedIn Recommendation: A written compliment from one of your connections that you can display on your LinkedIn profile. There's no limit to how many recommendations you can give or request.

List Broker: A person who rents mailing lists.

Mashup: A content mashup contains multiple types of media drawn from pre-existing sources to create a new work. Digital mashups allow individuals or businesses to create new pieces of content by combining multiple online content sources.

Meme: Used to describe a thought, idea, joke, or concept to be shared online. It is typically an image with text above and below it, but can also come in video and link form.

Metatags: Used to identify the creator of a web page, what HTML specs the page follows, and the keywords and description of the page.

Microblogging: Brief text updates that are usually less than 200 characters. These are published via SMS (short message service), the web, IM, email, or MP3 and can either be received by the general online community or a select number of individuals. The most popular microblogging service is Twitter.

Multimedia Messaging Services (MMS): A standard way to send messages that include multimedia content to and from mobile phones. It extends the core SMS (Short Message Service) capability that allowed exchange of text messages only up to 160 characters in length. Unlike text-only SMS, commercial MMS can deliver a variety of media including up to 40 seconds of video, one image, multiple images via slideshow, or audio plus unlimited characters.

Name Squeeze Page: A landing page, usually brief, designed to capture the user's email address, either in exchange for an offer of free content or as a condition of allowing the reader access to copy on a landing page or other web page. (Also known as a squeeze page.)

Outbound Marketing: Marketing messages distributed or broadcast by an advertiser to consumers or business prospects.

PDF Files: Adobe's portable document format (PDF) is a translation format used primarily for distributing files across a network or on a website. Files with a .pdf extension have been created in another application and then translated into .pdf files so they can be viewed by anyone, regardless of platform.

Per Diem: Fees charged by the day.

Permalink: An address or URL of a particular post within a blog or website.

PI (per inquiry advertising): Advertising for which the publisher or broadcast station is paid according to the number of inquiries produced by the ad or commercial.

Pinboard: A collection of pins on Pinterest. It can be organized by any theme of your choosing, and it can either be private or public. Some examples of pinboards: 50 Alternative Uses for Mason Jars, Short Hairstyles, My Dream Wedding, Easy Appetizers.

Pinned Tweet: A Twitter tweet that has been pinned to the top a Twitter profile page. Pinning a Tweet is a great way to feature an important announcement or one of your greatest hits. Everyone who views your profile page will see the Tweet; however, pinning a Tweet will not have an effect on its visibility in anyone else's timeline. To increase your reach and impressions, consider Promoted Tweets.

Pins: Favorite links stored on Pinterest are called pins. Each pin is made up of a picture and a description given by the user; when clicked, pins direct users to the image source page. Pins can be liked or repinned by other users. Users can also organize pins by theme or event into visual collections called Pinboards.

Pop-Over: A page that pops up on the screen when you visit a website or landing page, the purpose of which is to capture the email address of the visitor, usually by offering free content.

Pop-Under: A page that pops up on the screen when you attempt to leave a landing page or website without placing an order, the purpose of which is to capture the email address of the visitor, usually by offering free content.

Promoted Tweets: Native advertisements targeted to a specific audience available through Twitter ads. They look almost identical to organic tweets in users' timelines but include a small "Promoted" marker. Promoted Tweets are used by advertisers to reach an expanded audience.

Psychographics: Statistics relating to the personalities, attitudes, and lifestyles of various groups of people.

Pub-Set: Ads designed and typeset by the publication in which they will appear.

Real-Time Search: The method of indexing content being published online into search engine results with virtually no delay.

Repin: On Pinterest, if you find a pin on another user's Pinboard that you like, you can save it to your board by repinning it. If you like the pin, but don't want it to appear on your Pinterest page, you can like it instead of repinning it.

Responsive Web Design (RWD): Provides an optimal viewing experience—easy reading and navigation with a minimum of resizing, panning, and scrolling—on all devices, including desktop monitors, tablets, and mobile phones.

Return on Investment (ROI): A measurement of the effectiveness of an organization's investment in social media. Like any metric for ROI, social media ROI is calculated by dividing the total benefits of an investment by the sum of its costs.

Return on Relationship (ROR): A measurement of the value gained by a person or business from developing a relationship. Measuring ROR isn't easy; it involves not only analyzing connection growth, but also understanding the impact your customers' voices have on your brand and reputation. ROR is an alternative (or complementary) metric to social media ROI.

Retweet: When someone on Twitter sees your message and decides to reshare it with his/her followers. A retweet button allows them to quickly resend the message with attribution to the original sharer's name.

RSS (really simple syndication): Allows you to receive/syndicate information without having to constantly open new pages in your browser. As a content creator, RSS allows your content to be distributed.

RSS Feed: RSS is a family of web feed formats used to publish frequently updated content such as blogs and videos in a standardized format. Content publishers can syndicate a feed, which allows users to subscribe to the content and read it when they please, and from a location other than the website.

RSS Reader: Allows users to aggregate articles from multiple websites into one place using RSS feeds. The purpose of these aggregators is to allow for a faster and more efficient consumption of information. An example of an RSS Reader is Digg Reader (http://digg.com/reader).

Short Messaging Service (SMS): Text-only messages that can be sent to mobile phones from the internet or from other mobile devices; all phones are SMS capable.

Social Media Monitoring: A process of monitoring and responding to mentions related to a business that occur in social media. Also called "social listening."

Split Run Test: Two versions of an ad are run in different copies of a publication to test the effectiveness of one version against the other.

Squeeze Pages: See *Name Squeeze Page.*

Storyboard: Rough series of illustrations showing what a finished TV commercial will look like.

Sweepstakes: A sales promotion in which prizes are awarded by chance and the consumer does not have to make a purchase to enter.

Tag Cloud: A visual depiction of user-generated tags, or simply the word content of a site, typically used to describe the content of websites.

Targeting: Determining one's niche marketing audience of individuals within a group.

Teaser: Copy printed on the outside envelope of a direct-mail package.

Trade Advertising: Advertising aimed at wholesalers, distributors, sales reps, agents, and retailers rather than consumers.

Text-Based Email: An unformatted email that only includes text.

Thread: A strand of online messages that represent a conversation or part of a conversation. Threads begin with an initial message, then continue as a series of replies or comments. A thread provides both the specifics of the conversation as well as its context.

Timestamp: The date and time that a message is posted to a social network, usually visible below the headline or username. Clicking on a timestamp will usually bring you to the content's permalink.

Top Tweets: The most popular and engaging tweets for a given search query, as determined by a Twitter algorithm. Searches on Twitter return top tweets by default, but you can toggle to "All" results to see the full list of tweets that match your search.

Tracking: Measuring the success of a campaign by collecting and evaluating statistics.

Transaction Page: An order page.

Transfer Rates: The speed at which data is transferred across a network.

Trend: Social media trends are like fads that sweep through a social scene (in this case, the internet). Take, for example, Follow

Friday (#ff), a Twitter trend where users select other usernames and tweet them with #ff in their post, meaning they recommend following those Twitter users. Another example of a social trend would be cause-related tweet-a-thons, where users encourage their followers to tweet about and donate to a particular charitable cause over a specific period of time.

Triage: The process of prioritizing, assigning, and responding to inbound social media messages. Incoming messages are filtered, assigned to the right people, evaluated for urgency, and possibly escalated so that the organization can provide the appropriate response through the most appropriate channel(s).

Tweet: The accepted term for a Twitter message. A tweet can contain up to 140 characters of text, as well as photos, videos, and other forms of media. They are public by default and will show up in Twitter timelines and searches unless they are sent from protected accounts or as direct messages.

Twitter: A microblogging platform allowing individuals to communicate directly with their followers.

Twitter Card: A media-rich Tweet that includes an embedded video, photo gallery, page summary, or other interactive element beyond the text of the message. Twitter Cards help your tweets stand out and encourage your followers to engage with your content directly from their timelines.

Unfollow: The action of unsubscribing from another Twitter user's account.

Universe: The total number of people who are prospects for your product.

Unstructured Supplementary Service Data (USSD): Works on all existing GSM (Global System for Mobile Communications) phones, and provides session-based communication, enabling a variety of applications.

URL Shortener: An online tool that condenses a URL into a shorter (and more social media-friendly) format, known as a *short link*. Users who click on a short link are redirected to the original URL.

User-Generated Content (UGC): Media that has been created and published online by the users of a social or collaboration platform, typically for noncommercial purposes. User-generated content is one of the defining characteristics of social media.

Vertical Publication: Magazine intended for a narrow special-interest group.

Wireless Application Protocol (WAP): A set of standards that allows web access on mobile devices.

Word Cloud: Also known as *Tag Clouds* or *Weighted Lists*; word clouds are a visual representation of text, where the frequency of a word determines its size in the word cloud. This is a great tool for identifying words (and the ideas they represent) that are most common.

ABOUT
THE
AUTHOR

Bob Bly is an independent copywriter and marketing consultant with over 35 years of experience in business-to-business and direct response marketing. McGraw-Hill calls Bob Bly "America's top copywriter," and he was American Writers and Artists Inc.'s (AWAI) 2007 Copywriter of the Year. Clients include IBM, the Conference Board, PSE&G, AT&T, Embraer Executive Jet, Intuit, ExecuNet, Boardroom, Medical Economics, Grumman, RCA, ITT Fluid Technology, and Praxair.

Bob has given presentations to numerous organizations, including National Speakers Association, American Seminar Leaders Association, American Society for Training and Development, U.S. Army, American Society of Journalists and Authors, Society for Technical Communications, Discover Card, Learning Annex, and New York University School of Continuing Education.

He is the author of 85 books, including *The Copywriter's Handbook* (Henry Holt), *The White Paper Marketing Handbook* (Thomson), *Public Relations for Dummies* (IDG Books), and *Business-to-Business Direct Marketing* (NTC Business Books). Bob's articles have appeared in *Cosmopolitan, Writer's Digest, The Writer, Successful Meetings, Amtrak Express, Direct, City Paper, Bergen Record, DM News,* and many other publications. Bob is a columnist for *Target Marketing.* The *Direct Response Letter,* Bob's monthly enewsletter, has over 65,000 subscribers (www.bly.com/reports).

Awards include a Gold Echo from the Direct Marketing Association, an IMMY from the Information Industry Association, two Southstar Awards, an American Corporate Identity Award of Excellence, Marketer of the Year from *Early to Rise*, and the Standard of Excellence award from the Web Marketing Association. He is a member of the International Association of Business Communicators (IABC), Business Marketing Association (BMA), and the American Institute of Chemical Engineers (AIChE).

Prior to become a freelance copywriter, Bob was advertising manager of Koch Engineering and a staff marketing writer for Westinghouse Defense. He holds a BS in chemical engineering from the University of Rochester and is trained as a Certified Novell Administrator.

He can be reached at:

Bob Bly

31 Cheyenne Dr.

Montville, NJ 07045

Phone: (973)263-0562; Fax: (973) 263-0613

Email: rwbly@bly.com

Web: www.bly.com

INDEX